To Danny,
Let's hope this is not
Best wishes,
Keith

ROYAL HISTORICAL SOCIETY

STUDIES IN HISTORY

New Series

MANAGING THE SOUTH AFRICAN WAR, 1899–1902

POLITICIANS *v.* GENERALS

MANAGING THE SOUTH AFRICAN WAR, 1899–1902

POLITICIANS *v.* GENERALS

Keith Terrance Surridge

THE ROYAL HISTORICAL SOCIETY
THE BOYDELL PRESS

First published 1998

A Royal Historical Society publication
Published by The Boydell Press
an imprint of Boydell & Brewer Ltd
PO Box 9, Woodbridge, Suffolk IP12 3DF, UK
and of Boydell & Brewer Inc.
PO Box 41026, Rochester, NY 14604–4126, USA

ISBN 0 86193 238 2

ISSN 0269–2244

A catalogue record for this book is available
from the British Library

Library of Congress Cataloging-in-Publication Data
applied for

This book is printed on acid-free paper

Printed in Great Britain by
St Edmundsbury Press, Bury St Edmunds, Suffolk

Contents

		Page
Acknowledgements		vii
List of maps		viii
Abbreviations		ix
Introduction		1
1	Managing the Boer threat: 1895–9	15
2	The final crisis: June – October 1899	40
3	War, defeat and reform: October 1899 – November 1901	57
4	The conquest of the Boer republics: December 1899 – September 1900	75
5	Police and refugees: May – December 1900	93
6	Battling for supremacy: December 1900 – July 1901	112
7	Kitchener's victory: July 1901 – March 1902	133
8	Managing the peace: the Treaty of Vereeniging: December 1901 – June 1902	155
Conclusion		175
Biographical appendix		185
Select bibliography		190
Index		201

Publication of this volume was aided by a grant from the Scou-
loudi Foundation, in association with the Institute of Historical
Research. It was further assisted by a grant from The Isobel
Thornley Bequest Fund of the University of London

Acknowledgements

For permission to examine collections of documents in their care, I would like to thank the following individuals and institutions: Birmingham University Library; the Bodleian Library and the Warden and Fellows of New College, Oxford; the British Museum and the staff of the British Library; the marquess of Salisbury and Dr R. Harcourt-Williams at Hatfield House; Hove Central Library; the Trustees of the Liddell Hart Centre for Military Archives, King's College, London; the National Army Museum, Chelsea; and the Controller of Her Majesty's Stationery Office for permission to use Crown copyright documents held in the Public Record Office, Kew. I would also like to thank the Historical Association for permission to use material originally published in their journal *History*. Unfortunately, the papers of the fifth marquess of Lansdowne became available too late to be used in this work.

This book began as a PhD thesis thanks to the financial help provided by a British Academy three-year research grant. The expert supervision of Professor Andrew Porter ensured the thesis was completed, and thanks to his continuing generosity I was able to use the map of South Africa in the *Atlas of British overseas expansion*. I would also like to acknowledge the publishers, Routledge, for their consideration as well. My thesis examiners Dr David Killingray and Dr Iain R. Smith made invaluable suggestions and criticisms, as did my editorial adviser Professor Martin Daunton, whose enthusiasm for the project is gratefully recorded. Dr William Philpott was also kind enough to give constructive advice on part of the manuscript. However, any mistakes and blemishes that remain are solely mine.

For their help and guidance at various times I am indebted to the staff at the Institute of Historical Research, particularly Bridget Taylor, the members of the Imperial History Seminar, Dr Kelly Boyd, Dr Peter Catterall, Caroline Johns, Dr Rohan McWilliam, Jennifer Ridden, Dr Jane Samson, Tim Wales and Dr Glenn Wilkinson. Dr Gareth Prosser kindly lent his time to help with the maps, as did Dr Stuart Carroll. The illustration for the cover, from the Scarlet Gunner Collection, Tenterden, Kent, is reproduced by kind permission of Colonel Peter Walton. I would also like to thank Christine Linehan for her editorial guidance.

Finally I am very grateful to all my friends outside the academic world, who were always on hand to offer their advice and support. Most of all, I dedicate this book to my family, especially to my mother and the memory of my father.

Keith Surridge
January 1998

List of Maps

Map 1.   South Africa 1899–1902   x

Map 2.   The Natal Triangle 1899–1902   24

Abbreviations

CAB	Cabinet papers
C-in-C	Commander-in-Chief
C-in-C(SA)	Commander-in-Chief (South Africa)
CO	Colonial Office
DMI	Director of Military Intelligence
GOC	General Officer Commanding
GOC SA	General Officer Commanding, South Africa
HW	*History Workshop*
HP	Hamilton papers
JC	Joseph Chamberlain papers
JICH	*Journal of Imperial and Commonwealth History*
KP	Kitchener papers
MP	Milner papers
OFS	Orange Free State
ORC	Orange River Colony
PRO	Public Record Office
RCWSA	Royal Commission on the war in South Africa
RD	Rawlinson diary
RP	Roberts papers
SAC	South African Constabulary
SJB PRO	St John Brodrick papers
VMP	Violet Milner papers
WO	War Office
WP	Wolseley papers

Note on Usage

For clarity I refer to the Dutch-speakers of Cape Colony as Afrikaners throughout the book, to distinguish them from those in the Boer Republics.

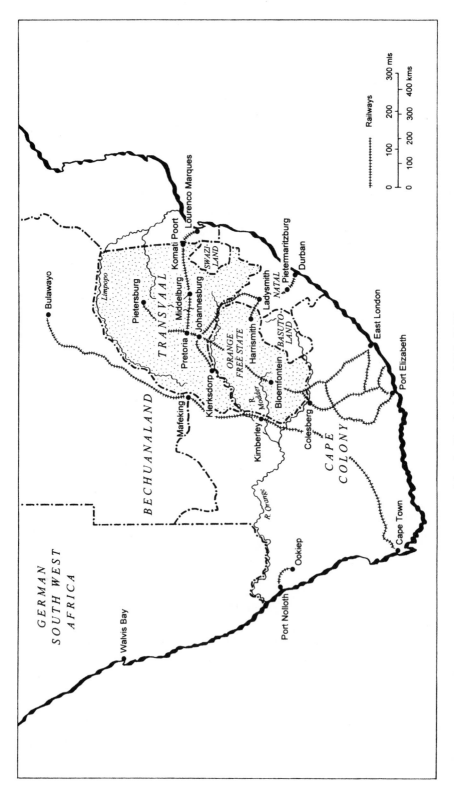

Map 1. South Africa 1899–1902

Introduction

I

The second South African war was the largest and most costly war fought by Britain between 1815 and 1914. It provided the Victorian army with its greatest test, provoked enormous interest in the nature of Britain's imperial expansion, and affected in varying degrees the societies of all the participants. This book explains how such a war had a profound impact on British civil–military relations, as the politicians and generals sought to resolve a conflict that was going badly wrong; and how its unexpected character exacerbated pre-war tensions over army administration and reform, and generated new difficulties at the same time. By focusing on those individuals at the highest level (the leading politicians, administrators and generals in both Britain and South Africa), this book provides the first proper account of the higher strategic management of the South African war.[1]

This study offers a comprehensive survey of British civil–military relations for two important reasons: first it helps us understand how the late Victorian state prepared for war at a time when enormous changes had transformed both society and the political process. The growth of a mass, urban-dwelling electorate, easily accessible to a wide-ranging, popular media, meant that governments had to consider more than ever how foreign policies were formulated and the effect they might have on what was considered to be an excitable population. Moreover, according to Andrew Porter, the proliferation of foreign and imperial issues during the latter part of the nineteenth century, beginning with Gladstone's 'Bulgarian horrors' and Midlothian campaigns, intermixed with the advent of jingoism between 1876 and 1880, 'appeared to confirm the disastrous effect of democratic party politics in the sphere of foreign affairs, and awoke in statesmen, particularly conservative ones, an abiding fear of public opinion's unpredictability, of its fits of irrationality rather than its ultimate reasonableness'. Furthermore, 'policy-makers began to fear and grew in the conviction that if the beast of "public opinion" was to be disturbed by a diplomatic pin-prick in any one of its many joints, the whole might wake from its slumber with uncontrollable results'.[2] Joseph

---

[1]   There has been a study of this kind undertaken by S. B. Spies, *Methods of barbarism?: Roberts and Kitchener and civilians in the Boer republics January 1900–May 1902*, Cape Town 1977. Spies, however, focuses on the treatment of Boer civilians by the British army, such as the use of concentration camps and farm burning.

[2]   A. N. Porter, *The origins of the South African war: Joseph Chamberlain and the diplomacy of imperialism 1895–9*, Manchester 1980, 18–19, 27. For a brief look at the development of

Chamberlain, who in 1895 became the colonial secretary, was well aware of this problem, but felt that the new working-class-dominated electorate, which to him constituted 'public opinion',[3] could be harnessed if approached carefully. At a time when Britain appeared to be faced with a plethora of foreign and domestic difficulties, Chamberlain, himself a convinced imperialist,[4] sought to promote closer ties with the empire as a way of offsetting Britain's problems. To Chamberlain the electorate needed to be made aware that the security of the empire was vital to Britain's future well-being. The fortuitous outbreak of the crisis in South Africa thus allowed Chamberlain the opportunity to 'educate' public opinion and propagandise on behalf of the empire, mainly by using parliamentary Blue Books, the press and extra-parliamentary speeches.[5] The message would then, Chamberlain believed, somehow filter down to the electorate. Only when public opinion was considered to be educated enough would the government then act one way or the other to preserve British interests.[6] Throughout the South African crisis and conflict, politicians, and one or two soldiers, constantly referred to the needs or attitudes of public or popular opinion, or even the people. Few, if any, actually sat down and defined what they meant. Nevertheless, to them public opinion was real enough and its views and moods had to be interpreted somehow. What criteria they used in this instance seems largely unknown, but even before the South African war began the perceived requirements of public opinion, alongside the interests of party, were major considerations in the decision-making process, factors which the generals themselves also needed to ponder.[7] In this respect the pre-war crisis is particularly illuminating because it simmered for four years and thus provides a good opportunity to evaluate how Britain's politicians and generals formulated military policy, and how far the generals were attuned to the constraints under which the politicians operated.

These considerations were just as prominent during the war itself and further complicated the government's relations with the generals, as did the fact that the war dragged on far beyond pre-war expectations. War usually

public opinion during the mid nineteenth century see Jonathan Parry, *The rise and fall of Liberal government in Victorian Britain*, London 1996, ch. i.

[3] Porter, *Origins*, 64.

[4] Ibid. ch. ii; Peter Marsh, *Joseph Chamberlain: entrepreneur in politics*, London 1994, 406–8; Iain R. Smith, *The origins of the South African war 1899–1902*, London 1996, 72–5.

[5] For more on how politicians used public speech-making and the press see H. C. G. Matthew, 'Rhetoric and politics in Britain, 1860–1950', in P. J. Waller (ed.), *Politics and social change in modern Britain: essays presented to A. F. Thompson*, Brighton 1987, 34–58. For a view on the growing importance of the press in shaping the 'public sphere' see James Vernon, *Politics and the people: a study in English political culture, c. 1815–1867*, Cambridge 1993, ch. iii, esp. 142–60.

[6] See also A. N. Porter, 'Lord Salisbury, Mr Chamberlain and South Africa, 1895–99', *Journal of Imperial and Commonwealth History* i (1972), 3–26.

[7] For a discussion of this problem in the late Victorian period see W. S. Hamer, *The British army: civil–military relations 1885–1905*, Oxford 1970, ch. ii and pp. 223–4.

confuses, and often blurs, the boundaries between civil and military responsibility, especially when extraneous political factors emerge and oblige the government to take a keener interest in the management of that war. This leads us to the second important factor. In South Africa a difficult constitutional question arose which, as Robert Blake notes, also occurred during the First World War: 'How could the ultimate responsibility of the Cabinet be reconciled with the need to give military experts freedom to make military decisions?'[8] This question is of course one of supreme relevance in a parliamentary democracy. In fact, it is a perennial problem and explains why civil–military relations were often problematic throughout the conflict in South Africa.

For historians of the late Victorian army the study of civil–military relations has usually meant looking at the persistent controversies arising from the army reforms enacted between 1870 and 1872.[9] This is perhaps understandable since the continual balancing act between the requirements of party politics and the demands of the army are inherent in Britain's parliamentary system. Thus attention has been fixed firmly on peacetime disputes to the detriment of our understanding of civil–military relations under the strain of war.

That this is so should come as no surprise when it is remembered that colonial warfare remains the poor relation of British military history.[10] Where work has been done on civil–military relations during wartime, the focus has been on the two world wars of the twentieth century, particularly the First World War,[11] which has rather overshadowed anything that happened before 1914. A further manifestation of this tendency can be seen in the works of those scholars interested in the Edwardian period. For them it is the consequences of the South African war which are important, for the light shed on the formative years of institutions such as the general staff and the committee of imperial defence and how Britain prepared for a future European conflict.[12]

It is generally forgotten, however, just how extensive the South African war was. The renowned military thinker and Boer war veteran, J. F. C. Fuller, classed the South African war as one of the 'roots of armageddon',

---

8 *The private papers of Douglas Haig 1914–1919*, ed. Robert Blake, London 1952, 33.
9 Hamer, *British army*, passim; E. M. Spiers, *The late Victorian army 1868–1902*, Manchester 1992, chs i–iii, vi; Paul Smith (ed.), *Government and the armed forces in Britain 1856–1990*, London 1996, chs i–iii.
10 A point made recently by James Belich in *The Victorian interpretation of racial conflict: the Maori, the British, and the New Zealand wars*, Montreal 1989, 12.
11 See, for example, David French, *British strategy and war aims, 1914–16*, London 1986, and *The strategy of the Lloyd George coalition, 1916–18*, Oxford 1995; D. R. Woodward, *Lloyd George and the generals*, Newark, Del. 1983.
12 N. J. D'Ombrain, *War machinery and high policy: defence administration in peacetime Britain 1902–1914*, London 1973, ch. i; John Gooch, *The plans of war: the general staff and British military strategy c. 1900–1916*, London 1974, chs i–ii.

acknowledging it as an early rehearsal for events between 1914 and 1918.[13] Indeed, it ought to be emphasised that the war stood at the watershed of military development, in which aspects of both the traditional and the modern reacted together. The South African war therefore stands out in two ways: as a precursor of the First World War; and as the last of the great colonial conflicts.

The South African war demonstrated that the late Victorian way of preparing for, and conducting, warfare was generally no longer applicable. The scale and duration of the conflict revealed that the existing arrangements, so arduously constructed and bitterly fought over by politicians and generals beforehand, had largely failed when confronted by the realities of a major conflict. Thus a radical overhaul of Britain's defence apparatus was called for, one that would fit the new diplomatic and strategic realities of the early twentieth century. In consequence, not only did the South African war lead to the reform of administrative structures, it also proved to be the catalyst for a fundamental reform of the army itself, which ensured that Britain was prepared both for a major colonial conflict and the possibility of war in Europe.

Moreover, the war was also a tactical laboratory in the sense that the British were fighting an enemy armed with the latest weaponry, which was used with skill and finesse, and which allowed European observers the opportunity to assess, almost for the first time, the new technology in action. Although the Boers were not the first to dig trenches and use barbed wire, they were certainly the first enemy Britain had faced that used them in conjunction with smokeless powder, magazine rifles and rapid-firing artillery. Much of the tactical baggage the British army carried with it on colonial campaigns was no longer relevant and the army had to adapt accordingly. Overall, this transition was achieved remarkably quickly.[14]

The South African war therefore has several distinctive features. One other, which made the situation more complex, was the existence of political authorities other than the British government. The high commissioner for South Africa wielded substantial political authority in his own right and in the case of Sir Alfred Milner this authority was used to further distinct personal aims. In addition to the two Boer republics there were also two semi-independent British colonies whose interests could not be ignored.

S. E. Finer has pointed out that warfare expands the political powers of the military, which is best demonstrated when politicians have tried to oppose the army's conduct of war.[15] In essence, the military became another 'political' authority in South Africa which meant that four interests competed in varying degrees for influence and the right to be heard. Moreover relations between Milner and General Lord Kitchener were embittered further by an

---

13 J. F. C. Fuller, *The conduct of war 1789–1961*, London 1979, 139–40.
14 For a summary of these developments see Spiers, *Late Victorian army*, 314–18.
15 S. E. Finer, *The man on horseback: the role of the military in politics*, 2nd edn, London 1988, 64.

ideological dispute over the future of South Africa itself. Thus the controversial question of control is central to this study: that is, how far were the politicians prepared to let the soldiers exercise complete control over the conduct of operations; and how far were the generals prepared to resist what they regarded as undue interference. This issue was complicated greatly by the onset of guerilla warfare which blurred the distinctions between military and political responsibility. The generals, however, had one great advantage: they were popular heroes and public opinion refused to believe they were anything else. This factor significantly handicapped the politicians in their attempts to over-rule the generals and has not been stressed before. In evaluating the major role played by the army in the decision-making process during the South African war, this study will add an extra dimension to the political histories of the period.

II

Throughout the nineteenth century the British empire continued to grow. From the 1870s, however, much of this expansion was taken up in response to the perceived threat posed by European rivals, who were now empire-building themselves. By the 1890s many in Britain were concerned about how the empire – the world's largest – could be maintained and defended in the face of foreign competition which not only menaced the imperial frontiers, but was also undermining Britain economically. By the end of the century it was now obvious to many commentators and interested parties that Britain was no longer the pre-eminent world power.[16]

The British empire was spread throughout the globe, and the political structures of the imperial domain were as diverse and disparate as the empire itself. There was no overarching form of imperial government because the empire had been acquired and developed in a number of ways. By 1899 there were three main forms of imperial administration: foremost were the white, self-governing dominions and colonies; then there was India, ruled by a viceroy and with its own government; lastly, there were the tropical colonies ruled by British officials both directly and indirectly.[17] Some of the imperial governors were considered to be so powerful they were given the unofficial title of 'proconsul', which denoted their semi-independence and 'extraordinary capacity to shape the periphery'.[18] Through force of personality, ready

[16] For a useful summary see Peter Marshall (ed.), *The Cambridge illustrated history of the British empire*, Cambridge 1996, chs ii–iii. More specifically see Ronald Hyam, *Britain's imperial century, 1815–1914*, 2nd edn, Basingstoke 1993; Bernard Porter, *The Lion's share: a short history of British imperialism 1850–1983*, 2nd edn, London 1984, chs i–v.

[17] For more on this see A. J. Stockwell, 'Power, authority, and freedom', in Marshall, *Cambridge illustrated history*, 147–84.

[18] John Benyon, 'Overlords of empire? British "pro-consular imperialism" in comparative perspective', *JICH* xix (1990), 164–202 at p. 165.

opportunity and their 'portmanteau' commissions which gave them considerable local authority, these men, of whom Lord Cromer in Egypt, Lord Curzon in India and Sir Alfred Milner in South Africa were the most prominent at the time, ensured their territories became 'significant power-systems or proto-states in their own right'.[19] There were several factors which enabled the proconsuls to develop the importance of their territories and at the same time their own position: first was the strategic value of the territory, second, 'the presence of serious communal cleavages' within the territory which required rigorous imperial supervision, thirdly, frontiers which had not been properly defined or closed and therefore were 'turbulent', fourthly, the proximity of a rival European power, and lastly, the fact that proconsuls had the requisite authority to intervene 'in the interests of regional security'.[20] The proconsuls were consequently very powerful officials, more so it seems than ordinary governors of less prestigious locations. At times, the British authorities found it difficult to keep these men under control and were obliged to endorse proconsular initiatives which London first thought either ill-advised or too thoughtless. The policies of Lords Lytton and Curzon on the Indian frontiers with Afghanistan and Tibet in 1878 and 1904 respectively fall into this category; as does Sir Bartle Frere's policy in regard to Zululand in 1879 and, to a certain extent, Milner's actions in South Africa in 1899.

The era of imperial expansion meant the British army found itself in almost continuous employment against colonial enemies, and for all its modern trappings the South African war was essentially a colonial war and the last of many campaigns which had punctuated Queen Victoria's long reign. According to Colonel Charles Callwell's authoritative text-book on colonial warfare, there were three main classes of campaign. The first consisted of campaigns of conquest and annexation, which meant the invasion of a foreign territory or external war. The second class comprised campaigns to suppress rebellion or internal wars, fought on British territory. Finally, the third class constituted punitive expeditions to redress a grievance or to remove a dangerous threat, which in theory meant that the campaign was of short duration and involved the immediate evacuation of enemy territory.[21]

In principle at least, once the decision for war was made the military were considered supreme and completely in charge. This had much to do with the fact that the British army fought, and was expected to fight, in numerous regions with a wide variety of terrains and climates, which ultimately precluded contingency planning. The commanding officer was thus personally responsible for ensuring every aspect of the army's requirements for a particular region and also for the conduct of the campaign itself. With one or two

19 Ibid. 165–70.
20 Ibid. 170–1.
21 Colonel Charles Callwell, *Small wars: a tactical textbook for imperial soldiers*, 1906 edn, repr. London 1990, 25–33; Brian Bond, 'Introduction', in Brian Bond (ed.), *Victorian military campaigns*, 2nd edn, London 1994, 3–29 at pp. 17–18.

exceptions most Victorian commanders were free from close political scrutiny during a campaign and could conduct it how they thought fit.[22] Limited communications were generally the main reason why this was so, but in certain cases politicians felt the need to interfere. Direct interference occurred on several occasions and could be applied in numerous ways: by the British government, by the Indian government, or by representatives on the spot, such as through a governor-general or high commissioner. Examples of each type can be seen during the first Boer war (1880–1), the Abyssinian expedition (1867), and the conquest of the Sudan (1896–8). The respective reasons for interfering were first to carry out secret diplomacy with the enemy; the desire to secure political representation and ultimately control over the expedition; and the need to ensure the expedition was as cost-effective as possible. Commanding officers usually resented such interference. In the examples mentioned above, the politicians prevented the army from inflicting a decisive defeat on the enemy following a series of minor but embarrassing reverses. In Abyssinia the presence of a 'political officer', who had authority to question military decisions and suggest alternatives, caused offence. In the Sudan civilian financial retrenchment meant the possibility of an inglorious end to a campaign. All these are examples of direct interference, but there was also the possibility of indirect hindrance as well. In 1884, the vacillation of the Liberal government beforehand severely handicapped the expedition sent to relieve General Gordon in Khartoum.

For most generals the successful command of an expeditionary force was the surest way to fame, fortune and rapid promotion. The fear of having their ambitions thwarted and, for that matter, their army possibly jeopardised, by the need to defer to political considerations which they might consider onerous and unnecessary, caused many commanders much anguish.

III

One last factor and one which is important in our understanding of civil–military relations is the question of personalities. The very nature of colonial campaigning, and indeed the British style of warfare, placed great emphasis on the role of individual commanders. Most campaigns were small-scale affairs with the commanding officer often leading from the front, aided by a small staff selected by himself. Colonial warfare was essentially personal warfare in that it was often fought at close quarters and demanded the presence of officers whose personal qualities were displayed for all to see.[23] In such

---

[22] Ibid. 19–20.
[23] Spiers, *Late Victorian army*, 112, 287–8, 299–300. For an examination of the continuing premium placed on individuals and the 'human battlefield' see Tim Travers, *The killing ground: the British army, the western front and the emergence of modern warfare 1900–1918*, London 1990, chs ii–iii.

campaigns the three main military protagonists of the South African war, Lords Wolseley, Roberts and Kitchener, gained vital experience of politicians and the factors which governed political decision-making. All three had varying experiences, although both the two great rivals, Wolseley and Roberts, were at one time or another let down by the political authorities of the time; whereas Kitchener was the only one to endure direct political supervision during the conduct of a campaign. The early years, therefore, provided the foundations upon which the generals subsequently managed their relations with politicians.

Lord Wolseley was the most experienced campaigner, in the field and in the War Office and, consequently, the most inveterate hater of politicians.[24] Yet, for the most part, Wolseley's military operations were free of political interference. This had a great deal to do with the fact that his wars were short: his main campaign against the Ashanti (1874) lasted about two months; the Egyptian war (1882) three weeks; and the Sudan operation (1884–5) about five months. Moreover, Wolseley was often granted full political powers, a common occurrence owing to poor communications with London or the lack of local imperial and colonial authority. Soldiers were often used in political capacities, their prestige expected to overawe or charm recalcitrant natives or colonists. In south-east Africa (1879–80), Wolseley was given power in order to pacify Zululand after the recent war and quieten disgruntled Boers in the Transvaal, who were agitating against the annexation of their country in 1877.

Two colonial episodes intensified Wolseley's hostility towards politicians: first, the Transvaal crisis (1880–1) and secondly the Gordon relief expedition (1884–5). In December 1880 the Transvaal Boers rebelled when the new Liberal government refused to restore their independence.[25] Wolseley's successor, General George Colley, turned out to be a poor choice owing to his lack of both political and military skills. In the first weeks of 1881, he suffered a series of defeats and on 27 February was killed at Majuba Hill and his force routed. During the crisis, Colley's relations with the colonial secretary, Lord Kimberley, were never straightforward. For nearly a month he was kept in the dark about government attempts to negotiate with the Boers, owing to divisions within the cabinet and the need for secrecy. Colley only learned of these moves towards the end of January 1881, when the government used him as an intermediary with the Boers. Kimberley and Gladstone were angered, however, by Colley's apparent reluctance to negotiate properly and his continuing military operations. His conduct during this time has generated some debate amongst historians: did he intentionally frustrate chances

---

24 For a detailed account of Wolseley's career as an army reformer see Halik Kochanski, 'Field-Marshal Viscount Wolseley: a reformer at the War Office, 1871–1900', unpubl. PhD diss. London 1996.

25 Joseph Lehmann, All Sir Garnet: a life of Field-Marshal Lord Wolseley, London 1966, 278–9.

of peace in order to redeem his reputation and that of the country? Or did he make justifiable military decisions in the wake of the government's indecision which left him confused about the direction of policy?[26] Whether Colley acted properly or not, for Wolseley the defeat at Majuba was still a major embarrassment, particularly as Colley was considered an outstanding member of Wolseley's ring of favoured officers. But what really upset Wolseley was the government's decision to send his rival, Roberts, to succeed Colley rather than himself. Wolseley rightly complained that he had experience of South Africa, whereas Roberts did not. Wolseley later described the decision as 'the greatest blow I had ever received'. To make his misery complete the government concluded a peace settlement with the Boers without avenging the defeat at Majuba.[27]

In Egypt (1882) and the Sudan (1884), Wolseley was given licence to proceed as he saw fit. The Egyptian campaign culminated in Wolseley's stunning victory at Tel-el Kebir and the accolade that he was Britain's 'only general'. Events did not go as smoothly in the Sudan where Wolseley commanded the relief force ordered to rescue General Gordon in Khartoum. It was during this ill-fated expedition that Wolseley actually received a direct order from the government which interfered with his management of a campaign. Fearful of Wolseley's impetuosity, the government forbade him to lead the relief force itself and for the first time he had to direct his army rather than lead it from the front.[28] Throughout the Gordon relief expedition, Wolseley's journal and letters home revealed him to be an inveterate hater of Gladstone and the radicals. His diatribes, described by one historian as 'an almost pathological hatred of representative government',[29] reflect more his overstrained mind and political predilections (he described himself as a 'jingo of the jingos'), rather than any frustrations caused by political interference during the campaign. Wolseley was a close friend of Gordon and had called for an expedition months before Gladstone's ministers finally gave the necessary orders. Such political dilatoriness infuriated Wolseley, who berated Gladstone and the radicals, in one instance, for being 'churchwardens and parish vestrymen more than Englishmen'.[30] Moreover, for a second time, Wolseley lost a

---

[26] For a view condemning Colley see D. M. Schreuder, *Gladstone and Kruger: Liberal government and colonial home rule 1880–85*, London 1969, 109–10, 114–18, 122, 130–3; for alternative views see Joseph Lehmann, *The first Boer War*, 2nd edn, London 1985, 162, 230–5; Brian Bond, 'The South African war, 1880–81', in Bond, *Victorian military campaigns*, 199–240 at pp. 219–20, 222–4.

[27] Lehmann, *First Boer War*, 265. Wolseley still harped on about the peace settlement when in the Sudan: *The letters of Lord and Lady Wolseley 1870–1911*, ed. Sir George Arthur, London 1922, 154

[28] *In relief of Gordon: Lord Wolseley's campaign journal of the Khartoum relief expedition 1884–1885*, ed. Adrian Preston, London 1967, p. xxxvi; Lehmann, *All Sir Garnet*, 366–7.

[29] See *The Gladstone diaries*, ed. H. C. G. Matthew, Oxford 1990, x, p. lxxx.

[30] Cited in Lehmann, *All Sir Garnet*, 282. For more of Wolseley's vituperation see *In relief of Gordon*, entries for 4, 5 Dec. 1884, 17, 19 Feb. 1885, at pp. 80–1, 147, 149. See also Wolseley to his wife, 24 Nov. 1884, in *Letters of Lord and Lady Wolseley*, 131.

favoured subordinate: General Herbert Stewart was killed leading the Gordon relief column, which although it did not carry the humiliation attached to Colley's death, was nevertheless personally painful.

Thereafter, Wolseley spent the rest of his career in the War Office (apart from an interlude in 1890–5 as the commander in Ireland), filling a number of high military posts which culminated in his promotion to commander-in-chief in 1895. Wolseley reached the pinnacle of his career an embittered man. Not only had politicians let him and the country down in 1881 and 1884–5, they had also proved unreceptive to his ideas regarding army reform. He deplored both Liberal and Conservative governments' reluctance to provide funds needed to ensure the efficiency of the army, and the growing influence politicians exerted over its administration. To him, politicians were beholden to the electorate and none the wiser for it. Thus, writing in 1890 he said:

> Party government nowadays does not mean the leading or the endeavour to lead public opinion so much as the following of public opinion and the giving effect to it. The worst side of it is the controlling of public opinion, diverting it into side issues so as to avoid expenditure which would be inconvenient from a party standpoint.[31]

When experts like himself offered advice on military matters which did not correspond with the policy requirements of the government, it was usually ignored. Consequently he grew ever more intolerant of politicians and the party system which was to have dire results when he had to work closely with the government during the South African crisis.[32] By then Wolseley was at the tail-end of his career, although the crisis presented a last opportunity to redeem not only his reputation, but that of his 'ring' and the reforms he so heartily endorsed.

IV

By 1895 Lord Roberts was Wolseley's only rival to the claim of being the greatest general of the late Victorian period. Unlike Wolseley, Roberts had spent the vast bulk of his career in India, which culminated in his promotion to commander-in-chief, a post he held for eight years (1885–93). In 1895 Roberts succeeded Wolseley as commander-in-chief in Ireland. Despite Roberts's ability and desire to acquire the friendship and patronage of politicians, his relations with some were at times problematic.

Roberts achieved lasting fame during the invasion of Afghanistan between 1878–80, but at the same time fell foul of politicians from both parties.

---

[31] Cited in Hamer, *British army*, 219.
[32] Spiers, *Late Victorian army*, 154–6.

During the early stages of the war, he commanded the Kurram Field Force and was given full political powers throughout the territory occupied by his army. These he failed to use properly when he made promises to local chiefs which the viceroy and the British government had no intention of keeping. Lord Lytton, the viceroy and Roberts's chief backer, admonished him for his injudicious remarks, and when Roberts occupied Kabul in December 1879 during another phase of the campaign, Lytton took no chances and sent him a political adviser. According to Roberts's most recent biographer 'Roberts was not wrong in seeing this as a reflection on his conduct of political affairs hitherto ... [and] he did not cease to resent his [the political officer's] appointment.'[33] While in Kabul, Roberts tried and executed a number of Afghans for the earlier murder of the British representative and his mission. In Britain, some radicals in parliament accused him of committing an atrocity and then launched a personal attack on him because he was associated with Lytton, the nominee of the Conservative government. When the Liberals took office in April 1880, the attacks continued and following the end of the war the government showed their disapproval of the affair by granting a financial reward which Roberts considered derisory.[34] Ironically perhaps, both Roberts and Wolseley fell out with Gladstone's government at about the same time. Roberts later complained that: 'It would seem as if I had been made the scapegoat of party strife, partly from the antagonism of the present Government to the policy which brought about the Afghan War, and partly also from an unfounded belief that I had allied myself to their opponents as a political partisan.'[35] Matters were not helped when Roberts was appointed to succeed Colley in South Africa. He arrived in Cape Town to discover the government had made peace and that his services were no longer required: such was his disgust that he did not even set foot on South African soil but stayed on the boat until it returned to Britain. Roberts was mortified by the government's decision not to avenge Majuba,[36] which was a major reason behind his continual requests for employment in South Africa in 1899.

Roberts's last campaign in Asia was in Burma between 1886 and 1887, although from his point of view it could hardly be dignified by the term campaign. He spent only three months in Burma but managed to organise local operations and a military police force against the activities of rebels and bandits or dacoits. Roberts's spell in command was characterised by good relations with the political officer, Sir Charles Bernard, and with the viceroy

[33] *Roberts in India: the military papers of Field-Marshal Lord Roberts 1876–1893*, ed. Brian Robson, Stroud 1993, 113–14; for Lytton's earlier reprimands see pp. 46–8, 97.
[34] Evidently it was less than Wolseley received for his services in Ashanti. Ironically, Wolseley felt he had received a derisory reward from Disraeli's outgoing government in 1880, despite his considerable services as an administrator in Natal (1875–7) and Cyprus (1879), in addition to his efforts in Zululand and the Transvaal mentioned earlier: Lehmann, *All Sir Garnet*, 283.
[35] Cited in David James, *Lord Roberts*, London 1954, 174. See also pp. 140–5.
[36] Lehmann, *First Boer War*, 281.

himself.[37] In reality, the Burma operations were but a footnote to his long service in India.

In 1885 Roberts was promoted commander-in-chief thanks largely to the Conservatives taking office in June. Normally he would have held the post for five years but in the end did not leave India until 1893. The circumstances of his departure were not entirely happy because he returned to Britain without an active command. In 1890 Roberts had lost the chance to succeed Wolseley as adjutant-general, having been offered the post by the Conservative government, which then rescinded the offer when it proved too difficult to find a suitable successor. Roberts was asked to extend his period as commander-in-chief for two years, to which he agreed and therefore lost the chance of becoming adjutant-general. Thereafter, the government proved to be both inconsiderate and unaccommodating, denying him home leave and then asking him to extend his service in India once again. This time he refused and instead of being offered a prominent position in the War Office, he was asked to become the governor of either Gibraltar or Malta. As these were semi-retirement posts Roberts declined the offer.[38] Despite the clamour in the press to find him suitable employment, it was two years before he was given a fitting appointment, this time the Irish command. However, with Wolseley now the commander-in-chief in Britain, Roberts's prospects looked bleak: for all he knew his career was over.[39]

Despite the ungracious treatment meted out by both parties, Roberts maintained his political contacts, managing to gain the confidence and friendship of several viceroys from Lord Lytton onwards. Lord Dufferin described himself as Roberts's 'true and faithful friend', and his successor, Lord Lansdowne, became a close and personal friend who corresponded with Roberts until the latter's death in 1914.[40] The connection with Lansdowne would bear much fruit for Roberts in 1899.

V

Lord Kitchener was the most recent addition to the Victorian military pantheon when the South African war commenced in 1899. Compared to his illustrious colleagues, Kitchener was an inexperienced general, his one major command being the conquest of the Sudan between 1896 and 1898. During that time Kitchener had enjoyed a close working relationship with Lord Cromer, the British resident in Egypt and effective overlord of Egyptian affairs, in whom Kitchener gained an assiduous backer but a miserly and overbearing master. Cromer's oppressive demands did not however cause Kitchener too

---

37 James, *Lord Roberts*, 201–3; *Roberts in India*, 364.
38 *Roberts in India*, 233, 330; James, *Lord Roberts*, 222–6.
39 James, *Lord Roberts*, 240–8.
40 Ibid. 221–2.

many problems. Like Cromer, Kitchener shared the same determination to reconquer the Sudan as cost-effectively as possible, and such was his diligence that he earned from Cromer the encomium that he was 'cool and sensible and knows his job thoroughly and is not at all inclined to be rash'.[41]

Be that as it may, there were times when this partnership was seriously disturbed. For Cromer the war, far from being an opportunity for fame and glory as it was for Kitchener, was nothing more than an ugly intrusion into his ordered world of finance and politics.[42] Completely unwilling to relax his tight control of the purse strings, Cromer imposed such constraints on Kitchener that even he, normally the most economical of soldiers, eventually rebelled. In late 1897 relations between the two reached their nadir when Kitchener asked for more money to consolidate his territorial gains. Fearing this would upset all his achievements, Cromer refused and told Lord Salisbury that: 'In moments of retrospection I tear my hair over the hurried decision of March 1896 [the decision to invade the Sudan]. It has upset all my calculations and introduced an entirely new factor into Egyptian politics.' Furthermore, he even felt it unnecessary to advance on Khartoum, as the anticipated loss of life and money would not be worth it.[43] Kitchener was so frustrated by Cromer's indifference he even offered his resignation, although he later withdrew it. With his ambitions apparently thwarted by Cromer's obduracy, Kitchener's mental health suffered. He explained to a friend: 'You have no idea what continual anxiety, worry, and strain I have through it all. I do not think that I can stand much more, and I feel so completely done up that I can hardly go on and wish I were dead.'[44] Only when the enemy sent their forces against the Egyptian army in January 1898 did Kitchener finally get his way. After his victory, he was no longer willing to play second fiddle and tolerate the shackles of political control; he would not, in Magnus's words, 'be scolded like a schoolboy by Cromer'. Kitchener demonstrated his independence by ruling the Sudan on his own, without the benefit of Cromer's experience and advice.[45] By the time the Sudan was finally pacified in November 1899, the war in South Africa had raged for nearly two months. Such was his fame, Kitchener could expect fresh employment before very long. By the end of the year he was on his way to South Africa.

At the outbreak of the South African war, all three generals had reached a crucial point in their careers. For Wolseley, the crisis and war in South Africa provided a significant opportunity to redeem a career which had lost meaning. Here was the chance at last to avenge Colley's defeat and death at Majuba, to wipe out the stain on his and the army's honour, and show his

[41] Cited in Trevor Royle, *The Kitchener enigma*, London 1985, 106.
[42] This section is based on Philip Magnus, *Kitchener: portrait of an imperialist*, Harmondsworth 1968, 134–46.
[43] Ibid. 136–7.
[44] Ibid. 139.
[45] Ibid. 183–9.

detractors that the army reforms with which he was closely associated had been worthwhile. These sentiments were largely shared by Roberts, who hoped to erase his own South African humiliation and, in the process, revitalise a career heading for the doldrums. For Kitchener, employment in South Africa would provide pastures new for fame and glory, and, hopefully, without the restraining hand of a Cromer to hold him back. All three, therefore, had something to gain from the new crisis in South Africa, whether it be redemption, invigoration or distinction. For each general the critical lessons and experiences of the past would now determine the nature of their relations with the political authorities, and whether this was to mean success or failure.

1

Managing the Boer Threat: 1895–9

Lord Salisbury, the prime minister, once remarked 'I have the greatest respect for the advice of soldiers as regards the conduct of war, none whatever for their opinions as to the policy which dictates war.'[1] This view clearly enunciated the way in which the British government approached a succession of diplomatic crises with the Transvaal between 1895 and 1899. Each prompted attempts by soldiers and politicians to define the role and strength of the South African garrison in a possible conflict with either one or both of the Boer republics. Until 1895 the garrison's main function was the defence of Cape Town against seaborne attack by imperial rivals. However, from December 1895, as Anglo-Transvaal relations deteriorated, the garrison's role was directed away from the wider aspects of imperial defence and towards the Transvaal. For the British, this change in outlook accentuated divisions between the civil and military authorities. By 1899 these divisions had contributed to the formulation of a compromise strategy designed to deal with the Boers. Although this strategy neither united the politicians and generals, nor engendered real confidence in its ability to end Boer defiance, it nevertheless influenced the British reaction to the final crisis of 1899.

The persistent military dimension to the South African question has received little attention from historians, even though the generals were constantly consulted by the politicians as the crisis unfolded and contributed to the formulation of policy. The aim of this chapter, therefore, is to unravel the contribution of the government's military advisors, and highlight the growing dispute between the soldiers and politicians which affected the way Britain approached its greatest colonial crisis.

Gauging the threat

The economic power of the Transvaal, which developed following the discovery of gold on the Witwatersrand in the late 1880s, threatened the ties that bound Britain, Cape Colony and Natal, and promised the Boers political hegemony in South Africa.[2] The combined threat of a powerful and potentially hostile neighbour, and a Cape Afrikaner population still mindful of the

---

1 Quoted in Hamer, *British army*, 31.
2 Ronald Robinson and John Gallagher, with Alice Denny, *Africa and the Victorians: the official mind of imperialism*, 2nd edn, London 1981, 410–20.

war in 1880–1, increased British military concerns, particularly for the safety of the vital strategic position of Cape Town. In 1884 a War Office memorandum had argued, 'It is impossible, for political reasons, to create a Gibraltar out of the Cape Town peninsula, and [thus] the permanent retention of the peninsula . . . is dependent upon the maintenance of British ascendancy in all South African colonies.'[3] Nevertheless the strength of the garrison was not reviewed and, until 1896, it remained at between 3,500 and 4,000 men, divided almost equally between Cape Colony and Natal.[4] Conflict with the Boers was hardly considered as more pressing problems surfaced in other parts of the world.

British concerns were heightened, however, by the increased interest shown in the region by Germany and France, as the booming economy of the Transvaal formed a natural focus for investment. Cecil Rhodes, founder of the British South Africa Company (1889) and prime minister of Cape Colony (1890–5), also viewed these developments with alarm. He wished to create a British South African federation dominated by English-speaking colonists, and believed this might be achieved by overthrowing the Transvaal's government. In 1895, during an economic dispute with Cape Colony, the Transvaal demonstrated its power by preventing Cape goods from entering the country over the Vaal river railway bridges. This quarrel, the 'Drifts Crisis', obliged Rhodes to call on the help of the British government, which eventually forced the Boers to back down. However, to Rhodes it became a matter of necessity that the regime in Pretoria be removed. Rhodes therefore attempted to overthrow the Transvaal government by sparking an uprising in Johannesburg, the centre of the gold industry.[5]

Johannesburg was a city of foreigners, known as Uitlanders, whose industry and taxes had done much to create the Transvaal's wealth. Most Uitlanders were of British origin and their concentration in Johannesburg frightened the Boers into believing their numbers vast. Consequently, the Uitlanders were denied political rights which caused great resentment. The size of the Uitlander community was in turn exaggerated by the Uitlanders themselves as part of their demands for greater political autonomy. Kruger himself, the Transvaal President, exaggerated Uitlander numbers to convince the Boers that their homeland was under threat.[6] In December 1895 Rhodes and his co-conspirators in the mining industry attempted to use Uitlander resentment to ignite a rebellion, but the forces of his lieutenant, Jameson, were easily defeated by the Boers.[7]

Just before the Raid, a Unionist ministry had taken power in Britain. The

3 Schreuder, Gladstone and Kruger, 15.
4 Parliamentary papers (1904), xl, Cd. 1789, 'The Royal Commission on the war in South Africa', 21.
5 Porter, Origins, 55–6; Smith, Origins, 56–66.
6 For Uitlander numbers see J. S. Marais, The fall of Kruger's republic, Oxford 1961, 1–3.
7 Robinson and Gallagher, Africa and the Victorians, 438–61; Porter, Origins, 95–121; Smith, Origins, ch. iii.

new colonial secretary, Joseph Chamberlain, was fully conscious of the need for Britain to exert her supremacy in South Africa and elsewhere in the world. The defeat of Jameson, and the Kaiser's congratulatory telegram to Kruger, were keenly felt. Chamberlain urged Lord Salisbury to consider a vigorous act 'to soothe the wounded pride of the nation', and recommended as one response 'the immediate preparation of a force of troops for Capetown sufficient to make us the masters of the situation in S. Africa'.[8]

In early 1896 Chamberlain's deputy, Lord Selborne, considered southern Africa in the aftermath of the Jameson Raid. For Selborne, the government needed to formulate a policy by which British prestige and supremacy could be reasserted. In two memoranda Selborne established that Britain had to persuade Kruger to alleviate the lot of the Uitlanders, and mollify Cape Afrikaner opinion which had been antagonised by Rhodes and the Raid. In his view, the main long-term objective was to create a confederation, which might bind South Africa to Britain; he decided the time had come for Britain to assert its power before it was too late.[9]

Military officials also began to review the South African situation in a similarly individualistic manner; military responses were unco-ordinated and there existed no machinery to encourage a coherent appraisal. When the Unionists took power they inherited a scheme to reorganise the office of commander-in-chief (C-in-C). Since 1856 this office had been filled by the queen's cousin, the duke of Cambridge, who was the principal military adviser to the secretary of state for war and head of the army. Under the Cardwell reforms of 1870–2, the duke's powers were somewhat curtailed and the ultimate authority of the secretary of state over the army was officially recognised. Nevertheless, the duke still retained immense authority by dint of his royal connections, his virtually unassailable position in the War Office, and because he remained the sole source of official advice to his political chief, especially as he controlled virtually all sources of information. Despite his residual power and prestige, the duke's relations with the politicians were poor because he persisted in his hostility to Cardwell's reforms, such as short service, the localisation of regiments and the abolition of purchase. Moreover, to defend his authority he attempted to thwart any perceived intrusion by the politicians into what he considered professional and technical matters, as his squabble with Hugh Childers over the territorialisation of the regiments during Gladstone's second ministry testified. His continual complaints about Cardwell's system and his obstructionism meant that the duke, in Hamer's words, 'helped keep the attention of soldiers, politicians, and the service departments upon domestic issues and away from the broader

8 Chamberlain to Salisbury, 4 Jan. 1896, Hatfield House, Salisbury correspondence, fo. 43. South Africa was not the only area of concern; Britain and the USA were at loggerheads over British claims along the border between Venezuela and British Guiana.
9 Memo. by Selborne, [Jan. ?] 1896, in *The crisis of British power: the imperial and naval papers of the second earl of Selborne 1895–1910*, ed. George Boyce, London 1990, 30–2; Robinson and Gallagher, *Africa and the Victorians*, 434–7.

considerations of military policy and imperial defence. A dead horse was being whipped with a vengeance'.[10] The duke was finally eased out of office in 1895 by the incoming Unionist government after it became clear that his position and conservatism were hindering modern developments within the army. Consequently, the order-in-council of November 1895 limited the power of the C-in-C in order to secure civilian control over that office, and marked the end of a conflict that had started with Cardwell's reforms.

However, the government then had little alternative but to appoint Lord Wolseley in the duke's place, even though he shared his predecessor's views regarding the power and authority of the C-in-C's office: General Buller was lower in rank and less respected, although he had administered the army for many years; Lord Roberts had spent his career in India and could not match Wolseley's knowledge of the home army. Once appointed, however, Wolseley made no effort to accept his position and preferred to circumvent the constraints imposed by the order-in-council. He was helped in this by the fact that his duties were imprecise and ambiguous. The order-in-council stated that the C-in-C would now supervise the various military departments, under the adjutant-general, the quartermaster-general, the inspector-general of fortifications and the inspector-general of ordnance. But the government was unable to state clearly what 'supervision' meant. On paper, Wolseley was *primus inter pares*; in practice, as the senior officer in the British army and by virtue of his title and experience, this meant that others naturally deferred to his authority. General Wood, when adjutant-general, was actually ordered by Wolseley to consult him first before going to Lord Lansdowne, the secretary of state for war, on any matter.[11] As Wolseley had hoped to wield the same powers as his predecessor, his frustration and bitterness at being given a mass of administrative work without the requisite authority spilled over into his relations with Lansdowne. Wolseley could not accept being directly subordinate to a politician whom he considered an amateur meddling in army affairs, and probably kept Lansdowne unaware of military papers circulating in the War Office. Lansdowne resented Wolseley's refusal to co-operate and give the new system a fair trial. Each was unsympathetic to the other's viewpoint and unwilling to understand the constraints within which the other worked when dealing with the crisis in South Africa.[12]

As part of his office, Wolseley was directly responsible for the Intelligence Department. Unlike its European counterparts, the British army did not have a general staff and there was little in the way of investigation and planning. There were several reasons for this, despite Prussia's effective use of a general staff during the wars with Austria and France in 1866 and 1870–1 respec-

---

10 Hamer, *The British army*, 35–9, and chs i–ii passim; Spiers, *Late Victorian army*, 5–8, 30–3, 44–5.
11 Field-Marshal Sir H. E. Wood, *From midshipman to field-marshal*, London 1906, ii. 251–2; Captain Owen Wheeler, *The War Office: past and present*, London 1914, 257.
12 Hamer, *British army*, 148–73.

tively. In the first place, British involvement in a European war was considered negligible, and therefore extensive planning was thought unnecessary; secondly, the duke of Cambridge was against the idea because a chief of staff might undermine his own authority, a view shared by Wolseley himself who wanted to inherit the powers of the C-in-C intact; thirdly, civilians showed no interest because a general staff was deemed 'foreign' and inapplicable to Britain's needs, and because a chief of staff would merely be a C-in-C with another name; and fourthly, the Treasury believed a general staff would be too costly.[13]

Despite the fact that Britain now faced greater challenges to its world-wide position, little was done to provide comprehensive strategic advice to the Cabinet. Some forums did exist, and attempted to bring together interested departments and to formulate appreciations of imperial defence. The creation of a colonial defence committee in 1878, which lasted for a year and was then reinstated in 1885, was a response to the numerous imperial crises which arose during the last quarter of the nineteenth century. It was the only forum in which the Colonial Office, the War Office and the Admiralty came together to discuss defence issues. Basically, its main task was to help the colonies maintain their own defences. Other than that the committee lacked the power and authority to provide a coherent appreciation of imperial defence needs.[14] In 1895 the government established a defence committee of the Cabinet in order to bring together the two services in an attempt to produce some form of co-ordinated defence planning. However, this body was not a success: overall, ministers lacked sufficient interest in its tasks or were too busy working on other matters; secondly, no records of its sporadic meetings were kept;[15] and thirdly it spent too much time trying to resolve interdepartmental disputes, mostly over finance. Basically, as Gibbs observed, the committee never performed its primary task: 'how to settle the broad principles of national and imperial defence upon the basis of information from all interested Departments, and then to lay down, again in principle, the size and composition of the military and naval forces necessary in peace to make such a defence policy possible'.[16]

Casting a shadow over the whole business of defence planning was the

---

13 Brian Bond, The Victorian army and the Staff College 1854–1914, London 1972, 212–13; Gooch, The plans of war, 1–20. A Royal Commission under Lord Hartington sat in 1888 and its second report in 1890 examined the question of military advice given to ministers. Its most radical recommendation was that after the duke retired, his office should be replaced by a chief of staff. For more see Spiers, Late Victorian army, 46–9, and Hamer, British army, ch. iv.

14 N. H. Gibbs, The origins of imperial defence, Oxford 1955, 9–12; Donald C. Gordon, The Dominion partnership in imperial defense, 1870–1914, Baltimore 1965, ch. v; Gooch, The plans of war, 6–7.

15 As Gibbs explains our knowledge of this body comes from the criticisms levelled at it after the South African War.

16 Gibbs, Origins of imperial defence, 16–17; Zara Shakow, 'The defence committee: a forerunner of the Committee of Imperial Defence', Canadian Historical Review xxxvi (1955),

Treasury, which looked askance at any measures which might cost large amounts of money. From the late 1880s the Treasury became increasingly concerned about the high levels of central and local government expenditure. As a bastion of Gladstonian financial orthodoxy, which advocated low taxation, low expenditure and balanced budgets, the permanent officials at the Treasury deprecated the growing calls from government departments for more money to spend on defence, imperial development and the alleviation of social problems.[17] Although many of Lord Salisbury's ministers were essentially 'Gladstonian' in outlook, few could ignore the claims of their officials for extra cash. Chamberlain, for example, faced a continual battle with the Treasury in his attempts to finance colonial projects.[18] For the War Office, the Treasury remained a formidable adversary and the military estimates were invariably lower than the amount sought, despite the army over-estimating its requirements in order to obtain a sum nearer its immediate demands. As Edward Spiers remarks, this process caused civil–military friction within the War Office because ministers, unable to account for every estimate, 'had to reduce the excessive demands within the overall limits imposed by the cabinet. Arbitrary economies, in short, took precedence over any criteria of military efficiency or the requirements of national security.'[19] Nevertheless, in the 1890s the Treasury was losing ground and fighting a desperate rearguard action, especially in the case of the defence estimates, which constituted the bulk of government expenditure, and which increased significantly owing to a new naval building programme.[20] The weakened state of 'Treasury control' was to become apparent following the outbreak of war in South Africa.

Within the War Office the Cinderella section was the Intelligence Department, which was responsible for gathering information. Its task, however, was not to issue advice and influence policy; the department only collected and collated military intelligence; nor were its officers assigned to help Wolseley prepare plans for future contingencies. Although other crises erupted in the late 1890s, in the Sudan and Niger valley, the department's duties and resources were neither specialised nor increased. Indeed throughout this period, the Intelligence Department received only £11,000 *per*

36–44; Franklyn A. Johnson, *Defence by committee: the British Committee of Imperial Defence 1885–1959*, London 1960, 34–5; David French, *The British way in warfare 1688–2000*, London 1990, 153–4.

17 E. H. H. Green, *The crisis of Conservatism: the politics, economics and ideology of the British Conservative party*, London 1995, 48–53; Green states (p. 49) that between 1870 and 1895 expenditure, as a percentage of GNP, increased from 9% to 19%.

18 See Marsh, *Joseph Chamberlain*, 412–19. For Salisbury's conduct of foreign policy under 'Gladstonian' restrictions see A. N. Porter, 'Lord Salisbury, foreign policy and domestic finance 1860–1900', in Robert Blake and Hugh Cecil (eds), *Salisbury: the man and his policies*, London 1987, 148–84.

19 Spiers, *Late Victorian army*, 37–9; Johnson, *Defence by committee*, 14.

20 Aaron L. Friedberg, *The weary titan: Britain and the experience of relative decline 1895–1905*, Princeton 1988, 89–106, 128–34.

annum, whereas the Transvaal government spent £90,000 on its intelligence services.[21]

The department's Section B was responsible for gathering information relating to the colonies. It had to cover all aspects of the empire's military needs, except India, but usually had a staff of only two officers and a clerk. The department as a whole was neglected by both the civil and military authorities. Civilians were suspicious and stingy, regarding an Intelligence Department as a short step from a general staff and unfettered militarism; Wolseley gave little help, showing no appetite for work as a chief of staff.

Wolseley sent Lansdowne a minute that combined two aspects which greatly concerned the military establishment: European conflict and the Boer threat. Wolseley's appreciation of the South African problem was more intuitive than reasoned, and this owed much to the nature of his office and relationship with Lansdowne. Although Wolseley's minute was designed to obtain an increase in the numerical strength of the British army, his growing anxiety about South Africa was evident. As yet, however, the Boer menace was not considered sufficient to warrant a substantial increase in numbers; Wolseley envisaged an addition of about 3,500 men, two battalions of which (roughly 2,000 men) would be positioned in Cape Colony, the rest in Natal. This small addition to the Natal garrison would be sufficient to have a 'steadying effect on the Boers' and would enable the force to take up forward positions along the frontier if necessary. Considering the modest strength of the Natal garrison, this confidence in its ability to overawe the Boers revealed Wolseley's contempt for Boer military abilities. Even so, Wolseley realised that more was needed to uphold British prestige:

> To anyone who knows South Africa well, it must be evident that the present state of things, the existing distribution of power in South Africa cannot long continue. To give any future redistribution of it an English character, we should be strong there. At present, and indeed ever since we pulled down our flag after our defeat at Majuba, the Africander, has believed the Boer power to be superior to ours, and Dr. Jameson's recent surrender, and the policy it has forced upon us, will inevitably tend to strengthen this belief.[22]

At the same time, officers of the Intelligence Department also provided appreciations of the situation in South Africa. Officers were able to produce memoranda as and when they deemed them necessary, and could prepare them for any office of state. In fact, Lansdowne often by-passed Wolseley and approached General Ardagh, Director of Military Intelligence, personally. As a result, intelligence appreciations were circulated around the various departments and to various ministers.[23]

The first appreciation was written by Major Altham, currently in the

21 T. Fergusson, *British military intelligence 1870–1914*, London 1984, 109–12.
22 Wolseley wrote this on his own initiative: 22 Feb. 1896, RCWSA, xl, Cd. 1789, 225–6.
23 For Ardagh's relations with other departments and with Wolseley see ibid. xl, Cd. 1790,

Intelligence Department but about to go to South Africa as military secretary to General Goodenough, the general officer commanding, South Africa (GOC SA). Altham was to undertake intelligence work whilst there and probably felt it beneficial to produce an evaluation before leaving. He believed the Boers would take the offensive, as they had more arms and coveted the port of Durban. He urged that Goodenough should be sent some strategic guidance, and suggested stressing the points to be defended by the garrison. Altham preferred to defend the bridges across the Orange river, vital to the advance of any main army arriving in South Africa. He stated that the Natal frontier, particularly Laing's Nek, was not worth defending but offered no reason for this, although he must have been aware of its isolation. However, he felt that Durban and Pietermaritzburg ought to have garrisons for reasons of prestige. Furthermore, Altham suggested that the Uitlanders might be encouraged to carry out acts of sabotage to supplement regular operations.[24]

The second memorandum was provided by Ardagh, who drew official attention to the possibility of a conflict with the Orange Free State as well as the Transvaal. As DMI and adviser to both Wolseley and Lansdowne, Ardagh's views carried some weight. Although, as he later confessed, his rank was not high enough to guarantee influence with his superiors, he felt duty bound to inform them of his views.[25] In 1889 the Boer republics had signed a defensive alliance,[26] and Ardagh wondered if Bloemfontein would co-operate with Pretoria should war occur between Britain and the Transvaal: this, he argued, should be known on the outbreak of hostilities. Ardagh wanted the OFS given two alternatives; the first, that it should be benevolently neutral, allowing the British to pass through its territory; the second, war. According to Ardagh there was no alternative to an invasion of the OFS, no matter what its attitude. The Natal route into the Transvaal was inadequate: it was serviced by only one small section of railway; and the border country was difficult to traverse, owing to its mountainous nature. Ardagh concluded: 'The remarkable and unprecedented spectacle afforded by the Transvaal must, so long as present conditions last, inspire us with apprehension, and compel us to regard armed intervention as a possibility which may be forced upon us, however conciliatory our attitude may be.'[27]

Lansdowne's response to Wolseley's advice was not altogether dismissive but showed him concentrating on short-term solutions. He explained that he

210; for those with Lansdowne, for whom he had previously worked in India see ibid. xli, Cd. 1791, 502.

[24] Memo. by Altham, 11 June 1896, WO 32/7844/079/8501.

[25] RCWSA, xl, Cd. 1790, 5045–6, 213.

[26] In March 1897 Presidents Steyn and Kruger reaffirmed the alliance.

[27] Memo. by Ardagh, Oct. 1896, Ardagh papers, PRO 30/40/16. The memorandum dealt chiefly with the Transvaal Boers military capacity, Ardagh believing the Boer rifleman was degenerating into 'an untrained yeoman' owing to the lack of space in which to trek and shoot game.

could not agree to a substantial rise in army numbers unless the necessity for the expenditure was fully proved, and this he said Wolseley had not done. Lansdowne was not interested in strengthening the garrison in South Africa. Wolseley's recommendation of two battalions as a deterrent and the nucleus of an expeditionary force was inadequate and would not do for either task. He reminded Wolseley that the garrison in Natal was only temporary as it had been agreed that in 1898 the Natal government should be responsible for its own defence, five years after the grant of self-government. Lansdowne's response to the evaluations provided by Altham and Ardagh is unknown.[28]

Nevertheless, in 1896 the garrison was increased, although the surviving evidence in the War Office files does not state when the decisions to reinforce it were made. As, however, the returns printed in the Royal Commission give half-yearly figures it is possible to gain some idea of when it was decided to send out extra troops. In December 1895 the garrison numbered 3,588 men;[29] in June 1896 the garrison had been increased by 1,000 men; by December the garrison stood at 5,409, with the greater proportion concentrated in Cape Colony, an extra increase of about 800 men. These figures confirmed that Wolseley's recommendations were acknowledged. Evidently, the garrison in 1895 had been at its lowest level at a time of international tension.[30]

Selborne, though, considered the time had come to increase the numbers of the Cape garrison. He told Chamberlain he had been impressed by a memorandum from George Fiddes,[31] which showed Britain unable to assert its interests with the force currently in South Africa. Selborne believed that the Boers had not been overawed by the recent increase in the garrison, and that only a major expeditionary force would do that. To ensure that British power was evident, to the Boers, to the colonials, and to the Cape Afrikaners, required the largest garrison in South Africa compatible with Britain's defensive requirements.[32]

This may have influenced Chamberlain who pressed Lansdowne to increase the garrison by an extra 5,000 men. Lansdowne, using Wolseley's figures, informed him at some length that this would mean recruiting more troops, and would be difficult because it would require the sanction of parlia-

---

28 Memo. by Lansdowne, 10 July 1896, CAB 37/42/32. In his evidence before the Royal Commission Lansdowne, when asked whether Altham's and Ardagh's papers had ever been put before him replied, 'I do not think so; I may have seen some of them': RCWSA, xli, Cd. 1791, 21085–8, 502.

29 Including the ½ battalion assigned to Mauritius, part of the South African defence establishment, and then stationed in the Cape because barracks in Mauritius were awaiting completion: ibid. xl, Cd. 1789, 153.

30 Ibid. 21. Wolseley himself seemed to be unsure about the decision-making process: 'we went on adding to it [the garrison] bit by bit. That was on the strong recommendations I made from time to time': ibid. 8719, 365.

31 Private secretary to Sir R. Meade, permanent under-secretary at the Colonial Office.

32 Selborne to Chamberlain, 6 Oct. 1896, in Crisis of British power, 40–1.

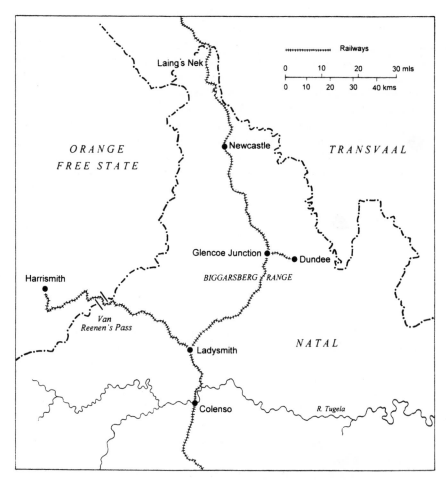

Map 2. The Natal Triangle 1899–1902

ment to alter the army estimates.[33] Chamberlain nevertheless insisted on presenting his proposals to the Cabinet. He explained that from information received from South Africa it appeared the Boers were preparing to throw off British suzerainty and invade British territory. To counter this, Chamberlain stressed the diplomatic advantages of strengthening the garrison; of demonstrating British resolve; and of fortifying the resolve of the loyalists. Chamberlain believed that a display of military strength had always impressed the Boers and had, on several occasions, prevented serious consequences; he mentioned General Warren's expedition to Bechuanaland in 1885 as a prime example. An increase in the garrison would be a sensible defensive measure on its own, gaining time, in the event of hostilities, for the arrival of reinforcements. However, Chamberlain, perhaps impressed by the reservations of the War Office, tempered his appraisal by stating that the problem was not urgent, but a matter of policy requiring the agreement of the military authorities to spare 5,000 men for garrison duty in South Africa for a year or two. He was prepared to drop the matter, moreover, if all this was dependent on an increase in the army and on a vote of money in parliament.[34]

Lansdowne later summarised the military position, and informed ministers that minor increases to garrisons abroad were required throughout the empire. The international situation was the main reason for this together with, as Lansdowne explained, the inability of the Admiralty to guarantee the safety of various naval bases. The Admiralty had stated that its first priority was to secure command of the sea in home waters; until this was achieved naval bases would have to fend for themselves. In this case Lansdowne agreed that the Cape garrison ought to be strong enough to defeat a seaborne assault, and emphasised that it should not be responsible for the land frontier, stating that he would have to ask the Cabinet 'whether the two extra battalions . . . are to be regarded as permanently quartered there'.[35] Lansdowne then was still not convinced about the necessity of increasing the garrison to counter the Boer threat: it might be asked whether Lansdowne thought a Boer threat even existed.

At the end of 1896, therefore, the South African garrison could still be regarded as a defence against seaborne attack. Despite the evaluations presented by the Intelligence Department, a clear, comprehensive survey of the situation, which had been altered by Jameson's Raid, was still lacking. Nevertheless, the promptings of the Colonial Office and the soldiers had highlighted the potentiality of a Boer threat. The following year this threat became more pronounced.

---

33 Lansdowne to Chamberlain, 6 Nov. 1896, Birmingham University library, Joseph Chamberlain papers (JC) 5/51/20; Wolseley's Minute, 5 Nov. 1896, JC 5/51/19. There is no copy of Chamberlain's letter to Lansdowne in the Chamberlain papers.
34 Memo. by Chamberlain, 10 Nov. 1896, CAB 37/43/45.
35 Memo. by Lansdowne, 4 Dec. 1896, RCWSA, xl, Cd. 1789, 238–9.

The crisis of 1897

Desiring to limit the numbers of Uitlanders in the Transvaal, Kruger's government, early in 1897, attempted to impose an Aliens' Immigration Act which restricted both the number of immigrants and their right to become citizens of the republic. Chamberlain's desire to strengthen the empire and to educate the British public into supporting his ideals meant that such an insult – as he and others perceived it – could not go unanswered. Moreover, a strong response was required to convince the British element in South Africa that London would and could uphold their interests. Furthermore, as the Transvaal was now becoming very dangerous owing to the large import of arms since the Raid, it was necessary for the British government to win a diplomatic victory which might discredit Kruger's policy and, with luck, his regime. In the process, significant divisions amongst soldiers and politicians were revealed, which decisively affected the military response to the Transvaal's intransigence.

On 5 April 1897 the Colonial Office informed the War Office that the disagreement between Britain and the Transvaal had reached a point where it was necessary to present certain despatches to Kruger, regarding his government's breaches of the London Convention of 1884.[36] It was emphasised that these despatches were not an ultimatum; but owing to the Transvaal's enhanced military capability and the comparatively defenceless state of the British colonies, a Boer military response could not be ruled out. An initial Boer victory, it was felt, might add to British difficulties by securing the support of many Afrikaners. The Colonial Office thought the Boers were likely to attack Kimberley which meant the covert or manifest support of the OFS would be required, which might also lead to the destruction of the Orange river bridges. British forces were wholly inadequate to defend the frontiers, a position which risked the hostility of the loyalists. Chamberlain wanted his views put before Lansdowne who was reminded that he had 'the responsibility of deciding what military measures should be taken, to safeguard the interests of the Empire in South Africa at the present juncture'.[37]

There were two questions to be answered before a coherent policy could be produced. First, the politicians, with their military advisers, had to decide what strategy the Boers were likely to employ should war break out; and second, how many troops were required to defeat the Boers?

On 8 April Chamberlain called a Cabinet meeting to discuss the crisis. With Salisbury away, the meeting comprised Chamberlain, Lansdowne, Hicks Beach, the chancellor of the exchequer, Balfour, Salisbury's deputy, and Goschen, the first lord of the Admiralty. All admitted that there was a possibility of the Boers launching an attack, but thought it was unlikely;

---

[36] This convention had finally settled the differences between Britain and the Transvaal following the war in 1880–1.

[37] Colonial Office (CO) to War Office (WO), 5 Apr. 1897, WO 32/7844/079/8234.

nevertheless they acknowledged that an early Boer success might win over the OFS and many Afrikaners. Again Chamberlain stressed the need to support the loyalists who were 'alarmed at the apparent indifference of the British government to their danger', and advocated the immediate despatch of 3,500 men. Evidently, Lansdowne favoured doing nothing, but Chamberlain and the rest wanted something done for political reasons because they believed the Boers would back down in the face of British determination.[38]

After consulting his military advisers, Lansdowne acknowledged that the garrison was inadequate both to meet a Boer offensive on a wide front and to launch an offensive.[39] Lansdowne doubted the Boers would actually attack; he believed they were preparing to meet a British offensive, as evidenced by the building and stocking with 'guns of position' fortresses at Pretoria and Johannesburg. He also felt the Boers would not relish the prospect of leaving their homes for long to conduct a military campaign outside their borders. Nor did Lansdowne think the Boers would make a dash into Cape Colony to stir up support, as this would 'exasperate the loyal colonists'. (The thought that it might provoke an Afrikaner rebellion and undermine British plans does not seem to have occurred to him). Even if the Boers destroyed the bridges the soldiers did not believe this would seriously jeopardise operations. Lansdowne added that Chamberlain wanted something done for political reasons, primarily to bolster the loyalists as the weak garrison had undermined their confidence. Unconvinced by this, Lansdowne preferred to send an ultimatum followed 'by an overwhelming force when the moment for putting our foot down had arrived'. The main force to be sent 'would probably be not less than 40,000 men', although the prevalence of rinderpest meant that providing transport animals might be a problem and the main army might then be tied to the railway. However, none of these difficulties was expected to hinder the advance through the Boer republics.

Lansdowne further explained that the soldiers were divided on the issue; Wolseley supported Chamberlain, whilst Buller and Wood (adjutant-general and quarter-master-general respectively) agreed with Lansdowne. The latter preferred to wait and felt the British could do so longer than Kruger: the British, he contended, were already 'in the wrong' over the Jameson Raid, and it would add to their difficulties to precipitate a crisis.[40]

At a further meeting between Lansdowne, Wolseley, Buller and this time Milner (recently appointed high commissioner for South Africa and governor of Cape Colony) a new military action was proposed.[41] Instead of preparing for an invasion of the OFS it was agreed that the British should send an

---

[38] Chamberlain to Salisbury, 8 Apr. 1897, JC 5/67/76.

[39] Lansdowne to Salisbury, 9 Apr. 1897, Salisbury correspondence, fos 248–54.

[40] Wolseley noted in his diary that he continued to insist that the garrison at the Cape be increased, and that while Chamberlain agreed, Lansdowne remained opposed: Sir Frederick Maurice and Sir George Arthur, *The Life of Lord Wolseley*, London 1924, 315.

[41] Lansdowne to Chamberlain, 13 Apr. 1897, JC 5/51/25.

immediate force to Natal, to hold the strategic position of Laing's Nek. Apparently Milner objected to an invasion of the OFS because, according to Lansdowne, he did not like the thought of pushing the OFS into the arms of the Transvaal. Milner's ability to change the plan suggests the others were undecided about it anyway. The decision to change, however, completely altered the focus of British strategy; hitherto the OFS route had been considered vital owing to the nature of the country and the number of railways that could be used to bring troops and supplies to the frontier and then support the invasion. Now this strategy had been superseded. Instead of using an 'overwhelming force' and operating in advantageous country, the British had decided to rely on a small addition to the garrison and place them in terrain which favoured the Boers. Evidently the soldiers agreed but no evidence has survived of the reasons given; Lansdowne favoured this change because it seemed to secure military objectives within the financial limit of £200,000 imposed by Hicks Beach.[42] Thus it was agreed that the new military objective was for British troops to occupy Laing's Nek, to block any attempted Boer invasion, and provide a springboard for a possible offensive against the Transvaal, without recourse to an invasion of the OFS.

Not all military opinion favoured such a move. Ardagh reiterated the danger posed by the OFS. He believed that even if it remained neutral, an estimated 5,000 Free Staters were likely to join the Transvaal; this action alone warranted a declaration of war. Ardagh warned his superiors that, 'Procrastination and delay in settling this important question of policy at the critical moment will be most prejudicial toward us.' He added that the Boers could easily seize strategic locations, such as Laing's Nek, and damage the railway upon which a British advance depended.[43] Ardagh's opinion was supported by Wood, who had missed the meeting with Milner. Wood condemned the idea of occupying Laing's Nek, as it could easily be dominated from adjoining positions; provided the Boers had not already seized Laing's Nek beforehand.[44]

The advice proffered by the military thus involved two contrasting strategic scenarios. One recommended that British reinforcements should be deployed near the OFS border, and that OFS hostility ought to be assumed. Invading the OFS would facilitate the advance of the main expeditionary force, which would number some 40,000 men. The second scenario envisaged the deployment of British troops in Natal, where there was a common

[42] Lady Victoria Hicks Beach, *Life of Sir Michael Hicks Beach*, London 1932, ii. 51.

[43] Memo. by Ardagh, 15 Apr. 1897, WO 32/7844/079/8234. General Goodenough refused to move forces to Laing's Nek. He felt it was a bad strategic position and knew the Natal ministry, which feared provoking the Transvaal, shared his view. Eventually, as a compromise gesture, troops were moved from Pietermaritzburg to Ladysmith, a move also designed to improve the health of the troops: Goodenough to Ardagh, 21 Apr., 14 July 1897, and Ardagh to Goodenough, 3 Sept. 1897, WO 32/7844/079/8270.

[44] Lansdowne to Chamberlain, 20 Apr. 1897, JC 5/51/27. Lansdowne wanted to await Salisbury's opinion (he was in France) before making a decision.

border with the Transvaal in country of great strategic importance to both sides. British conjectures were based on a small force holding an isolated position to deny access to Natal and to facilitate a future advance. Disadvantages arising from such a course were numerous: the position chosen, Laing's Nek, could easily be isolated and dominated from neighbouring heights; the Boers could get there first if their suspicions were aroused or the political situation deteriorated.

While Lansdowne was discussing the issue with his military advisers, his colleagues were expressing their views. Balfour recommended that the government ought to accede to Chamberlain's demands because he had been allowed to goad the Boers. Although Balfour considered a Boer attack improbable, he reckoned that if the Boers believed the British were determined to attack them, they might attack first. As the committee investigating the Jameson Raid was about to consider sensitive documents, Balfour thought this would eventually antagonise the Boers, 'and it is a nice point whether the sending out of 3000 or 4000 men will prove to be a sedative or a stimulant'.[45] Hicks Beach was more concerned about costs. He complained to Chamberlain that his main worry was to persuade the War Office to cut their own estimates for the increase in the garrison, especially as he had to consider further expenditure on the navy.[46]

The final decision rested with Lord Salisbury. He was quite agreeable to Chamberlain's viewpoint, recognising that he had considered the problem for a long time. Nevertheless, he was concerned lest any precipitate action should have a bad effect on European politics. He was especially worried that a war against the Transvaal would see an alliance made between Germany and Holland against Britain. However, Salisbury made one telling observation; he felt that sending troops to South Africa would appear provocative to public opinion in England. He therefore thought the best course, politically and strategically, was to take up Lansdowne's suggestion of sending troops to Natal. As he told Chamberlain, it was the correct political decision because 'No one could find fault with us for defending such an important point in the face of Kruger's excessive armaments. Merely sending 2 regiments to the Cape will not appeal to English opinion in the same way, or seem so defensible: for they would be of little use against a surprise.'[47]

Faced with such reasoning, especially that relating to public opinion, Chamberlain was prepared to accept the Natal alternative.[48] Chamberlain knew Lansdowne appreciated his concerns regarding the position of the OFS, but Lansdowne had convinced himself the Natal option was the best one to

---

45 Balfour to Salisbury, 10 Apr. 1897, Salisbury correspondence, fo. 168.
46 Hicks Beach to Chamberlain, 11 Apr. 1897, JC 5/51/24.
47 Salisbury to Chamberlain, 16 Apr. 1897, JC 5/67/77.
48 Chamberlain to Salisbury, 19 Apr. 1897, Salisbury correspondence, fo. 89.

follow. Consequently, the Natal garrison was increased from 1,881 men to 4,347 in June 1897.[49]

This switch to Natal had two effects. It obscured the necessity of examining the attitude of the OFS, and it perpetuated the idea that a small show of force would ensure a Boer climbdown. Regarding the first, Ardagh's and Chamberlain's expressions of concern on the uncertainty of the OFS standpoint, and Wood's objections to the Laing's Nek position went largely unheeded. Clearly Lansdowne achieved his objectives by finding a position that appeared strategically viable, yet required only a small force to make it secure, and, just as important, kept costs within Treasury limits. It also had the added advantage of being acceptable to British public opinion which Chamberlain had been unable to educate fully at this stage.

Lansdowne's political position was apparently enhanced once the crisis had passed. The Boers did seem to back down, as the extra troops, coupled with a naval demonstration in Delagoa Bay, indicated Britain's intention to uphold the cause of the Uitlanders. Moreover, Chamberlain's intervention and his demands for military action were driving an even bigger wedge between Lansdowne and Wolseley. It seemed the latter relished the opportunity to oppose Lansdowne and side with another member of the Cabinet.

According to his biographers, from 1896 Wolseley's greatest concern was how to avoid war with the Boers.[50] He believed strongly that the best way to ensure peace was to increase the military presence in South Africa. This view had wider implications because Wolseley's demands for more troops in South Africa were also demands for extra troops for the home army; in fact he was saying one could not be achieved without the other. Chamberlain's vociferous demands for a strong British response to Boer intransigence gave Wolseley both an ally and further occasions to propagate his own ideas.

Lansdowne's suggestion regarding Natal scuppered any 'alliance' that might have formed between Chamberlain and Wolseley because it fulfilled all government requirements in one fell swoop. The War Office reply to the Colonial Office's letter of 5 April reflected the War Office's success. The note criticised the Colonial Office for leaving 'considerable room for doubt with regard to the attitudes of the Transvaal', and for trying to predict Kruger's future actions, especially as the Cabinet had not decided what action to take if the Transvaal's response to British demands was unsatisfactory. As for the need to make a military demonstration to impress South African opinion, Lansdowne was aware of Chamberlain's views, but said it was for the government to decide what course to follow; it remained only 'for the War Office to provide whatever force is best suited for the purpose'. Evidently, Lansdowne was not averse to 'strengthening our diplomacy' and had consulted the soldiers as to 'what steps would, within the financial limits, be most effectual

[49] Lansdowne to Chamberlain, 16 Apr. 1897, JC 5/51/26; RCWSA, xl, Cd. 1789, 21.
[50] Maurice and Arthur, Life of Wolseley, 314.

both as a demonstration and as a reinforcement'.[51] Sending a few troops to Natal had, it seemed, done the job admirably.

There seemed little doubt that sending reinforcements was effective. Conyngham Greene, the British agent in Pretoria, informed Selborne that the Boers would not fight to remove the Convention, and he was strengthened in this belief by the arrival of the troops, which 'will have a splendid effect and will be our best guarantee against having to use them. The Boers are accustomed to deal forcibly with those whom they know to be weaker than themselves, and this is the line of treatment they best understand'. According to Greene, the 'first fence had been carried', and it was essential Britain should continue to be firm and forceful.[52]

Milner, now firmly settled in Cape Colony, was also sure that reinforcements had had a good effect. Having discussed the issue with leading South Africans, including some sympathetic to the Transvaal, he was convinced the military and naval response had impressed Boer opinion, which 'regarded [it] as a clear indication that we meant business & that they must yield or fight'. Milner believed those who said the Boers would not fight if faced by a clear demonstration of British determination. Although he favoured conciliation it had to be from a position of strength: 'And from war with England, I believe even the most violent reactionaries will shrink, as they have shown already, if such a contingency stares them fairly in the face.'[53]

The crisis of 1897 had emphasised a discernible trend in the way the British approached the South African question. If the British appeared ready to go to war, then the Boers backed down especially after troops had been sent to Natal. What was not considered was the reason why the Boers pulled back. On the surface, the British had overawed their opponents; but few British officials seemed to appreciate that the Boers might not be quite ready to accept a challenge and were biding their time. In 1898, the British discovered how transitory their response had been.

A certain eventuality

The re-election of Kruger as the Transvaal president, with an increased majority, convinced Milner that 'There is no ultimate way out of the political troubles of S.Africa except reforms in the Transvaal or war. And at present the chances of reform in the Transvaal are worse than ever.'[54] Milner's pessimism owed much to a letter from Conyngham Greene, who informed him that the Boers were arming rapidly, paying for their weapons from the taxes provided by foreigners, i.e. the British residing in the republic. He stated that

51 WO to CO, 29 Apr. 1897, WO 32/7844/079/8234.
52 Conynghame Greene to Selborne, 18 June 1897, in *Crisis of British power,* 52.
53 Milner to Chamberlain, 2 Aug. 1897, JC 10/9/10.
54 Milner to Chamberlain, 23 Feb. 1898, JC 10/9/18.

in 1895 the Transvaal spent £61,903 on arms, which in 1897 had risen to £256,291: 'it is a matter of common gossip', he explained, 'that it is the aim of the Transvaal Government to arm the Free State Burghers and such of the Colonial Boers as may eventually be induced by their offers'.[55] For Milner, Kruger represented a major stumbling block to his dreams of a consolidated South Africa firmly under British control. Like Chamberlain, Milner felt that the empire was vital to Britain and in this respect South Africa was 'the weakest link in the Imperial chain'. If he failed, Milner believed that Afrikaner nationalism would win and, as Iain Smith states, 'would powerfully assist the centrifugal forces at work elsewhere in the world which were tending to dissolve the British empire into separate nation states and thus to undermine the basis of Britain's position as a world power'. Milner was now determined that Kruger should be coerced not cajoled.[56]

Obviously alarmed at the worsening political situation, the Colonial Office continued to send such information to the War Office, in the hope of stirring some response. So concerned were Colonial Office officials that even Milner's despatches were passed on, notably those which dealt with the dearth of military transport in the area following the Basutoland crisis in late 1897.[57] Milner was anxious that the transport deficiency might hamper future operations against the Boers. He suggested that a small nucleus of transport be maintained and, as there would be a need for civilian help, a standing contract for transport be negotiated forthwith.[58]

The debate regarding the provision of military transport highlighted the continuing apprehension and uncertainty still prevalent within the British government. For the soldiers, however, this debate went beyond the number of wagons and horses; for them it meant a change in perspective. The crisis of 1897 had almost brought war between Britain and the Transvaal; in 1898 the soldiers expected a war to come sooner rather than later. Although the military continued to think a Boer war would be a corollary of a European conflict, military attention was now firmly focused on the need to prepare for a war in South Africa. Military evaluations produced during the transport debate, although as before more the product of individual concern than departmental, clearly showed that a war against the Transvaal at least was considered a 'certain eventuality'. Lansdowne, though, did not see beyond the immediate discussion and confined his decisions to the numbers and cost of wagons and horses. The almost total breakdown in outlook between the civil and military elements in the War Office completed the division between Lansdowne and his military advisers.

[55] Conynghame Greene to Milner, 7 Feb. 1898, WO 32/7844/079/8501, enclosed in CO papers sent to the WO.
[56] Smith, *Origins*, 148, 184–94.
[57] *The Milner papers*, ed. C. Headlam, London 1931–5, i. 156–8.
[58] CO to WO, 11 Mar. 1898, enclosing Milner to Chamberlain, 1 Feb. 1898, WO 32/7844/079/8487.

An indication of military concern was provided by a further comment on Boer intransigence by the DMI, who echoed Conyngham Greene's concern over the scale of Boer arms-buying. Ardagh stressed that the Boers themselves seemed to have a 'definite policy' underlining their military preparations

> which will build up a Dutch Oligarchy in South Africa strong enough to shake off the English suzerainty when a favourable opportunity offers, and, perhaps, even to carry out the larger dream of a great Dutch independent state reaching from the Zambezi down to the Hottentot Holland mountains, and with Delagoa Bay as its seaport.[59]

Again, the Colonial Office copied to Lansdowne Milner's despatches which continued to emphasise the growing intransigence of the Transvaal. For good measure a copy of Ardagh's report, referred to above, was also sent, for 'facility of reference'. The Colonial Office stated that the Transvaal appeared to be waiting for Britain to become involved in a dispute with other European powers, either to denounce the London Convention, or to attack the British colonies. Apparently Chamberlain wanted Lansdowne to consider whether the garrison in South Africa needed augmenting in order to meet the growing crisis; at the same time, he reminded him of the lack of transport in Cape Colony.[60]

In reply, the War Office appeared unwilling to authorise expenditure on a nucleus of military transport. Nevertheless they were prepared to negotiate a standing contract, especially if the Cape government would contribute some of the money.[61] This financial diffidence was not appreciated at the Colonial Office and the minutes show a developing sense of frustration and annoyance: one noted, 'Notwithstanding the warnings of their Intelligence Department, the WO seem to grudge every penny in S. Africa.'[62] The Colonial Office deprecated the financial stringency shown by the War Office at a time of growing political crisis. The importance of having an efficient garrison was stressed again, both for its political and military value, and it was emphasised that costs ought not to stand in the way of military efficiency.[63]

Lansdowne's attitude is difficult to fathom. He seemed reluctant, or unable, to appreciate Chamberlain's pessimistic view of the British position. Although he had agreed to 'forceful measures' in 1897, he remained unconvinced. He had chided Chamberlain after the crisis for remarking in parliament that the reinforcements were to remain permanently, because it 'appears to me to go beyond what was intended'. Lansdowne believed the intention had been to respond to a passing difficulty with a temporary

59 Ardagh to CO, 17 Mar. 1898, WO 32/7844/079/8501.
60 CO to WO, 6 Apr. 1898, ibid.
61 WO to CO, 14 Apr. 1898, CO 417/252/8358.
62 CO Minutes, 18–20 Apr. 1898, ibid.
63 CO to WO, 5 May 1898, WO 32/7844/079/8520.

measure.[64] However, on hearing of Milner's 'strenuous resistance' to any attempt to reduce the garrison, backed by Wolseley 'and other high military authorities', Lansdowne eventually acknowledged the need to keep a larger garrison in South Africa permanently; but he still hoped the Cape would assume responsibility for defending its own land frontiers sooner rather than later.[65] Thus, in early 1898, Lansdowne revealed how reluctant he still was to commit the War Office to expensive and permanent adjustments to the defence establishment in South Africa.

When the War Office wrote again in June some action had been taken. Lansdowne, 'on the recommendation of his military advisers', had finally authorised General Goodenough to purchase sufficient vehicles and to negotiate a standing contract to supply the animals within seven days of notification. Furthermore the GOC SA was allowed to negotiate for enough vehicles and animals to be supplied to make the whole garrison mobile thirty days following notification.[66] The recommendations of his military advisers seemed to have had some effect on Lansdowne's judgement.

Ardagh felt the Natal garrison, combined with local forces, was adequate for defensive operations, but he was still disturbed by the state of the Cape garrison. Dispersed amongst a hostile population, and lacking in cavalry, artillery and transport, he felt the garrison could do little should hostilities commence. Returning to a favourite theme, he noted that much would depend on the attitude of the OFS, if the Cape garrison was to help Natal by menacing the Transvaal from Bechuanaland. Ardagh advised that the Cape garrison should receive equipment to enable it to operate independently of the railway.[67]

Wood, now adjutant-general, complained that he had told the War Office civilians of the deficiency in transport eighteen months ago when, in collaboration with the GOC SA, he had urged that a standing contract be made with Weil & Co; his attempt to help the garrison in Natal by requesting that reserve supplies be stockpiled in Ladysmith, was also refused by Lansdowne. Wood was prepared to play down the Boer threat by stating that their leaders (most of whom he had met in 1881 when negotiating peace) were unlikely to be adventurous in their strategy. He expected them to wait until Britain was in conflict with a European power before declaring war, and even then send only raiding parties into British territory. Nevertheless, the garrisons needed to be efficient and ready to combat raids and able to mobilise within two

---

[64] Lansdowne to Chamberlain, 5 May 1897, JC 5/51/28.

[65] Memo. by Lansdowne, 6 Oct. 1897, CAB 37/45/33.

[66] WO to CO, 9 Jun. 1898, CO 417/252/13057. This was a concession to the Colonial Office which wanted all forces capable of rapid mobilisation, 'this being the object of chief importance from a political point of view': CO to WO, 25 June 1898, ibid.

[67] Ardagh to Wolseley, 14 Apr. 1898, WO 32/7844/079/8501.

weeks.[68] Armed with these opinions, Wolseley entered the fray and wrote that:

> As long as there is a probability of our having trouble with either France or Russia, there may be some good reason why more troops should not be sent to South Africa, but there can be no valid reason why we should not send the stores and supplies & transport which I believe to be necessary in order to make us safe until troops could be sent from home both to Natal and Cape Town.[69]

Only under the combined weight of military and Colonial Office opinion did Lansdowne agree to the measures indicated above. Yet these measures hardly did more than make the garrison more efficient. Although the military power of the Boers was still underestimated, the manner in which the British authorities gradually increased their military presence had little to do with a coherent appreciation of the situation. It seemed that the decisions taken in Whitehall were more to do with interdepartmental politics and personal rivalry than the needs of the British position in South Africa.

Enter and exit General Butler

If anyone hoped that these limited measures would indicate to the Boers Britain's resolve then they were mistaken. Major Altham, having returned to the Intelligence Department in a permanent capacity in March 1897, informed the War Office that nothing had changed in South Africa. British military preparations were still inadequate; the Transvaal continued her military preparations, 'and the condition of affairs in South Africa has practically now become that of an armed neutrality, which may last for years or may culminate in a war at very short notice'. The defence problem was still serious, especially in the Cape because of the hostile population, 'and its difficulty will be enhanced by the fact that any mistake or lack of firmness at the outset would seriously affect subsequent operations'. Altham explained that the Cape garrison consisted of only three and a half battalions (roughly 3,500), but two battalions were the war garrison of the Cape peninsula and half a battalion was for Mauritius; the remaining battalion was divided between Grahamstown and King Williamstown. Practically the whole of the Cape force was placed near the coast, hundreds of miles from the frontier: only the Cape Regulars were of any use to the army, the Volunteers having disgraced themselves in recent operations in Bechuanaland. The force available, barely 5,000 men, was required to defend a frontier of 320 miles, from Fourteen Streams to the Basutoland border. Altham pointed to the lack of planning, as nothing had been done to ensure a rapid mobilisation nor to integrate the

---

68 Wood to Wolseley, 17 Apr. 1898, ibid.
69 Wolseley to Knox (permanent under-secretary, War Office), 20 Apr. 1898, ibid.

recent transport arrangements into any plan, either in Natal or Cape Colony. Altham argued that defence schemes ought to be submitted by the military authorities in South Africa and urged

> That the arrangements which would be made for the despatch of reinforcements from England and for the provision of supplies and transport be worked out fully by the War Office; and that the General Officer Commanding, South Africa, be informed what action under the arrangements would be required of him on the outbreak of war.[70]

Owing to ill-health General Goodenough was replaced by General Butler in November 1898 and at almost the same time the political situation deteriorated, making defence planning for South Africa more important. In November Major Altham followed up his earlier memorandum by drafting a letter to General Butler in which he hoped to clarify the question of frontier defence. In addition, to help the GOC SA draw up his own comprehensive plans (all GOC SA's were required to submit plans during their tenure in office), Colonel Stopford of the Mobilisation Subdivision of the Intelligence Department, informed the C-in-C that the officers 'concerned in the questions affecting mobilization in South Africa' had met and come to the conclusion 'that the quickest & most satisfactory way of harmonizing the various instructions which have been issued to the GOC South Africa is to send to him a secret letter giving him full information on the situation which would exist if war were to break out in that country'.[71]

Both views went to Butler in a combined letter outlining the current appreciation of Boer military power, and recognising the incompleteness of British military plans. Stopford explained that OFS burghers were expected to join the Transvaal in the event of war even if the OFS remained neutral. This had been one of the major lessons from the first war and would give the Boers a fighting force of 27,000 men, after allowing for units to watch the Uitlanders and natives. However, a large-scale Boer incursion was not anticipated against either British colony: 'Raids . . . of 2,000 to 3,000 men may be expected, and it is against such raids that a careful preparation on your part is necessary.' Interestingly, Stopford remarked that any plans would be better prepared if the line of advance of the main army was known, but said the C-in-C thought 'the plan for offensive operations must depend upon the political and military situation of the moment, and cannot be definitely fixed'. Nevertheless, Butler was expected to bear in mind an advance in preparing his plans, and to base them only on existing resources and arrangements. Once his plans were prepared he was to send copies to London.[72]

These were the first instructions Butler had received. Even before his

---

70 Memo. by Altham, 21 Sept. 1898, ibid.
71 WO Minutes, 15 Nov., 9 Dec. 1898, WO 32/6369/266/Cape/30.
72 Stopford to Butler, 21 Dec. 1898, ibid. The Colonial Office, shown this letter on 23 Dec. 1898, felt the figure of 27,000 exaggerated as the War Office had used a Boer publication –

departure he had been given no directions as to what was expected of him, save for a friendly chat with Chamberlain which clarified nothing. Stopford's instructions, however, offered no real help. Under Queen's Regulations Butler was obliged to plan with only the forces at his disposal which were then woefully inadequate to defend both British colonies.[73] Even if the Boers were only going to raid, their commandos would cause much damage, especially with the garrison split between Cape Colony and Natal. How to defend important points and leave neither colony bereft of defensive cover presented a substantial headache for any commander. Consequently Butler, between March and April 1899, visited the frontiers of both colonies in order to gauge the situation for himself.

By May 1899, however, Butler had still not informed even the War Office of his plans and officials there became steadily more concerned, especially after the breakdown of the Bloemfontein talks between Milner and Kruger on 5 June. Evidently Butler had been prompted twice, once in February and again in early May to consider two schemes emanating from Natal for local and frontier defence. On 8 June 1899 Butler was ordered to provide the information requested in December.[74]

Butler's reluctance to forward his plans owed something to his lack of confidence in certain unspecified War Office personnel. He was convinced some of the staff, if not the whole department, were out to provoke war with the Transvaal. In his memoirs he complained about the lack of orders and instructions on his appointment and believed matters had been arranged beforehand; he was told nothing, 'still less with the development of plans and purposes which I knew to have been then matured and arranged'.[75] In fact, the War Office had nothing prepared except General Goodenough's overall plan which dated back to 1896 and was based on the premise that the main army, when it arrived, would advance through the OFS. Goodenough intended to use his scarce resources to secure the bridges over the Orange river, having had them placed nearby before the outbreak of war, although not close enough to arouse OFS suspicions.[76]

As mentioned above, Butler had toured the frontiers to see the ground for himself. This had taken up a good deal of his time, but once ordered to comply, he sent his plans on 14 June. In his 'observations' Butler raised a number of pertinent points that had still not been fully addressed by the government.

---

the *Staats Almanack* – for their figures; they felt 15,000 nearer the mark: CO Minutes, 27 Dec. 1898, CO 417/252/29002.

[73] See paragraph 168, *The Queen's regulations and orders for the army*, London 1899, 49. On 1 Dec. 1898 the garrison in South Africa stood at 8,456 men.

[74] Everett to Butler, 8 June 1899; DMI [Everett] to Butler, 6 June 1899; Butler to DMI [Everett], 7 June 1899; WO Minutes, 8 June 1899; Everett's Minute, 3 July 1899, WO 32/6369/266/Cape/36, 38. Everett was Ardagh's deputy and filling in whilst Ardagh was at the Hague Conference.

[75] Sir William Butler, *An autobiography*, London 1911, 389.

[76] Goodenough to WO, 30 Sept. 1896, WO 32/6369/266/Cape/1.

The first was the attitude of the OFS; the second that moving troops to the frontier might precipitate a crisis which diplomacy had been trying to avoid or delay. This was equally true for the Natal front, especially as the press had excited public opinion to such an extent that troop movements anywhere, no matter how innocuous, were likely to 'create false impressions'. Nevertheless, in the event of hostilities, Butler anticipated moving the Natal garrison forward to Glencoe, the Biggarsberg range, Ladysmith and Pietermaritzburg. Unlike Lansdowne, Butler thought Laing's Nek impracticable, especially as it had no water supply. In Cape Colony he proposed to occupy De Aar, Naauwpoort and Molteno thus garrisoning the important railway junctions, while a strong detachment guarded the bridge over the Orange river, ready to support Kimberley also. For good measure he reiterated his conviction that the attitude of the OFS was the important factor.[77]

Butler was in fact depressed by the whole situation. He continued to warn the War Office of the dangers facing the British in South Africa if war broke out. He tried to show how Rhodes and other capitalists were influencing the Boer mind against a peaceful solution, their aim 'the forcing of a racial war in this country', the result of which would be the destruction 'of the social body itself'.[78] Such was Butler's anxiety that when Lansdowne requested information regarding transport animals and asked for further observations,[79] he was unable to restrain himself any longer. Although Lansdowne had wanted general military comments, Butler offered political remarks instead: 'Persistent effort of a party to produce war forms in my estimation graver elements in situation here.' A war, he believed, between the 'white races' would be calamitous for South Africa.[80]

Naturally, Butler was admonished for his outburst by Lansdowne and was told, 'it is your duty to be guided in all questions of policy by High Commissioner, who is fully aware of our views, and whom you will of course loyally support'.[81] This transgression into politics was not enough to warrant Butler's sacking. No real harm had been done in addressing his views to his superiors, as he had not blatantly publicised his opinions. To Milner these remarks were an affront; they hindered Butler's efficiency and made him a 'source of weakness'. Milner asked outright, 'Would it be possible to find some pretext for summoning the General home immediately, say for consultations, and then finding him another post?'[82] Chamberlain had to explain the unpalatable truth that to recall Butler was inadvisable and would give ammunition to Milner's critics, as well as embarrass Chamberlain. Milner was reminded that

77 Butler to WO, 14 June 1899, WO 32/6369/266/Cape/36.
78 Butler to Knox, 21 June 1899, WO 32/7850
79 Lansdowne to Butler, 21 June 1899, WO 32/7849.
80 Butler to Lansdowne, 23 June 1899, ibid.
81 Lansdowne to Butler, 27 June 1899, ibid.
82 Milner to Chamberlain, 24 June 1899, JC 10/9/37. Butler had actually shown Milner his observations: Butler, *Autobiography*, 449.

Butler would be superseded anyway, should substantial reinforcements be sent out.[83]

Not long after this episode Butler received a letter from London telling him how unpopular he was in the War Office and in some newspapers. The writer, whom Butler never revealed, told him to resign if the stories about him were true. On asking Milner if he had ever been a 'hinderance or an embarrassment', Milner told him he had.[84] Consequently, on 4 July 1899, Butler offered his resignation.

Faced with Milner's hostility, forced to follow the policy of the high commissioner and unable to convince the authorities at home about the role of Rhodes and his confederates, it is not surprising Butler finally resigned. It was not until the 8 August that Lansdowne informed him that his resignation had been accepted, that he was to return to Britain, and that General Forestier-Walker was to replace him. By August, however, events in South Africa meant that Butler's return home was hardly noticed.

By mid 1899, relations between the generals and politicians in Britain had deteriorated significantly. Little consensus existed about the nature of the Boer 'threat' and consequently the best method to deal with Boer intransigence. The government believed it had formulated a policy which successfully overawed the Boers: strong words, complemented by minor increases to the South African garrison, appeared sufficient to enforce British demands. To the politicians, the Boer 'threat' was negligible. However, since early 1898, most generals agreed that war was inevitable. They felt that the correct response to Boer stubbornness was the despatch of substantial reinforcements to South Africa as a clear message of British impatience and resolve. This reaction would then either deter the Boers completely, or defeat them if they risked a war with Britain. Continual Boer defiance had convinced the generals that the government had failed to use its policy effectively. From June 1899, as the last crisis gradually unfolded, British civil–military relations deteriorated further.

[83] Chamberlain to Milner, 26 June 1899, JC 10/9/36.
[84] Butler, *Autobiography*, 451; Edward McCourt, *Remember Butler: the story of Sir William Butler*, London 1967, 228.

2

The Final Crisis: June – October 1899

In December 1898 the killing of a British miner by a Johannesburg policeman enabled Chamberlain and Milner to promote Uitlander grievances as a major issue.[1] Throughout most of the following year, pressure was applied on the Transvaal government to meet Uitlander demands and as the political situation deteriorated military matters became more prominent. Milner was particularly concerned about the defence of the British colonies and took a lively interest in the size and disposition of the army garrison. On 31 May 1899 Milner and Kruger met at Bloemfontein to discuss the problems besetting South Africa. When the talks collapsed on 5 June, the crisis between Britain and the Transvaal worsened and eventually led to war. The British government attempted to impose their demands for Uitlander rights on the Boers by utilising the diplomatic tactics used in preceding crises. However, the Boers did not respond as expected and forced the British government to increase the military pressure until a complete army corps of 50,000 men was mobilised for service in South Africa. Until the very end the British authorities never believed the Boers would fight, even though each British demand was systematically rejected. Throughout this period civil–military relations deteriorated as the generals failed to comprehend the government's desire to explain their policy to British and colonial public opinion at each stage of the crisis, and to give the Boers every chance to back down. The failure of the civil–military authorities to formulate a policy acceptable to generals and politicians alike led to serious flaws in the British response which were to have grave implications once war broke out. Despite these differences, however, ministers and soldiers were united by one factor; a complete underestimation of Boer military power.

The anxiety of Lord Wolseley

Three days after the conclusion of the Bloemfontein conference, Wolseley, on his own initiative, presented a memorandum to the Cabinet outlining his ideas on the situation in South Africa. He explained that, in addition to the garrison in South Africa, a complete army corps of 50,000 men would be required to fight the Transvaal. Wolseley felt the government should consider

---

[1] Butler, who stood in for Milner during this episode, thought the furore greatly exaggerated. Milner was in Britain until February 1899: Butler, *Autobiography*, 400–3.

'to what extent shall we at once prepare for this contingency', and whether preparations should be open or secret. He favoured mobilising the army corps on Salisbury plain, under the general who would command it in South Africa. This would reveal British determination, and could be done without calling out the reserves, thus avoiding consulting parliament.[2]

The Cabinet, however, rejected outright military preparations. Salisbury told the queen that public opinion, in Britain and Cape Colony, was not ready to support a war with Kruger. Instead, the Boers would be pressed steadily by diplomacy and nothing like an ultimatum would be presented.[3]

Kruger was coerced by a combination of official publications and speeches. On 13 and 14 June Chamberlain published correspondence relating to Uitlander grievances, which included Milner's famous 'Helots' despatch of 4 May. On 26 June Chamberlain himself launched the verbal assault on Kruger, by emphasising the importance of securing Uitlander rights. It was the only way, he argued, to maintain peace in South Africa. These tactics, particularly Chamberlain's speech, were considered highly successful by ministers, yet the government still lacked sufficient confidence to increase the garrison as Milner demanded, even though he felt the publications had created a sensation in South Africa. In fact, Colonial Office officials were irritated by Milner's views, Chamberlain minuting that he would not be hurried and did not believe an Afrikaner rising was imminent in the Cape, as Milner had suggested. Selborne told Milner that the publications had not won over the public sufficiently enough.[4]

As Chamberlain's speech had been favourably received, the Cabinet felt able to make some military preparations. It was agreed to send special service officers to South Africa to enhance defences in Cape Colony. Cabinet assent was given to General Butler to make minor transport arrangements for the garrison, and extra supplies of ammunition were also sent.[5] In addition, sometime in early June, General Buller was appointed the commander of an expeditionary force should one be needed.[6]

Prompted by a combination of public confidence arising from Chamberlain's speech, and the need to do more in case the Boers were unresponsive, Lansdowne asked Wolseley and Buller about the possibility of more overt military preparations. Buller was summoned to the War Office on 3 July and Lansdowne told him he was contemplating the despatch of 10,000 men to

2 Memo. by Wolseley, 8 June 1899, CAB 37/50/38.
3 Salisbury to the queen, 13 June 1899, CAB 41/25/12.
4 Milner to Chamberlain and CO Minutes, 16 June 1899, CO 48/542/fos 466–7; Selborne to Milner, 25 June 1899, in *Crisis of British power*, 83–5; Porter, *Origins*, 217–23.
5 Lansdowne to Wolseley, 16 June 1899; Wolseley's comments, 17 June 1899; Lansdowne's decision, 18 June 1899, WO 32/7846; Salisbury to the queen, 20, 27 June 1899, CAB 41/25/13, 14.
6 Milner's military secretary, Hanbury-Williams, said Buller's appointment was well received: 'I am told his name is a terror to the Boers': Hanbury-Williams to Altham, 27 June 1899, CO 417/275/fo. 433.

South Africa.[7] The following day, Lansdowne asked Wolseley to prepare 10,000 men for service in South Africa, in case the negotiations should collapse. Wolseley was advised to consider such matters as transport, equipment and costs.[8] Whether doubling the garrison was felt to be a sufficient indication of British resolve, or whether 10,000 men was the number the military could mobilise at short notice is not indicated. Equally, it is not clear if this was Lansdowne's idea, or one taken by the Cabinet. But as the generals' opinions were put before the Cabinet, it is likely the decision was not Lansdowne's alone. On 6 and 7 July 1899 Lansdowne received Buller's and Wolseley's views. Buller was hostile to the idea of sending troops from the main field force. He had taken this position two years before; he knew the Boers well and probably realised that only an 'overwhelming force' would either intimidate or eventually defeat them. He preferred to send the whole complement once hostilities were inevitable; in the meantime he wanted defensive preparations made in the Cape and Natal. Buller also wanted a decision made about the OFS, as 'the route to be adopted in operations against Pretoria must chiefly be decided on with regard to our relations with the Orange Free State', especially as this route would make it easier to obtain supplies and transport.

Wolseley broadly agreed with Buller's comments and endorsed his plea that the position of the OFS be clarified. But, as in 1897, Wolseley did not share Buller's views regarding the 10,000 reinforcements. He considered it a good idea 'being an open demonstration of a warlike policy, and also an efficacious method of strengthening our present military position there'. Apart from this Wolseley and Buller were in complete accord.[9] However, on 12 July, Lansdowne informed Wolseley that 'There is now I think a general agreement that if there is to be a serious demonstration it should take a different shape. The proposal need not be further pursued.'[10]

The plan was altered by a change in the political situation. On 7 July the Boers issued tentative proposals that offered the prospect of revitalising diplomatic negotiations. Unwilling to appear intransigent themselves, and genuinely optimistic, the British government gladly deferred making overt military preparations. The Cabinet now saw the chance of getting concessions from the Boers without the use of force or more expenditure. Wolseley, however, feared Kruger was playing an intricate game, having found the measure of the British Cabinet, especially their desire to avoid war until public opinion clamoured for it. Rather contemptuously, he thought the

---

7   Buller to brother, 3 Nov. 1899, and Memo. by Buller, c. 1903, 1–2, Buller papers, PRO, WO 132/6, 24.
8   Lansdowne to Wolseley, 4 July 1899, WO 32/7847.
9   Memo. by Buller, 6 July 1899, and Wolseley's comments, 7 July 1899, CAB 37/50/43.
10 WO Minutes, 12 July 1899, WO 32/7847.

politicians only desired to forestall war and let a future government incur the odium of fighting the Boers.[11]

Wolseley's anxiety was perceptive: Kruger was tantalising the Cabinet. Salisbury explained to the queen that he was 'much impressed with the more pacific tone of the Cabinet': most ministers felt Britain should be circumspect in its actions as public opinion was still unfavourable.[12] The government's determination to hold back was further strengthened when, on 18 July, the Transvaal Volksraad clarified the Boer proposals by carrying an amendment reducing the residence qualification from nine years to seven. The apparent Boer climb-down seemed to indicate that if the government used diplomatic and military tactics similar to those employed between 1896 and 1898 then the Boers, for all their obduracy, would eventually retreat. Moreover, the apparent relief at being able to drop military preparations at a stroke revealed the trend in civil–military relations throughout June and July. Each time public opinion appeared favourable, military estimates and preparations were asked and called for, until the next Boer diplomatic initiative seemed to turn public opinion in the other direction.

Milner was astounded by the government's prevarication, especially as Chamberlain appeared to believe the offer was genuine. So alarmed was he by Chamberlain's telegrams that he suspected 'He seems now to *wish a patch-up.*'[13] Yet Milner realised the weakness of this policy: the government left themselves with little room to manoeuvre. A forthright note to Chamberlain revealed the nub of his argument. Milner stated that as the Boers were so powerful militarily, the present garrison of nearly 10,000 men was totally worthless. More troops were needed to intimidate the Transvaal, to make them honour their side of the bargain. He explained that if the crisis was resolved without the stipulation of Transvaal disarmament, the Boers would be free to abrogate any treaty whenever they wished. 'Public opinion would surely approve action directed to prevent establishment of military power overshadowing S. Africa.'[14]

Milner's protestations emphasised the fact that the government had not considered how agreements were to be implemented and enforced. Intimidating the Boers had seemed easy; ensuring that intimidation lasted was not so simple. Milner tried to remedy this defect in government policy; whether it was his pleas that awoke the government is unclear; but Salisbury at least suddenly realised the importance of keeping military pressure on the Boers, to stop them 'back-sliding' in the future. However, his suggestion that troops

---

11 Wolseley to his wife, 11 July 1899, Hove Central library, Wolseley papers (WP) 28/38.
12 Salisbury to the queen, 11 July 1899, CAB 41/25/16.
13 Milner to Selborne and Selborne to Milner, 12, 27 July 1899, in *Crisis of British power*, 89–92. Selborne assured Milner that public opinion was being won over – gradually. Salisbury, he explained, wanted steady military pressure to be applied.
14 Milner to Chamberlain, 16 July 1899, in *Milner papers*, i. 511.

be positioned on the Transvaal's northern border, away from the politics of the Cape, lacked subtlety.[15]

Securing Natal

Following the Boer announcement on 18 July, the Cabinet declared publicly that now the Boers had offered concessions they would not tolerate any turning back, and equated any such move as a threat to British supremacy. To reinforce their stand, ministers, in reply to the Boer proposals, advocated the formation of a joint commission to investigate how the proposals might work in practice.[16] Yet while government rhetoric was aimed at the British public, it did not impress politicians in Natal. Between late July and early August opinion within the Natal ministry began to exert a significant influence over British policy.

The attitude of the Natal government was important for Milner. As the only colony with a British majority, opinion in Natal, if cultivated properly, was a considerable asset. Milner, unable to rely on the loyalty of the Afrikaner Bond ministry in Cape Colony, had to use Natal as the mainstay of his loyalist support. Without the backing of this important sector of colonial opinion, Milner's attempts to persuade the British that colonial loyalty was at risk would have little credibility. But as Natal offered the Boers access to the sea it was likely to become a major, if not the main, battlefield in the event of war. Even if the capture of Durban was beyond the Boers' capabilities Natal, nevertheless, offered them the opportunity of gaining early victories. Milner had realised this factor earlier and in May had told Selborne that an initial Boer success would induce the OFS to join the Transvaal and spark a rebellion in the Afrikaner north-eastern districts of Cape Colony. Milner wanted to see an *overwhelming* British force in Natal *before* the outbreak of war, and favoured the early occupation of Laing's Nek: 'My view has been and still is, in spite of all these alarms and excursions, that if we are perfectly determined we shall win without a fight or with a mere apology for one.' But it would be necessary to have a large force in South Africa to complement 'diplomatic pressure of steadily increasing urgency'. This would have the double effect of preparing for a hostile Boer response while denying them the chance of an early victory. Even so, the Boers proximity to the strategic positions of Laing's Nek and the Biggarsberg meant that in all likelihood they would achieve that opening success, but the important thing for Milner was that British forces should hit back immediately. Having a strong force in South Africa would also be the only way to deter the OFS.[17] Boer numerical superiority and ability to concentrate numbers quickly meant they might easily defeat a smaller

15 Salisbury to Chamberlain, 19 July 1899, JC 5/67/114.
16 Porter, *Origins*, 223–33; Smith, *Origins*, 305–15.
17 Milner to Selborne, 24 May 1899, in *Milner papers*, i. 400–4.

British contingent, and over-run much territory before British reinforcements arrived. The propaganda value of Boer victories was something both Milner and the Natal government were loath to contemplate.

To secure Natal's support, therefore, Milner instructed the governor, Hely-Hutchinson, to inform ministers 'that it is out of the question that any invasion of Natal should be tolerated by Her Majesty's Government. Such an event is highly improbable, I think: but Natal would be defended with the whole force of the Empire, if it occurred, and redress would be exacted for any injury to her.' Milner told Chamberlain that he hoped this would make the Natal government 'overtly [take] our side on the Uitlander question'.[18] Consequently, Milner was keen to humour the Natal government whenever possible. So when ministers became apprehensive about the colony's defence, and wished to be informed about military plans, Milner lobbied for them vociferously and successfully.[19] Milner attempted to use the Natal government's anxieties in a bid to get the reinforcements he craved. Yet, paradoxically, his lobbying did not soothe the Natal government; in fact it made their anxiety worse. Informed of the plans, ministers discovered that the area to the far north, known as the 'triangle', was to be abandoned owing to the lack of troops. General Symons, then in command of British forces in Natal, only intended to defend the Glencoe/Dundee coalfields and forsake the defence of Newcastle and, more emotively, Laing's Nek. As Hely-Hutchinson explained, Symons would need far more troops to defend the whole colony.[20] Symons had informed the governor that 1,600 men were required to render Natal safe from raids and to hold Newcastle, while 5,600 men were required to defend the colony from Laing's Nek.[21] This information made the Natal ministry call for reinforcements, and remind Milner of his promise of 25 May; furthermore they added that if negotiations with the Boers collapsed, 'such steps may be at once taken as may be necessary for the effectual defence of the whole colony'.[22]

The Colonial Office responded enthusiastically to Natal's request. The Boers had not been forthcoming in their answer to Chamberlain's joint enquiry proposal, and therefore needed some prompting. Natal now provided the arguments for increasing the military pressure on Kruger, and assisting Britain's bargaining position by an addition to the garrison. Clearly, officials had in mind earlier Boer retreats when troops were sent to South Africa.

[18] Milner to Chamberlain, 25 May 1899, WO 32/7850. Chamberlain endorsed Milner's action.
[19] Milner to Chamberlain, 16 July 1899, CO 417/263/fo. 685. Wolseley, however, was against this arguing it would increase the difficulties of the GOC SA. Wolseley did not trust colonial governments and said telling them military plans, 'amounts to throwing one's cards on the table': Wolseley to Knox, 27 July 1899, WO 32/6369/266/Cape/41.
[20] Hely-Hutchinson to ministers, 24 July 1899, CO 179/205/fos 858–9.
[21] Symons to Hely-Hutchinson, 21 July 1899, CO 179/205/fos 863–4.
[22] Hely-Hutchinson to Chamberlain, 25 July 1899, CO 179/205/fos 791–2, 796–7.

Selborne wanted 5,000 troops sent, and argued it was the cheapest way to conclude negotiations successfully.[23]

Milner pointed out that reinforcements would make Natal secure and 'be in a position of advantage almost compelling submission'. He also stated that for once Natal was actually asking for troops rather than opposing the idea: 'It is an opportunity that may never recur.'[24]

In the end, the Cabinet decided to send only 2,000 troops to Natal immediately, slightly more than Symons wanted to make the colony safe from Newcastle and safe against raids, but not enough to make the whole colony secure.[25] Apparently Lansdowne had recommended the figure of 2,000 and was supported by Hicks Beach who was against any unnecessary expenditure. Salisbury had wanted to send 5,000, but eventually agreed with his chancellor and war minister. Treasury control of the spending departments had, it seems, created a mentality of economy whereby ministers were loath to recommend extraordinary expenditure.[26] Undoubtedly this played a part in the decision-making process, but Treasury control, actual or influential, was not the only reason for limiting the number of reinforcements. Ministers were following precedent, as the earlier discussion of previous crises has shown. Lansdowne told Wolseley 'The object of such an addition would be to strengthen our own position, to reassure the colonists, and, above all, to strengthen our diplomacy during the new phase which is commencing.' Lansdowne was swayed by several arguments for recommending the lesser figure. First, as he explained further, this small addition was not designed to occupy Laing's Nek as this would require a lot more men, especially as a Boer invasion was not expected, 'and we are not asked to provide against it'. Secondly, he could refer to the precedent of 1897. Thirdly, the Natal ministry was expected to supplement the regular army by calling out the volunteers. Wolseley welcomed the addition to the Natal garrison even though it would not make the colony entirely safe, but 'it will make our position north of the Tugela River, and at Ladysmith particularly, much more secure than it is at present'.[27] Nevertheless, Wolseley remained unconvinced that this was a proper answer to Boer obduracy and told Edward Hamilton, a Treasury official, that 'Kruger intends to play the game of bluff for some little time longer – he has not yet put us to sufficient trouble and expense – and that he will then climb down'.[28] Thus the government had dealt with the Boers as they had done in the past; all that remained was for the Boers to take the hint.

[23] CO Minutes, 26 July 1899, CO 179/205/fo. 790.

[24] Milner to Chamberlain, 30 July 1899, CO 417/264/fos 238–9.

[25] Salisbury to the queen, 1 Aug. 1899, CAB 41/25/17.

[26] M. M. Yakutiel, ' "Treasury Control" and the South African War 1899– c. 1905', unpubl. DPhil diss. Oxford 1989, 12–13.

[27] Lansdowne to Wolseley and Wolseley to Lansdowne, 2 Aug. 1899, RCWSA, xl, Cd. 1789, 264–5.

[28] Sir Edward Hamilton's diary, cited in Smith, Origins, 345.

Cajoling the Boers

Early August was an anxious time for the British government. As the Boers seemed unwilling to respond further to British overtures, drastic measures had to be contemplated once more. The pattern of the period following the Bloemfontein conference was repeating itself as Boer non-compliance appeared very real. In view of the fact that 'a new phase was commencing', Lansdowne, at the behest of the Cabinet, presented a memorandum on 12 August which provided information 'as to the time which would elapse between the occurrence of an event rendering hostilities with the Transvaal inevitable and the concentration in the north of Natal of the force which we should probably send out, viz., an Army Corps and a cavalry division'.[29]

Lansdowne told his colleagues how difficult it was to get the timing right when ordering full mobilisation. If all was in readiness, the army corps would take less than a month to embark for South Africa. Unfortunately, it would not only cost large sums of money to get everything ready, but as nothing had yet been done, the mobilisation would take far longer. The army, in fact, lacked transport, equipment and supplies; and it would take three months to remedy these defects. Furthermore, the Natal railway was so inadequate it would take an extra six weeks for the army to move troops, equipment and supplies to the railhead. Lansdowne estimated it would take four months before the army corps was ready for action in South Africa. He calculated that over £1m. would have to be spent to reduce that period by a month. However, Lansdowne's concluding paragraph ended optimistically because he did not believe the Natal garrison was in danger: 'The long delay anticipated in this Memorandum would therefore not involve any risk of a military reverse although its political effect might be serious and inconvenient.'

Lansdowne was later asked why he did not make any recommendations. He said it was 'because I cannot dissociate my position as Secretary of State for War from my position as a member of the Cabinet. I placed the Cabinet in full possession of the problem which lay before us. I gave them this "time table", so that they might know what risk was incurred by the postponement of the expenditure.'[30] The Cabinet had no intention of mobilising the army corps; it was merely time to consider options. The extent of the government's military policy was revealed by the despatch of 2,000 troops to Natal. To begin ordering the mobilisation of the army corps, when public opinion was unfavourable, would merely show the government to be war-mongering. Moreover, the Boer response to the reinforcements had not been appreciated. Cabinet policy was well settled at that stage; the Boers were to be gently prodded, not goaded into retaliation.

That Lansdowne did not need to make a recommendation can be seen in Salisbury's reaction to his memorandum. Salisbury, perhaps speaking for the

---

29 Memo. by Lansdowne, 12 Aug. 1899, CAB 37/50/49.
30 Question 21154, RCWSA, xli, Cd. 1791, 508.

Cabinet, revealed the political thinking at the time. He did not consider it worth spending £1m. just to reduce the army's preparations from four to three months. For Salisbury, the 'wiser plan' was to spend money only when war was inevitable.[31] None the less, the politicians were now aware of the requirements should they decide to use the army corps; it remained for them to judge when the moment was politically suitable.

A week later, the Cabinet confirmed that the time for a full-scale mobilisation had not yet arrived by rejecting a new memorandum from Wolseley,[32] written without the approval of his political superiors, who were away on holiday. Wolseley focused on the weak garrison in Natal and echoed Milner's views that such a situation offered the Boers the chance of an early victory, particularly if they occupied the 'triangle', which would dismay loyalist opinion. He suggested the immediate despatch of 10,000 men drawn from the army corps. Once in position they could easily hold the 'triangle' and facilitate the future deployment of the main force.

The Cabinet spurned Wolseley's request because there had again been a dramatic change in the political situation. The Boers had despatched a new set of proposals (known as the Smuts Proposals, after the Transvaal's attorney-general who had been instrumental in formulating them), which seemed to offer the British a diplomatic victory. Chamberlain informed Lansdowne that these justified 'some delay in proceeding with preparations which would involve heavy expenditure'. Chamberlain was conscious that the proposals, like others before them, might amount to nothing, and suggested that the War Office prepare reinforcements as he expected the next British demand to be an ultimatum.[33] For Chamberlain these remarks hid, for the time being, his belief that the Boers had finally backed down.

There was a hint of irritation in Lansdowne's reply to Wolseley because, after all, the situation did seem to be changing for the better. Lansdowne told Wolseley he should have spoken out earlier, preferably at the beginning of the month when the situation was more critical. Lansdowne did not elaborate on this point and it is difficult to judge which predicament was the more critical of the two. Perhaps the appeals of the Natal ministry made it seem so; or Lansdowne was just exasperated with Wolseley for speaking out when he and other ministers were on holiday. Relations between the two were worse than ever owing to Wolseley's reluctance to use British troops from India as a source of reinforcements. Wolseley hated the Indian army for two reasons: first, Indian army troops had, to him, lost the battle of Majuba in 1881; second, they were associated more with his detested rival Lord Roberts. Lansdowne, however, reminded Wolseley that troops from India could reach South Africa earlier than those from Britain, and then proceeded to give him a lesson in strategy. Lansdowne, referring to Wolseley's favourable attitude

31 Salisbury to Chamberlain, 16 Aug. 1899, JC 5/67/115.
32 Memo. by Wolseley, 18 Aug. 1899, CAB 37/50/52.
33 Chamberlain to Lansdowne, 18 Aug. 1899, JC 5/51/63.

towards deploying troops in Natal, said British forces would be better disposed in Cape Colony as a complete force. They would then be ready for an advance through the OFS, should the OFS prove hostile, and added that he knew Wolseley endorsed this route: the troops from India, which were earmarked for Natal, meanwhile, could act as a valuable diversion. Lansdowne did not share Wolseley's anxiety about the safety of northern Natal and thought the present garrison quite capable of looking after itself.[34]

For an 'amateur' such as Lansdowne to tell the professional what was good or bad about a particular strategic scenario was something Wolseley could never let pass and Lansdowne's note did not go unanswered for long. Four days later Wolseley reminded him that Kruger's stalling was likely to cost more than any overt military preparations owing to the continual unrest. Indeed, on 21 August, only two days after presenting their proposals, the Boers had hastily put conditions on their acceptance, and were obviously 'backsliding' again. British strength in South Africa was such that if war came 'we shall surrender the initiative to Kruger; and in no recent case that I can think of would, or, at least, if properly handled, could that initiative be more likely to seriously injure our national prestige, or be more hurtful to the party in office, if I may venture upon such a political comment'. To secure peace, therefore, it was necessary to have a show of force in South Africa.[35]

As the Boers appeared to have promised so much and then backed down again, ministers now had to consider the possibility of altering their tactics. Public opinion had to be gauged carefully, and two questions needed consideration in attempting to measure the trend of public support: had ministers exhausted the diplomatic option sufficiently? Or was the time ripe for overt and substantial military measures to be ordered? As the recent addition to the Natal garrison had obviously not intimidated the Boers, Chamberlain felt strongly that they had been accommodated long enough and it was time for a substantial demonstration of British strength and resolve. As the views of Milner and Wolseley coincided, Chamberlain felt there was a point in sending out substantial reinforcements to support British demands. He concluded that if the Boer conditions to the Smuts proposals proved unacceptable, then they must be compelled towards a settlement, and that 10,000 troops ought to go to South Africa. He also wanted it made public that the army corps would soon follow.[36] Lansdowne too was moving towards this view, although a little reluctantly: the Boer proposals 'seem to me to merit benevolent examination'. But, on hearing that Conyngham Greene believed the Boers were likely to reject Chamberlain's demands, he concluded that the Indian

34 Lansdowne to Wolseley 20 Aug. 1899, CAB 37/50/53; to Chamberlain, 21 Aug. 1899, JC 5/51/67.
35 Wolseley to Lansdowne, 24 Aug. 1899, CAB 37/50/56.
36 Chamberlain to Lansdowne, 24 Aug. 1899, JC 5/51/70. Chamberlain endorsed Lansdowne's view that India should send the reinforcements as this was the cheaper option. Milner wanted 5,000 troops in northern Natal in order to quell any signs of rebellion and give heart to loyal colonists: Milner to Chamberlain, 23 Aug. 1899, JC 10/9/48.

contingent should be sent sooner rather than later.[37] Thus, 2,000 troops had proved incapable of altering Boer intransigence; the precedent set by earlier crises had failed. The time had now arrived for the government to increase diplomatic pressure and consider Wolseley's favoured option – the despatch of 10,000 troops to South Africa. All that remained was for public opinion to endorse such a measure.

On 28 August Chamberlain told the Boers he could not accept their conditions as they stood, although he left enough leeway for the Boers to make some arrangement. Nevertheless, on 2 September the Boers withdrew the Smuts Proposals altogether. For the British, the military option was now of paramount importance. The lull in preparations, evident in late August, made Milner fear that nothing would be done until the last moment. To Selborne, Milner wrote vehemently that it was time for stronger action: 'My own absolute conviction is that it is worth those millions to settle for ever, as you would, the South African question. If the plunge cannot be taken *now*, it will be too late.'[38] The only problem facing the politicians now, as Chamberlain acknowledged to Milner was that 'the technical *casus belli* is a very weak one', which hindered preparations and resolute action.[39] Consequently, in order to discuss and consider the situation, ministers decided to hold a special Cabinet meeting on 8 September. Although ministers were prepared to contemplate increasing the military pressure, they had failed to anticipate sufficiently the need for any rapid moves in talks with their military advisers, and there was a looming gap between what the politicians suddenly wanted and what the military could provide.

On 5 September General Buller interrupted the political debate and awoke the Cabinet to this problem. He requested that before the government decided on an ultimatum 'the military should be in a position to enforce it'. At the same time he wrote to Wolseley, and expressed his concern over future strategy. Buller had to assume the army corps would be based in Natal as the attitude of the OFS remained unclarified. His major concern, however, was the length of time needed for the reinforcements to arrive; as far as he was concerned the present garrison could defend itself, but not the whole colony. He urged therefore that any ultimatum be delayed until adequate numbers of troops had arrived in Natal.[40]

Wolseley endorsed Buller's views in a note to Lansdowne, which represented the difficulties facing the soldiers. While condemning the fact that preparations had not been made sooner, Wolseley asked: 'Can we not stave off actual hostilities for five or six weeks to enable us to collect in Natal the

[37] Lansdowne to Wolseley, 27 Aug. 1899, CAB 37/50/57; to Salisbury, 1 Sept. 1899, Salisbury correspondence, fos 431–2.
[38] Milner to Selborne, 30 Aug. 1899, in *Crisis of British power*, 93–4.
[39] Chamberlain to Milner, 2 Sept. 1899, JC 10/9/50.
[40] Buller to Salisbury, 5 Sept. 1899, CAB 37/50/62; to Wolseley, 5 Sept. 1899, CAB 37/50/66.

military force I have all along recommended should be sent there?' Wolseley's irritation centred on the belief that the Boers were now in a better position to strike the first blow: they had, he said, been given 'the initiative'. Wolseley wanted immediate reinforcements sent to Natal; his biggest fear was that the government would precipitate a crisis before the army was ready, under the impression that it was. It was time, he added, for the soldiers and the politicians to work hand in hand.[41]

With the Boers proving obdurate and unlikely to make any major concessions, Chamberlain's views moved closer to those of Milner and the soldiers. He was anxious about loyalist fidelity, and used the arguments of the generals to support his case. Chamberlain was concerned not to overstate his argument, particularly to fellow politicians who were wary of taking military opinion at face value. He qualified his assertions by saying he thought the soldiers' opinions somewhat exaggerated when they declared the garrison to be weak or in danger. By so doing, he was able to offer the Indian contingent as a compromise; he could placate the military by sending troops and accommodate the politicians by not making overt military preparations. For Chamberlain the Indian contingent was the best of both worlds. He argued that if military preparations were necessary 'has not the time arrived ... when we should increase our demands and make a final settlement?' The following day he emphasised his views more forcefully. He reminded his colleagues that the only time the Boers backed down was when the British supported their demands with force; and if Britain failed to resolve the crisis now 'we shall have to maintain permanently in South Africa a very large garrison, at a great expense to the British taxpayer, and involving the utter disorganization of our military system'.[42] Chamberlain, in fact, echoed what Milner had been saying for the past three months. He, like Milner, worried that an early Boer victory might have disastrous results, with the government held responsible. As a result, the Cabinet decided to send 10,000 reinforcements to Natal, exclusive of those sanctioned in August; this, as Salisbury explained to the queen, was done after considering messages from Natal because there were signs the Boers might strike first. They also resolved to test the OFS by demanding President Steyn maintain a strict neutrality should war occur between Britain and the Transvaal. Meanwhile, another note was sent to Kruger offering him the chance to reconsider, and to allow for the period required for the reinforcements to arrive: if Kruger's reply was unsatisfactory the next communication would be an ultimatum.[43]

---

41 Wolseley to Lansdowne, 5 Sept. 1899, CAB 37/50/69.
42 Memos by Chamberlain, 5, 6 Sept. 1899, CAB 37/50/63, 70.
43 Salisbury to the queen, 8 Sept. 1899, CAB 41/25/18; Hely-Hutchinson to Chamberlain, 6 Sept. 1899, CO 179/206/fos 226–8. Evidently, the Natal ministry was still anxious about abandoning Laing's Nek, and feared that a successful Boer invasion would dishearten the loyalists and the natives. Consequently, one Colonial Office official wrote that it was far

The Cabinet had, apparently, met the requirements of the military. Although Buller had second thoughts and wanted even more troops sent to Natal, Wolseley told Lansdowne 'that he will stake his reputation that after the reinforcements have arrived we shall be safe as to anything S[outh] of the Biggarsberg'. Any delay, he added, in preparing further reinforcements would be an inconvenience, nothing more.[44]

One effect of the government's decision was that ministers proved reluctant to order immediate preparations for the mobilisation of the army corps, despite Milner's pleas for them to do so. Ministers were concerned lest they should either appear aggressive by not giving the Boers a chance to consider their note of 8 September, or provoke them unduly. Such reticence, however, went unrewarded. Kruger rejected the Cabinet's overtures, and it became clear to ministers and soldiers alike that the army corps would have to be mobilised. Lansdowne, after consulting Wolseley and Buller, thought it best to wait until Natal 'should be thoroughly safe'. Moreover, he explained that the army corps' transport would take thirteen weeks to collect in South Africa, whereas the troops themselves would take only nine weeks to mobilise and arrive in Cape Town. Thus the four weeks delay was necessary to synchronise the arrival of the troops with the collection of their transport. Lansdowne, therefore, wanted Cabinet authorisation to purchase and arrange transportation and supplies immediately. This he believed would not provoke the Boers, as purchasing for the garrison was already taking place.[45]

On 23 September, the day after Kruger was warned finally that if he did not respond the next note would be an ultimatum, the Cabinet authorised Wolseley to spend £640,000 on transport for the army corps, something he believed should have been done in July. Wolseley did not share the government's concern with public opinion and had little sympathy for, or understanding of, Cabinet policy. As he explained to General Ardagh:

> We have lost two months through the absolute folly of our Cabinet & the incapacity of its members to take in the requirements & the difficulties of war ... It is no wonder we never achieve much in war & have to struggle through obstacles created by the folly & war ignorance of civilian ministers & War Office clerks.[46]

more important 'from a political point of view' to defend Natal; he did not believe the Boers would attack Cape Colony, probably because of the Afrikaner Bond ministry and generally sympathetic population: CO Minutes, 7 Sept. 1899, CO 179/206/fos 223–4.

[44] Lansdowne to Chamberlain, 9 Sept. 1899, JC 5/51/80; Thomas Pakenham, *The Boer war*, London 1982, 97.

[45] Milner to Chamberlain, 19 Sept. 1899, in *Milner papers*, i. 540–1; Lansdowne to Salisbury, 21 Sept. 1899, Salisbury correspondence, fos 433–9.

[46] Wolseley to Ardagh, 23 Sept. 1899, PRO 30/40/3/61–5; to his wife, 22 Sept. 1899, WP 28/55.

Ardagh shared Wolseley's frustration and felt Cabinet policy had not inspired terror or respect in the Boer leaders: 'I cannot, from what I know, defend their attitude as being the course most likely to end in peace with honour.'[47]

Strategic options

The next matter for ministers to consider was the campaign strategy. As early as 3 June 1899 Major Altham had compiled a memorandum recommending an invasion of the OFS as the best route to Johannesburg and Pretoria. On 8 August Altham reiterated his view that as the OFS was likely to side with the Transvaal, British military preparations ought to ensure they were based 'on the definite hypothesis of a hostile Free State'.[48]

This aspect enabled the South African command to intervene in the political debate. The garrison commanders had largely been forgotten by London, especially since Butler's resignation. The Cabinet and the military in London were too busy arguing amongst themselves to consider advice from the 'front' and felt, it seems, that the South African command was of little importance. In fact, Forestier-Walker was given no instructions before leaving Britain, nor left any information by Butler.[49] Similarly, General White, who had been appointed commander of the enhanced garrison in Natal, left Britain on 16 September also having received no instructions.[50] However, on 11 September, Forestier-Walker, who had only just arrived in South Africa, told Ardagh that it was virtually certain the OFS would join the Transvaal, as would Afrikaners living along the Cape Colony border with the OFS.[51] That same day Forestier-Walker informed Lansdowne that Milner was insisting that Laing's Nek be occupied at once, an operation he thought too risky under the circumstances. Lansdowne then informed Chamberlain that the military were against Milner's request to occupy Laing's Nek: Wolseley, Buller, Forestier-Walker and White were all averse to such an action.[52] The separation of the two commands in South Africa was an indication of the military preference for the Cape route. Their insistence that the Natal forces should not be moved further north than the Biggarsberg (which effectively abandoned the 'triangle' area) was meant to facilitate an advance into the OFS,

---

47 Ardagh to his wife, 24 Sept. 1899, PRO 30/40/3/66.
48 Memos by Altham, 3 June 1899 and 8 Aug. 1899, WO 32/7844 and WO 32/6369/266/Cape/42; the OFS had recently voted £34,370, or an extra 11% of its average annual expenditure, to be spent on arms.
49 Forestier-Walker evidence, RCWSA, xli, Cd. 1791, 13657–62, 93–4.
50 Ibid. 14720–2, 49.
51 Forestier-Walker to Ardagh, 11 Sept. 1899, WO 32/7855.
52 The Natal command was made distinct from that of Buller's, as he would be in Cape Colony. White though was subordinate to Buller.

and not risk the Natal garrison being cut off in the north. As Lansdowne stated, 'Whatever our private opinions . . . we must upon a point of this sort be guided by our military advisers.'[53]

On 25 September, Lansdowne discussed the problem with the Cabinet and presented notes by Wolseley and Buller (dated 24 and 25 September respectively) which supported the OFS move, and which he endorsed. If the OFS was ignored, and the Natal route decided upon, Lansdowne argued, 'we shall find it virtually impossible to alter our plans should the Orange Free State at the last moment declare itself hostile'. Hostility seemed likely given President Steyn's recent speeches.[54] Following a further note from Lansdowne which stated that the OFS route would save a week's preparations, as the army corps had less distance to travel, the Cabinet agreed to declare war on the OFS as well as the Transvaal. Moreover, they also agreed to mobilise the army corps and call up the reserves, a public message to the Boers, and British and loyalist opinion alike. The military recommended the reserves be mobilised on 7 October, and then parliament could meet on the 17th to sanction preparations. Despite the Transvaal's recalcitrance, the Cabinet still hoped that these preparations might prompt a Boer retreat. Kruger was given one last chance to back down.[55] Significantly, the Cabinet agreed to hold back any advance of the Natal garrison, in order to expedite the advance of the army corps. This was to be a key factor as the campaign unfolded.

The decision to mobilise the reserves and despatch the army corps occasioned relief rather than euphoria. Militarily, the British position seemed safe, and ministers did not believe the Boers would attack first.[56] Military opinion echoed that of the politicians. Wolseley was highly confident and felt the army corps was better led and equipped than the army sent to the Crimea in 1854.[57] Colonel Everett, temporarily in charge of the Intelligence Department, confidently stated that after the Transvaal had made troop deductions to watch over natives, Rhodesia and Johannesburg, only 9,000 men would be available for offensive operations. Similarly, the OFS, after their deductions, could only field 5,000 men.[58] Furthermore, Lansdowne

[53] Lansdowne to Chamberlain, 15 Sept. 1899; also enclosed is Forestier-Walker to Lansdowne, 11 Sept. 1899, JC 5/51/82.
[54] Memo. by Lansdowne, 25 Sept. 1899, CAB 37/51/73.
[55] Lansdowne to Salisbury, 30 Sept. 1899, Salisbury correspondence, fos 441–4; Salisbury to the queen, 29, 30 Sept. 1899, CAB 41/25/20, 21.
[56] Hicks Beach to Chamberlain, 4 Oct. 1899, JC 16/5/26; Chamberlain to Balfour, 3 Oct. 1899, JC 5/5/83.
[57] Wolseley to his wife, 29 Sept. 1899, WP 28/61.
[58] Memo. by Everett, 28 Sept. 1899, WO 32/6369. Altham's memo. of 3 June estimated a combined Boer force of 29,000, plus 4,000 Cape rebels. Everett deducted 15% from the Transvaal official figures to remove 16–18 and 50–60-year-olds. Likewise, 15% was deducted from the OFS figures supplied by his own department. The resulting figure was

showed Chamberlain notes from Buller and Wood which stated they were convinced the Boers would not attack Natal.[59]

Despite the apparent confidence within the ranks of the politicians and the soldiers, an important factor was emerging from the last days of peace. Whereas the Cabinet seemed content that everything had now been done to bring the crisis to a head and safeguard British interests in South Africa, doubts were materialising about government policy. Milner maintained that the interval between the arrival of the 10,000 reinforcements, who were expected to arrive in mid October, and the appearance of the army corps in late November/early December, was critical. Until then the Cape had few defenders and any Boer success might cause an Afrikaner uprising. Milner wanted units of the army corps sent out immediately in order to foster the impression that a steady stream of troops were arriving in Cape Town. Milner was prepared for the worst:

> and I foresee that if we met with any serious reverses in October, the fact of being without any prospect of further support till the end of November would discourage our men and give a tremendous impetus to the enemy. We might lose in a few weeks what it would take months to recover. Telegrams from home indicating long delay are doing mischief here.[60]

Indeed, British public opinion was beginning to turn in another direction. Selborne was concerned that only four-fifths of public opinion supported the government, not only due to the stalemate in negotiations, but, more ominously, owing to 'our hesitancy (militarily almost criminal) in making early preparations'.[61] In fact this problem had been pinpointed earlier by Brodrick, Salisbury's deputy at the Foreign Office. He believed that 'The Govt. have been courting disaster' because of the delay in authorising military preparations. 'I am not a jingo or a Milnerite, but it goes to my heart to see the risks we are running.'[62] The government was facing a particular difficulty as war approached: how to prevent public opinion becoming extreme and demanding massive military preparations. Now that the Cabinet had gained public support for war, they needed success to ensure that this support was not turned against them. Already, the obvious gap between the arrival of the reinforcements and the arrival of the army corps was pregnant with adverse possibilities. If military defeats should occur during that time, then the

55% of the total male population. Everett was in charge because Ardagh was ill and Altham was going to South Africa.
59 Lansdowne to Chamberlain, 4 Oct. 1899, JC 5/51/86. The notes are not included in the Chamberlain papers.
60 Milner to Chamberlain, 8 Oct. 1899, JC 10/9/71.
61 Selborne to Milner, 7 Oct. 1899, cited in Porter, Origins, 255.
62 Brodrick to Violet Cecil, 28 Sept. 1899, Oxford, Bodleian Library, Violet Milner papers (VMP) VM35/C176/45.

government would no doubt be assailed for delaying mobilisation. This was a possibility perhaps barely sinking into ministerial perceptions as the Boers presented them with their greatest public relations coup on 9 October, when they pre-empted a British ultimatum by tendering one of their own.

3

War, Defeat and Reform:
October 1899 – November 1901

With the outbreak of war on 11 October the British government had apparently achieved its aim of educating public opinion and gaining complete support for its policy. This of course was not the case because many Liberals and much of the Labour movement remained hostile to the war and the government's interpretation of its causes. The pro-Boers, as the opposition was termed, were however handicapped at the start by the Boer ultimatum and the belief that they were running against a jingoistic tide. Evidently, 'During the first year of the hostilities at least, the war's opponents were certainly outshouted, and by most politicians it was accepted that they were greatly outnumbered too.'[1] Thus as far as the government was concerned serious divisions within the country had been avoided, and although risks had been taken with the military situation and ministers had often differed seriously with their military advisers, warlike preparations appeared to be sufficient.[2] In all civil and military opinion appeared quietly confident.

It remained to be seen, however, if the military preparations were adequate. Having cultivated public opinion so assiduously and brought public belligerence to the surface, the government, for its own sake, had to deliver a quick and decisive victory. In fact, in this respect, the Boer ultimatum had done the government a disservice because it had greatly heightened public anger at Boer audacity. Popular expectations demanded the British army deliver a swift punishment, and when this failed to materialise, following a succession of military defeats, much of the press became extremely critical of the government, whose attempts to placate the nation's wrath were to have a profound affect on civil–military relations. Ministerial response was two-fold: first, ministers restructured the high command in South Africa by appointing Lord Roberts to lead the main campaign and by leaving Buller in charge of operations in Natal only; secondly, following a public rift with Lord Wolseley, the government was obliged to begin a series of administrative reforms which

---

[1] Bernard Porter, 'The pro-Boers in Britain', in Peter Warwick (ed.), *The South African war: the Anglo-Boer war 1899–1902*, Harlow 1980, 239–57 at p. 239, and *Critics of empire: British radical attitudes to colonialism in Africa 1895–1914*, London 1968, ch. iv. See also *The pro-Boers: anatomy of an anti-war movement*, ed. Stephen Koss, Chicago 1973, and A. Davey, *The British pro-Boers*, London 1978, 48–52 and passim.
[2] Chamberlain to the queen, 12 Oct. 1899, in *The letters of Queen Victoria*, ed. G. E. Buckle, 3rd ser., London 1932, iii. 406.

were to end after the war with the development finally of a permanent and more systematic forum of civil–military consultation.

Over before Christmas?

When war began such considerations were beyond the purview of politicians and soldiers alike and the level of expectation within official circles remained high. Chamberlain believed the Boers would not attack, but welcomed the prospect of them doing so. He later asked Lansdowne if Laing's Nek might be occupied simply to provoke the Boers into crossing the frontier.[3] Similarly, Wolseley wrote 'I rejoice beyond measure to think war must now come. Come it would most certainly sometime or other, & now is best for us. . . . Buller will, I am sure, end the war with complete success for England.'[4]

Press expectation was just as high. Having seen British armies defeat a succession of colonial enemies, the press had no reason to suspect the second war against the Boers would be any different. Prior to the outbreak of war, one commentator believed the Boer threat to be exaggerated, as was Boer confidence derived from the first conflict. He felt there was no basis for thinking a war would be lengthy or costly.[5] The military pundit, Spenser Wilkinson, later remarked that his editor on the *Morning Post* suppressed an article in which Wilkinson estimated the Boer forces at 50,000 men. His editor 'shared the almost universal opinion that a war with the Transvaal would be a small affair, resembling the autumn manoeuvres and lasting for a few weeks'.[6] Similarly, as war began, *The Times* stated:

> The military situation in Natal is a curious one, but there are no practical disadvantages. The positions held at Ladysmith and Glencoe are the best possible in the circumstances. If the forces there are not at present in sufficient strength to undertake offensive operations, they are ample to repel attack, which is most unlikely to be made, and they will suffice to prevent serious incursions into the territory behind them.[7]

But as the campaign in Natal progressed this optimism appeared misplaced. At the time Natal was the main theatre of operations and it was here the Boers concentrated the bulk of their forces. Hely-Hutchinson actually thought the position of Cape Colony more serious, 'but fortunately the Boers have a fad about getting Natal & have directed nearly all their energies on

---

3   Chamberlain to Balfour, 3 Oct. 1899, JC 5/5/83; to Lansdowne, 7 Oct. 1899, JC 5/51/88.
4   Wolseley to his wife, 11 Oct. 1899, WP 28/65.
5   Anon. [C. E. Callwell], 'A Boer war: the military aspect', *Blackwood's Magazine* clxvi (1899), 259–65.
6   H. S. Wilkinson, *Thirty-five years, 1874–1909*, London 1933, 238–9.
7   *Times*, 12 Oct. 1899, 9.

this side'.[8] With some 15,000 men in Natal, now that most of the reinforcements had arrived, optimism in London and South Africa was running high: yet the position was far from satisfactory.

As mentioned earlier, the Natal government had been depressed by the news that General Symons was unable to defend the whole colony. Symons felt that with the 2,000 reinforcements sent in August he could advance north to Glencoe, a move that was eventually sanctioned on 24 September by Hely-Hutchinson. Thus, at the outbreak of war, a British force of 4,000 men stood isolated at Glencoe: its nearest support was the 11,000 men (the reinforcements of 8 September and Natal contingents) then assembling at Ladysmith under General White.[9]

These dispositions had resulted from the desire to allay the fears of the Natal government (although Symons's over-confidence also had much to do with them). White had expressed his doubts about Symons's force being so far north without immediate support, but in an interview with Hely-Hutchinson, White was persuaded to leave Symons at Glencoe. The governor, with whom the Prime Minister concurred, stated that ordering Symons to withdraw would have grave political consequences; it would disgust the loyalists because of the abandonment of more territory and undermine the loyalty of the vast native population who believed in British power.[10]

During the opening phases of the campaign Hely-Hutchinson continued to bombard White with messages emphasising the fears of the politicians (including himself) at the situation. On one occasion he feared a Boer raid on Pietermaritzburg and Durban, and wanted troops sent from Ladysmith to defend these towns: 'I think if a successful raid were to take place Her Majesty's Government would be open to the charge of neglecting to perform a solemn engagement made with Her Majesty's loyal subjects in Natal.'[11] Also, a week later, on learning of White's unresponsive attitude, the governor reiterated his fears about the defenceless condition of Natal's two principal towns. This drew a testy response from White: 'I must earnestly request that pressure may not be put on me to reduce forces here.' White thought the reports of a raid misleading and felt he stood a better chance with his entire force intact, especially as Symons remained at Glencoe.[12] The Colonial Office was perturbed by Hely-Hutchinson's interjections, especially as

8 Hely-Hutchinson to Chamberlain, 13 Oct. 1899, JC 10/7/114.
9 Hely-Hutchinson to Chamberlain, 13 Sept. 1899, CO 179/206/fo. 273; Milner to Hely-Hutchinson, 24 Sept. 1899, WO 32/7863; Hely-Hutchinson to Chamberlain, 29 Sept. 1899, JC 10/7/112, and 30 Sept. 1899, CO 179/206/fo. 450.
10 Hely-Hutchinson to Chamberlain, 10, 11 Oct 1899, CO 179/206/fos 606–8. Both Chamberlain and Lansdowne agreed with the decision: CO Minutes, 11 Oct. 1899, CO 417/275/fo. 751. Later, Hely-Hutchinson said White could withdraw Symons's force if he thought it necessary; White now considered it would do too much harm: Hely-Hutchinson to White, 17 Oct. 1899, WO 32/7863.
11 Hely-Hutchinson to White, 17 Oct. 1899, WO 32/7863.
12 Hely-Hutchinson to White and White to Hely-Hutchinson, 25 Oct 1899, ibid.

Chamberlain felt that White alone was responsible for the military situation, and that he should not be pressured into changing his decisions.[13] As Hely-Hutchinson would not let the matter drop, Chamberlain noted, 'I wish Sir W Hutchinson would leave Gen. White alone. I have given him a hint & if this continues I shall have to give him distinct instructions.' Later, as Hely-Hutchinson became more disturbed by the defensive position, Chamberlain wrote 'I do not like Civil Governors meddling with Military Affairs. . . . The fault is entirely with the military authorities if they listen to civilians *against* their own military judgment. They ought to know that this responsibility is wholly with them.'[14] According to his latest biographer Chamberlain lacked the imagination to see that sometimes civilian interference might galvanise dithering generals.[15] In this respect he was not alone because like many politicians at the time he respected the reputations which British generals had gained on the imperial frontiers, and deferred to their professional competence. On this occasion, however, he was right to complain about political hindrance because White was perplexed enough without Hely-Hutchinson's ministrations. Nevertheless, Chamberlain's blind spot proved long-lasting, as Milner later discovered to his cost. The Colonial Office, therefore, was becoming increasingly aware of the political pressure on White and officials were conscious of this being blamed for the poor military situation, which steadily got worse. On 20 October Symons had been mortally wounded at the battle of Talana. His successor, General Yule, was forced to abandon Glencoe and retreat to the relative safety of Ladysmith. Eventually, despite minor victories at Elandslaagte and Rietfontein, White's force was cut off and besieged in Ladysmith. On 30 October White attempted to break the Boer siege, but part of his force was isolated at Nicholson's Nek and forced to surrender. By the beginning of November Natal virtually lay open to the Boers.

White's misfortune completely unbalanced the campaign strategy. Buller, who arrived in Cape Town on 31 October, felt he could not abandon White and some 15,000 British troops in Ladysmith. Even one of Buller's sternest critics later acknowledged that Buller had little choice but to rescue White's besieged army.[16] As a result Buller abandoned his plan to invade the OFS and instead divided his forces. He took the bulk of the army corps to Natal, leaving General Methuen in Cape Colony to relieve Kimberley, and General Gatacre to prevent the Boers advancing from the strategic railway junction at Stormberg. The British government showed no inclination to interfere in the conduct of operations as confidence in Buller remained high. Even so, Buller's own confidence was waning. On 25 November he had informed

[13] CO Minutes, 27 Oct. 1899; Chamberlain to Hely-Hutchinson, 27 Oct. 1899, CO 179/207/fos 114, 118.

[14] CO Minutes, 29, 31 Oct. 1899, CO 179/207/fos 264, 289.

[15] Marsh, *Joseph Chamberlain*, 484–5.

[16] Leo Amery (ed.), *The Times history of the war in South Africa 1899–1902*, London 1900–9, ii. 286.

Lansdowne that 'Up to date we are still hanging on by our eyelids.'[17] When he arrived in Natal and learned of the strength of the Boer position at Colenso, which blocked the route to Ladysmith, his pessimism increased.[18] Moreover, the actions of his subordinates in Cape Colony did nothing to allay his anxiety. Methuen was defeated at Magersfontein on 11 December, following General Gatacre's defeat at Stormberg the day before. Then, on 15 December, Buller's attempt to relieve Ladysmith failed at Colenso. These three defeats in five days became known as 'black week' and were a profound shock to the British public and authorities alike.

As a result of the poor performance of the British army, criticism of the government began to intensify. Wilkinson was particularly scathing. Before the outbreak of war, he had highlighted the danger inherent in government policy, principally the two-month period between the arrival of the reinforcements and the arrival of the army corps: 'The Cabinet has knowingly and deliberately taken upon itself the responsibility for whatever risks are now run. In this deliberate decision of the Cabinet lies the best ground for hoping that the risks are not so great as they seem.' Later he argued that White's task 'was disproportionate to his force' and blamed Lansdowne for his 'unbusinesslike way of playing with national affairs'. And on 8 November Wilkinson entitled one article, 'How weak policy leads to bad strategy'. Similar attacks by him continued well into the new year and concentrated on the government's, and particularly Lansdowne's, culpability for the military defeats.[19]

Indeed, since White's performance in Natal, public opinion was beginning to turn against the government. Brodrick believed the public was 'going through a great depression', and ministers themselves sensed this growing climate of disapproval, as Lansdowne felt the necessity to defend the government's diplomatic record and inability to synchronise diplomacy with military preparations.[20] 'Black week', in particular, brought forth much criticism of government policy, and also the current military system. Critics such as Major Arthur Griffiths and the ubiquitous Wilkinson blamed the government outright.[21] When ministers attempted to defend themselves, in and outside parliament, critics rounded on them even more. Balfour, particularly, was attacked for three crass speeches made at Manchester between 8 and 10 January 1900. In one he stated, 'I don't feel the need, so far as my colleagues and I are concerned, of any apology whatever.' To which *The Times* replied, 'There is need of apology on the part of the Cabinet for serious errors, both in

---

17 Cited in Lord Newton, *Lord Lansdowne: a biography*, London 1929, 161.

18 Pakenham, *Boer war*, 211.

19 H. S. Wilkinson, *Lessons of the war*, London 1900, 1–47, and 'On the art of going to war', in *War and policy*, 370–93.

20 Brodrick to Violet Cecil, 3 Nov. 1899, VMP VM35/C176/51; Lansdowne's Speech in the Cutlers' Hall, Sheffield, *Times*, 3 Nov. 1899, 7.

21 A. Griffiths, 'The conduct of the war', *Fortnightly Review* lxvii (1900), 1–10; Wilkinson, *Lessons*, 103–11; Brodrick thought 'the country is in fire & flame [against] the Govt.', Brodrick to Violet Cecil, 12 Jan. 1900, VMP VM35/C176/62.

policy and warlike preparation.'[22] Milner was informed that Balfour's speeches had disappointed everyone, more so than the military defeats: 'The nation has simply risen in wrath at the extraordinary superficiality & black ignorance wh[ich] they have betrayed.'[23] Another critic wrote, 'Mr Balfour's speeches show him to have been blind and indifferent to the danger; the plight of our army in South Africa, the half measures, the manifest hesitations, and the tardiness of the despatch of reinforcements, equally condemn Lord Lansdowne.'[24] As one reviewer pointed out, this criticism of the government found an easy and obvious target in Lansdowne.[25] The war, however, was now becoming a focus for a great many discontents. This owed something to the ministry's own failings before the conflict in South Africa. Up to 1898 they had enjoyed much success on the diplomatic front; but domestically the government had acted without distinction. In 1896 it had withdrawn its Education Bill, but just before the outbreak of war this issue had surfaced again owing to the Cockerton decision on secondary education. Certain ministers had proved disappointing, particularly White Ridley at the Home Office, and Henry Chaplin at the Board of Agriculture. Recently historians have argued that the Conservative/Unionist alliance of 1895 remained unimpressed by the size of its majority and did not take success for granted, adding that the Cabinet was pessimistic rather than optimistic. The war against the Boers, in fact, began to unravel the accommodation of interests made by Salisbury to keep the alliance together. As one historian has argued, 'A snapshot taken in 1900, gives a misleadingly favourable picture of the condition, prospects and self-confidence of Conservatism.'[26]

Not surprisingly, given the Unionists' poor performance, the critics singled out the politicians for blame. By contrast the soldiers escaped censure at this early stage. The explanation for this lies in more than political performance. The era of imperial expansion and cheap military victories had militarised British society to a significant degree, and popularised leading military figures. Recent historiography on this subject has identified conduits which led to militarisation. These include nationalistic and militaristic style teaching

22 B. Dugdale, *Arthur James Balfour*, London 1936, i. 304–5; *Times*, 10 Jan. 1900, 9. Lord Salisbury's attempt to defend the record of the government in the House of Lords was a disaster: Peter Marsh, *The discipline of popular government: Lord Salisbury's domestic statecraft 1881–1902*, Brighton 1978, 294–5.
23 Gell to Milner, 12 Jan. 1900, MP IV/B/213/27/fos 187–8.
24 An Englishman [H. W. Wilson], 'The causes of reverse', *National Review* xxxiv (1900), 830–42 at p. 836. See also H. W. Wilson, *With the flag to Pretoria*, London 1900, i. 205–15. Arthur Griffiths also blamed the government for an inadequate military system in the *Fortnightly Review* lxvii (1900), 214–23, as did the anonymous writer (the well known soldier, G. F. R. Henderson) of 'The war in South Africa', *Edinburgh Review* cxci (1900), 247–78.
25 A soldier [W. E. Cairnes] 'Some reflections on the war in South Africa', *MacMillan's Magazine* lxxxi (1900), 313–20.
26 B. Coleman, *Conservatism and the Conservative Party in nineteenth-century Britain*, London 1988, 200. See also M. Bentley, *Politics without democracy*, London 1984, 295; Marsh, *Discipline of popular government*, 247–90; Green, *The crisis of Conservatism*, chs i–iv.

in schools; cadet corps and boys' associations; and involvement in the various organisations connected with the army, such as the volunteers and militia. The subject matter of the music halls also conveyed an influence which heightened the nation's awareness of military matters and the role of the army in expanding the empire. Moreover, by taking recruiting figures for the army, the militia, the volunteers and the yeomanry between 1881 and 1898, M. D. Blanch calculates that just over 22 per cent of the entire male population between the ages of seventeen and forty had some form of military experience just before the outbreak of war. As Blanch suggests, 'we may conclude that powerful pre-war influences helped shaped popular response to the war itself'.[27]

This view contrasts with earlier work which sought to absolve the working class from the crude patriotism and jingoism which so disturbed J. A. Hobson in 1900. Studies by Pelling and Price argued that the working class was not particularly patriotic or imperialistic and was more concerned with 'knife and fork' questions and the problems of daily life.[28] Other historians, however, have suggested that working-class patriotism did exist, and that at times it was influenced by right-wing propaganda. Yet even so, the left offered a version of patriotism which accommodated a variety of ideas and interpretations. For some, joining the volunteers was considered patriotic because it would help ensure the continuation of traditional liberties; for others, the empire itself was justifiable as a great moral and beneficial force in the world; others still, as Paul Ward argues, believed in a 'social patriotism' which was predicated on the need to build a better and improved Britain. Although some on the left supported the war in South Africa, most did not. In the main this was not from a general anti-imperialistic outlook, but because they felt the government had provoked a war that had no moral rectitude.[29]

When all is said and done, it cannot be denied that expansive coverage of colonial wars by the press enhanced the careers and popularity of successful generals. These great heroes were imbued with an almost infallible quality and were lionised by press and public alike. Wolseley, 'our only general', was

---

[27] M. D. Blanch, 'British society and the war', in Warwick, The South African war, 210–38 at p. 215. See also John Mackenzie, Propaganda and empire, Manchester 1984, 1–14.

[28] J. A. Hobson, The psychology of jingoism, London 1901; Henry Pelling, Popular politics and society in late Victorian Britain, London 1968, ch. v; Richard Price, An imperial war and the British working class: working-class attitudes and reactions to the Boer War 1899–1902, London 1972, passim.

[29] Hugh Cunningham, 'The language of patriotism 1750–1914', History Workshop xii (1981), 8–33 at pp. 23–8; Anne Summers, 'Militarism in Britain before the Great War', ibid. ii (1976), 104–23 at pp. 106–7; David Feldman, 'Nationality and ethnicity', in Paul Johnson (ed.), Twentieth-century Britain: economic, social and cultural change, Harlow 1994, 127–48 at pp. 142–6; Paul Ward, 'Englishness, patriotism and the British left 1881–1924', unpubl. PhD diss. London 1994, also argues (pp. 7–11 and ch. iv) that 'social patriotism' was reciprocal in that the government could offer social reforms in return for patriotism; Miles Taylor, 'Imperium et libertas? Rethinking the radical critique of imperialism during the nineteenth century', JICH xix (1991), 1–23; Porter, Critics of empire, 176–90.

perhaps the most successful and well-known of the Victorian generals, and his image as an army reformer did much to endear him to the public as a 'scientific general'. As mentioned previously, Buller was very popular, and when in Natal, the famous correspondent Bennet Burleigh described him as a 'masterly leader of troops . . . an indomitable man of more than bulldog pertinacity'.[30] Correspondents such as G. W. Steevens not only helped the careers and reputations of officers like Kitchener, but eulogised the army as the vanguard of British civilisation. Moreover, certain officers, notably Havelock, Gordon and Roberts, were exemplified as Christian heroes, and given an 'intense aura of sanctity'. When war broke out in South Africa, Lord Roberts was the most conspicuous example of this type of officer: pious, professional and abstemious.[31] Roberts's popularity was further enhanced by the universal sympathy accorded to him and his family after the heroic death of his son at the battle of Colenso.

In all, leading generals had become figures of reverence, identified with the best aspects of British civilisation. To criticise these men publicly or insinuate their incompetence was a dangerous tactic. Balfour's Manchester speeches in January 1900 hinted at military incapacity and were a major reason for the criticism he received afterwards. Indeed, Wilkinson would not tolerate attacks upon the generals in South Africa as a means of deflecting criticism from the War Office or Cabinet.[32] Given the high esteem of military figures, the government had to face censure alone, even if members such as Balfour, with some justification, felt certain officers were as culpable as the politicians.[33]

'No more fitting appointment . . .'

The government did have one alternative with which to appease their critics: they could change the command in South Africa. This, however, was a difficult matter, with repercussions that might seriously damage government prestige. If Buller was dismissed outright his immense popularity meant the

[30] Quoted in Roger Stearn, 'War correspondents and colonial war, c. 1870–1900', in John Mackenzie (ed.), *Popular imperialism and the military 1850–1950*, Manchester 1992, 139–61 at p. 148. See also John Mackenzie, 'Introduction', ibid. 1–24; R. J. Wilkinson-Latham, *From our special correspondent: Victorian war correspondents and their campaigns*, London 1979, chs iv–viii.
[31] Roger Stearn, 'G. W. Steevens and the message of empire', *JICH* xviii (1989), 210–31; Summers, 'Militarism in Britain', 107–10, 117–20, and 'Edwardian militarism', in Raphael Samuel (ed.), *Patriotism: the making and unmaking of British national identity*, London 1989, i. 236–56 at pp. 249–50.
[32] Wilkinson, *Lessons*, 122.
[33] Brodrick told Violet Cecil that in a discussion with Balfour the latter 'tremendously blames the soldiers. . . . He thinks they should have advised us of necessity for heavier guns – for a tactical retirement on Colenso at outset': Brodrick to Violet Cecil, 24 Nov. 1899, VMP VM35/C176/54.

government might face a tirade of abuse. The politicians would be portrayed as sacrificing a soldier to cover their own mistakes. Buller's predicament was already being blamed on the poor defensive measures initiated before the outbreak of war.[34] The government was perceived as having been too ready to mollify Boer sensitivities and too reluctant to make hard military decisions. The unfortunate Buller was paying the price for political irresponsibility, an opinion which remained strong enough to survive the evidence of Buller's incapacity as a general. Whatever the reasons for his popularity the government was fully aware they still had to be circumspect in their dealings with him.

Fortunately for the government, the division of the army into 'British' and 'Indian' sections ensured there was an officer senior to Buller, and with a greater reputation. This facilitated a change of command in South Africa without necessarily demoting Buller. The appointment of Lord Roberts on 18 December 1899, as the new C-in-C(SA), marked the Cabinet's attempt to bring the war to a satisfactory conclusion. In fact, appointing Roberts was the most immediate palliative the Cabinet could offer the country before the opening of parliament in January. And by so doing the politicians were able to move with public opinion, which appeared to demand the utmost exertion be made to end the war. The sudden rush of volunteering and the establishment of volunteer bodies like the City Imperial Volunteers, testified to the resolution displayed by the British public to finish the war once and for all. By sending Roberts to South Africa the government demonstrated its own commitment to this ideal.

Why, it might be asked, was Roberts not appointed sooner? Roberts was a friend of Lansdowne's from their time in India, and he was also on friendly terms with Chamberlain. But to give Roberts command at the start of the war was virtually impossible. For one, he was considered too old at sixty-seven; and for another, his military career had been spent in India, making him unfamiliar with the administration of the home army. Moreover, Wolseley's rivalry with Roberts meant that he would consider anyone but him. As Buller's appointment was well received there was no justification for thinking he might fail. As Roberts was then C-in-C in Ireland, which was practically a retirement post, he appeared to have no chance of assuming command at the outset of war.

Even so, Roberts kept the government aware of his presence and interest. On 20 June 1899 he had informed Lansdowne of his ideas concerning a campaign against the Boers, adding 'I have marked this Private but you are welcome to show it to any member of the Cabinet if you think it desirable to do

---

[34] An officer, 'The government and the war', *Contemporary Review* lxxvi (1899), 766–92; Griffiths, 'The conduct of war', 1–4; Wilkinson blamed the government for Buller's predicament as early as November 1899: *Lessons*, 64–6.

so.'[35] Again on 8 December, with the war nearly two months old, Roberts wrote a long letter to Lansdowne explaining his views, this time more forcibly and with more emphasis on personalities than strategy. Roberts was aware of Buller's telegrams from Natal and became concerned at his gloomy assessment of the situation. He noted that Buller seemed weighed down by the responsibility of his command, and again offered his services:

> This letter would never have been written, did I not know I could depend from your knowledge of me, that I should not be misunderstood. It is for your eyes alone, unless, after reading it, you think my proposal worthy of consideration, then you are welcome to show it to the Prime Minister, and, if you wish, Mr Chamberlain.

Roberts asked Lansdowne not to show it to anyone else, especially in the War Office, 'for, impossible as it may seem, I am sorry to say I cannot help feeling they would prefer running very great risks rather than see me in command of a British Army in the field'.[36]

Undoubtedly Lansdowne would have liked to appoint Roberts, especially given his acrimonious relationship with Wolseley and Buller. But Lansdowne told Roberts that as Buller had made no mistakes, his pessimism was no reason for his replacement. Roberts insisted that one man could not possibly control all the forces in South Africa, given the size of the army and the scale of the operations. Despite Roberts's desire to assume control in South Africa there was nothing Lansdowne could do.[37]

Buller's defeat at Colenso on 15 December, and the subsequent tone of his telegrams to the Ladysmith garrison and the War Office, provided the excuse for Lansdowne to act, and to push the appointment of Roberts.[38] Lansdowne found a willing advocate in Balfour, who was the only other high-ranking Cabinet minister in London owing to the start of the Christmas holidays. Balfour agreed with Lansdowne's proposal to place Roberts in overall command, and won Salisbury's acquiescence by appointing Lord Kitchener as Roberts's chief of staff. That this moment gave Lansdowne the opportunity for revenge on one of the generals who had betrayed him and his colleagues cannot be doubted. The fact that neither Wolseley nor the queen were

35 Roberts to Lansdowne, 20 June 1899, National Army Museum, Roberts papers (RP) 7101/23/110/1/fos 146–9.
36 Roberts to Lansdowne, 8 Dec. 1899, RP 7101/23/110/1/fos 203–8.
37 Lansdowne to Roberts, 10 Dec. 1899, RP 7101/23/181; Roberts to Lansdowne, 11 Dec. 1899, RP 7101/23/110/1/fos 210–13. Lansdowne told Salisbury he did not know how Roberts knew so much about Buller's telegrams. He suspected the lord lieutenant of Ireland was confiding in him: Lansdowne to Salisbury, 11 Dec. 1899, Salisbury correspondence, fo. 480.
38 After the battle, Buller telegraphed Lansdowne and implied he would abandon White. Buller even suggested to White, via heliograph, that he should be prepared to surrender: Julian Symons, Buller's campaign, London 1963, 168–70; Pakenham, Boer war, 239–40. Lansdowne later wrote that the confidence of the War Office in Buller had been 'rudely shaken': Newton, Lord Lansdowne, 165–6.

consulted beforehand testifies to the government's determination to impose their own solution to the crisis. On 17 December 1899 Wolseley wrote to Sir Arthur Bigge, the queen's private secretary, informing him that the decision to supersede Buller had been taken without his knowledge and that he still considered Buller the best man for the job. Balfour told Salisbury that he had informed Bigge on the 19th, and once the queen's objections to her and Wolseley's treatment had been noted, stated 'it was impossible to consult the C-in-C upon such an appointment, as his well known jealousy of Roberts made his advice on such a subject perfectly worthless'.[39]

The respite gained by the appointment of Roberts was real, if only temporary: at last the government had done something right. The *Times* leader remarked, 'The action decided upon by the Defence Committee of the Cabinet . . . will command the warm approval of the British people. . . . No more fitting appointment would have been made, nor was any better calculated to satisfy the public and the Army.'[40]

Consequently, the government had found a way to relieve Buller of the responsibility of directing the war. The new situation was in some respects very much as before, with Roberts and Buller taking the roles of Buller and White. Not wishing to risk antagonising public opinion, the government kept Buller on as GOC(Natal), whilst Roberts took overall command in Cape Colony as a second army corps was mobilised and sent to South Africa.[41] Yet there was a certain disadvantage in the appointment of Roberts, something the government did not foresee. Roberts was the government's last hope of obtaining a quick and decisive victory; and to realise this ministers were obliged to back him all the way, despite any mistakes he might make. If Roberts proved unsatisfactory, the government could hardly supersede him. In effect the government had severely limited its options for it would have to sink or swim with Roberts, who, Cincinnatus-like, had been called to save the empire. The government would be obliged to defer to military exigencies perhaps more than was usual during a campaign. If not, they certainly had to be careful how they dealt with these officers, who were virtually the government's last hope of bringing the war to a speedy conclusion. In effect, Roberts's position was one which reduced the politicians' grip on the management of the war, despite the approbation the government had received for appointing him in the first place. However, the impact of that decision in South Africa had yet to be felt, and it was for Milner to face the consequences of that decision. Philip Gell warned of the changed circumstances 'Nobody

[39] Wolseley to Bigge, 17 Dec. 1899, in *Letters of Queen Victoria*, 437; Balfour to Salisbury, 19 Dec. 1899, Salisbury correspondence, fos 47–51; Lansdowne to Lady A. Roberts, 11 May 1921, RP 7101/23/181.

[40] *Times*, 18 Dec. 1899, 9.

[41] Buller was told the new arrangement would enable him to give the Natal campaign his complete and undivided attention: Lansdowne to Buller, 18 Dec. 1899, and Buller to Lansdowne, 20 Dec. 1899, accepting the situation, CAB 37/51/93.

believes much in them [the government] – except in Chamberlain. They believe in Roberts & in Kitchener, and I truly think in yourself, and acquiesce in the Ministry, so long as it gives Roberts what Roberts wants.'[42] Milner now had to discover how far the alteration to the civil–military balance in Britain, had changed relations in South Africa.

The empire's peril

Although somewhat marginalised by events in South Africa as the year 1899 ended, Wolseley still remained commander-in-chief and had to contend with the problems caused by the government's determination to boost the war effort. The realisation that the war was going to take longer to finish, and required a substantial input of troops and resources, meant that Britain's military capability now came under the spotlight. The dark corners illuminated revealed not so much a well-oiled war machine, as a creaking edifice whose structural integrity was being undermined by South African demands. For Wolseley and many others there was also the concern that foreign predators were awaiting the opportunity to strike when the edifice crumbled. Driven by these anxieties, Wolseley's relations with the government continued to remain problematic. From late 1899 through to mid 1900, he clashed repeatedly with ministers over the need to ensure Britain's security.

Wolseley began his fresh assault on the government after he was informed about the poor state of Britain's warlike stores. In December 1899 General Brackenbury, the inspector-general of the Ordnance, a leading member of Wolseley's ring and, ironically, a friend of Roberts, informed Wolseley 'That war has now disclosed a situation as regards armaments, and reserves of guns, ammunition, stores and clothing, and as regards the power of output of material of war in emergency which is, in my opinion, full of peril to the Empire'.[43] For the first three months of the war Brackenbury had worked incessantly to supply the army's ever-growing needs and had largely succeeded but, in the process, had exhausted all reserves. This revelation only increased Wolseley's anxiety because at the same time as Brackenbury revealed the perilous state of military supplies, the government sent two extra divisions to South Africa which left Britain seriously short of trained manpower. In fact Wolseley had expressed concern about this as far back as September and he became even more fearful as a continual stream of reinforcements was despatched to South Africa. Moreover, fear and anxiety were not confined to the higher echelons

---

42 Gell to Milner, 12 Apr. 1900, Bod. Lib., Alfred Milner papers (MP) IV/B/213/27/fo. 34.
43 Cited in J. F. Maurice and M. H. Grant, *Official history of the war in South Africa*, London 1906–10, i. 32. See also Clive Trebilcock, 'War and the failure of industrial mobilisation: 1899–1914', in J. M. Winter (ed.), *War and economic development: essays in memory of David Joslin*, Cambridge 1975, 139–64 at pp. 143–6. Brackenbury also informed Roberts, 17 Dec. 1899, RP 7101/23/11/fo. 151.

of the army. Boer successes produced much exultation abroad which caused consternation in Britain, and led directly to a widespread fear of invasion. As the troops left Britain public insecurity was increased by sections of the press, including the normally pacific W. T. Stead. Journalists and commentators called for a militia ballot, while one now felt that Britain was faced 'with a great and grave alternative which has been long approaching . . . and which cannot now be further evaded or ignored. We must either contract the boundaries of our Empire or we must expand our military forces'.[44] Such scaremongering continued well into 1900 and finally petered out in August. Nevertheless, while invasion fears were alive, public and official anxiety was great. Even Brodrick was caught up in the sensationalism and advised Wyndham that 'if your present schemes fail to produce the necessary men, some compulsion must be resorted to'.[45]

If a leading member of the government should advocate conscription to ensure Britain's security then one wonders how Wolseley reacted, especially as he was more informed than most. To a large extent Wolseley was unable, as often before, to take a detached and professional view of the situation and was caught up in all the excitement.[46] In a memorandum to the Defence Committee of the Cabinet he suggested that there was a possibility the French might be willing to settle old scores and take advantage of the fact 'that the greater portion of the small army on which we are content to rely for the defence of our shores, is no longer in the country'. Having been asked to consider an invasion Wolseley felt 'justifies me in assuming that its possibility is fully admitted'. The minimum requirement for home defence had been set at two regular and one militia army corps by the Stanhope Memorandum of 1888.[47] To ensure this was met, Wolseley argued that it was vital to find the men first and worry about the means after: 'Found they must be if the country is to be safe, and if compulsion or immense expense are necessary for this, one or other must be accepted.' Apart from embodying the militia Wolseley wanted thirty-two new regular battalions recruited from the 170,000 veterans he believed were still available. In all, he urged the enlistment of nearly 45,000 regulars, the embodiment of 50,000 militia and the purchase of additional artillery and stores.[48]

In preparing his reply Lansdowne took no chances and secured the advice of the other military departmental heads at the War Office all, of course,

---

44 Cited in Friedberg, The weary titan, 233. See also H. R. Moon, 'The invasion of the United Kingdom: public controversy and official planning 1888–1918', unpubl. PhD diss. London 1968, i. 129–42; Kochanski, 'Field-Marshal Wolseley', 235.
45 Brodrick to Wyndham (under-secretary of state for war), 16 Feb. 1900, Middleton papers (St John Brodrick [SJB]), PRO 30/67/5.
46 Moon, 'Invasion of the UK', i. 183.
47 For more on this see Ian Beckett, 'The Stanhope memorandum of 1888: a reinterpretation', Bulletin of the Institute of Historical Research lvii (1984), 240–7.
48 Memo. by Wolseley, 29 Dec. 1899, CAB 37/51/105; Kochanski, 'Field-Marshal Wolseley', 235.

junior to Wolseley. It was this type of procedure which Wolseley had fulminated against since 1895. However, once all the incoming information from the likes of Wood and Brackenbury had been collated, Lansdowne had a powerful counter-argument to present before the Cabinet. For all their difficulties at that time ministers were not going to take on board recommendations which, however genuinely offered, were largely unrealistic and Lansdowne showed how emotion had clouded Wolseley's judgement. For one, there was no guarantee that the men would come forward, despite the increased pay advocated by Wolseley. And conscription was an option which the country would not tolerate. Yet something had to be done to allay public fears and address tangible weaknesses in home defence. Accordingly Lansdowne offered the more obtainable figure of twelve new battalions comprised of men who would receive a bounty to join up and an opportunity to gain a pension. Paying 2s. 6d. a day – as recommended by Wolseley – was considered prohibitive as other troops would expect to receive the same rate. Embodying the militia was considered problematic also: they could not be housed and Lansdowne did not want them billeted; furthermore, it would be better to raise them in summer when they could be put under canvas.[49]

Three days later the Defence Committee decided to accept Lansdowne's recommendations. Wolseley minuted his disappointment although he was pleased something was being done, but even so he was not satisfied entirely.[50] In the War Office he continued to press the need for more troops but was told by Lansdowne that this was just not an option. Even before the Defence Committee made its decision, Wolseley was privately informed by Lansdowne that it was unlikely his recommendations would be accepted in their entirety. Wolseley said this was inadequate and that he might tender his resignation.[51] On 26 January he met Lansdowne and Balfour in order to persuade the government to accede to his demands and this time increased his recommendations. Two weeks later Lansdowne informed Wolseley that the government would not agree and when Wolseley stated that ministers 'had practically given me nothing' and offered his resignation Lansdowne accepted it.[52] Lansdowne, unable to arrange an immediate meeting of the Cabinet, promised to see Salisbury and Balfour over the issue which led Wolseley to tell his wife somewhat optimistically, 'I feel sure [they] will give me all I have asked for – if not, I go.'[53] What happened next is a mystery. All that we have on the issue are the words of Wolseley's biographers: 'Wolseley

---

[49] 'Note on the Commander-in-Chief's memorandum of 29th December', 17 Jan. 1900, CAB 37/52/4; Kochanski, 'Field-Marshal Wolseley', 236.

[50] Meeting of the Defence Committee, 20 Jan. 1900, Wolseley's minute, 23 Jan. 1900, CAB 37/52/5.

[51] Kochanski, 'Field-Marshal Wolseley', 237; Wolseley to his wife, 17 Jan. 1900, in *Letters of Lord and Lady Wolseley*, 379.

[52] Wolseley to his wife, 12 Feb. 1900, WP 29/16; to Lansdowne, 13 Feb. 1900, CAB 37/52/19, in which he reiterates his demands.

[53] Wolseley to his wife, 14 Feb. 1900, *Letters of Lord and Lady Wolseley*, 381.

only withdrew it [his resignation] upon assurance that proper provision would be made for home defence.'[54] What can we make from this episode? For one, it revealed that by February 1900 the government was more confident in its dealings with Wolseley. Ministers, it seems, were no longer willing to tolerate his outbursts and as he was approaching retirement anyway they felt able to risk accepting his resignation. Wolseley's views and demands, as outlined above, were emotional and excitable, almost irrational, and this too must have strengthened the government's hand. Moreover, with the war apparently going well in South Africa and with the government firmly hitched to Roberts's star, it was no doubt felt that Wolseley could now be safely discarded. In the long-running dispute between Wolseley and the government the pendulum had now swung firmly in favour of the latter.

Wolseley's last shout

For the rest of the year no great issue surfaced to disturb the fragile tranquillity which appeared to descend upon Wolseley and the government. As the last months of his term in office ebbed away Wolseley lost interest in his work and looked forward to his retirement.[55] Yet this happy prospect did not deter him from taking the opportunity to launch one last salvo in defence of his reputation and to lay the blame for the war's early disasters at the feet of the government. From being first a conflict by memorandum, the battle culminated in a public dispute in 1901, when Wolseley defended himself in the House of Lords. The outcome of his clash with Lansdowne was however to prove fruitful for the military. The government was obliged to investigate the workings of the War Office the result of which vindicated many of the army's complaints and consequently set in motion the complete reform of the inadequate consultative and administrative system employed hitherto.

In November 1900 the queen, after discussing the situation in the War Office with the new secretary of state for war, St John Brodrick, urged Wolseley, through Lord Salisbury, to encapsulate his criticisms of army administration for the benefit of the Cabinet.[56] In a stinging memorandum, Wolseley vented the frustrations of five years by attacking a system which he despised: the commander-in-chief according to Wolseley had lost direct control over the four branches of army administration, becoming in his words 'a fifth wheel to a coach'. The secretary of state for war had therefore become the head of the army having 'crushed out' the C-in-C between him and other departmental chiefs. As Wolseley explained:

---

54 Maurice and Arthur, *Life of Lord Wolseley*, 323.
55 Kochanski, 'Field-Marshal Wolseley', 246; Byron Farwell, *Eminent Victorian soldiers: seekers of glory*, London 1986, 237.
56 Maurice and Arthur, *Life of Lord Wolseley*, 295; Hamer, *British army*, 181.

the whole principle of army administration is that of working up through con-verging channels which finally meet in one man charged with the supreme military command, and if this command be properly exercised, this one man must be a soldier. It is idle to hope that any civilian, however eminent, can have the professional training and experience required to enable him to con-trol an army.

Transferring responsibility to the civil side had been 'a grave error'. The solu-tion rested in either restoring the C-in-C's authority, or abolishing the office altogether.[57]

The reply to Wolseley's lengthy diatribe was made by both the outgoing and incoming war ministers. Lansdowne's was naturally the more detailed and argued first that Wolseley had not been excluded from the control of the various branches, the evidence of which lay in the way he had frequently intervened in departmental business. Lansdowne argued that it was necessary for the secretary of state to receive full military advice, which was impossible for one man to give. Authority centred in one individual meant that he would be unable to take on board all aspects of military administration, which had been the case before 1895:

> under such an arrangement the Secretary of State would, in fact, obtain no real advice at all, but only expert advice at second hand, diluted and modified in accordance with the views or perhaps the prejudices of the Commander-in-Chief. [Moreover], I doubt whether the Commander-in-Chief can point to a case in which proposals made by him or any other high military officer have been 'burked' by the Secretary of State without sufficient investigation.

Lansdowne said Wolseley had performed his duty under a misapprehension of the 1895 order-in-council; that he did not understand the limits imposed by parliamentary government; and that he had not realised the strength of the opposition to a return to the old system.[58]

Brodrick's memorandum virtually repeated the views expressed by Lans-downe except that he began with a personal attack on Wolseley saying his work had been 'spasmodic' since his illness in 1897, and that it would have been ludicrous for him to assume more duties. Moreover, Brodrick, like Lans-downe, believed Wolseley had failed to perform his basic duties anyway, espe-cially as controller of the mobilisation and intelligence division, and had thus failed the War Office. Brodrick cited the disastrous concentration at Lady-smith as a prime example of Wolseley's failings.[59]

---

[57] Memo. by Wolseley, Nov. 1900, CAB 37/53/78.

[58] Memo. by Lansdowne, 17 Nov. 1900, CAB 37/53/73.

[59] Memo. by Brodrick, 20 Nov. 1900, CAB 37/53/75. The personal aspects in Brodrick's memorandum were dropped when all three were published the following year: Parliamen-tary papers (1901), xxxix, Cd. 512, 'Memorandum by Field-Marshal Viscount Wolseley, ad-dressed to the Marquis of Salisbury, relative to the working of the order in Council of 21st November, 1895'.

From this point the debate moved into the House of Lords in March 1901. Many of the points mentioned above were reiterated during proceedings, although it took Lord Salisbury's penetrating perception to put the whole matter in a nutshell. Summing up, Salisbury explained that it is easy to detect a desire that military problems shall only be resolved by military men; but any attempt to take the opinion of the expert above the opinion of the politicians must, in view of all the circumstances of our Constitution, inevitably fail.[60] It was a clear encapsulation of the limits imposed by a parliamentary system, which many soldiers preferred to ignore, and behind which many politicians liked to hide. Salisbury's ability to boil down a contentious issue and re-state political supremacy so neatly did not however solve the problem at hand. What was to be done about creating a system which was recognised by soldiers and politicians as the best way to achieve a consensus? Under the circumstances, with the war in South Africa showing no signs of abating, such wide-ranging considerations were too difficult to contemplate. Nevertheless, the government had already recognised the need to do something and started first with an investigation of the War Office, under the auspices of the leading businessman and friend of Milner's, Clinton Dawkins.

The report and recommendations of the Dawkins Committee, which sat for five months between January and May 1901, were, according to Hamer, 'a vindication of the grievances voiced by the soldiers for the past fifteen years'.[61] The committee found that there was no real administrative structure within the War Office; there were too many regulations which stifled the responsibility and initiative of the soldiers; and that soldiers and civilians remained too divided, evincing little in the way of co-operation.[62] Apart from changes to the administrative structures of the War Office which followed the Dawkins Committee's recommendations, the government was obliged to alter the position of the C-in-C, notably by giving many of his planning duties over to the newly created post of director-general of mobilisation and intelligence, although the C-in-C remained in overall control. This was the first step made towards the eventual establishment of a general staff and reflected the desire to harmonise civil–military relations.[63]

From this point there was indeed a substantial move towards bringing civilian and military interests together amicably. The administrative inadequacies revealed at the start of the South African war had shown all too clearly that to achieve a more constructive approach towards the formulation of policy, problems needed to be analysed and addressed in a far more systematic way. In the first instance, the Committee of Imperial Defence (CID) was set up in December 1902, in order to provide a forum in which the civil and military (both army and navy) authorities could discuss fully questions

---

60 Cited in Hamer, *British army*, 185.
61 Ibid. 187.
62 For a thorough survey of the committee's report and recommendations see ibid. 187–90.
63 Ibid. 190–2; Gooch, *The plans of war*, 22–6.

relating to imperial strategy. At these meetings, as John Gooch observes, 'the strategic proposals and policies of the two Services were tested by agnostic ministerial critics'.[64] Following on from this development, but related more to the immediate weaknesses revealed by the South African war, the government in 1903 established a royal commission to investigate the disastrous opening phases. The Elgin Commission, as it became known after its chairman the earl of Elgin, revealed all too plainly the shortcomings in the way Britain prepared for war. Criticising both the government and the military, the commission recognised the need for a more systematic method of consultation between the politicians and generals.[65] In 1904 a further committee, under Lord Esher, was established to examine the workings of the War Office in a far more radical and fundamental manner than before. The War Office Reconstruction Committee enhanced the efficiency of the CID by recommending it become a permanent organisation and that it appoint a secretariat. More controversially, the committee recommended the abolition of the office of commander-in-chief and the establishment of a general staff, all of which echoed suggestions made by the Hartington Commission in 1890. The Esher Committee reported early in 1904 and most of its findings were implemented almost immediately. Only the formation of a general staff was not so forthcoming owing to financial difficulties and bureaucratic delay, but was eventually created by the new Liberal government in October 1906.[66]

Thus, once Britain took up the Boer challenge in October 1899 few could have foreseen that seven years later the structure of the War Office and administration of the army would have been so radically altered. The confidence of those early months was quickly shattered to reveal that Britain's military might rested on crumbling foundations and that its administrative apparatus had proved incapable of making adequate preparations for a colonial war. Although these problems brought civil–military relations in Britain to a new low, as each side vilified the other, they did produce a climate for reform by exposing Britain's deficient system to open debate. In the end, these resulted in not only new structures but also, as Hamer has recognised, a new 'spirit' amongst the soldiers and politicians which infused the process by which policy difficulties were resolved.[67] All this though was for the future. Meanwhile, in South Africa, the spirit of co-operation remained weak.

64 John Gooch, 'Adversarial attitudes: servicemen, politicians and strategic policy in Edwardian England, 1899–1914', in Smith, Government and the armed forces, 53–74 at p. 55.
65 Hamer, British army, 201–9; Gooch, The plans of war, 32–5.
66 Hamer, British army, 223–46; Gooch, The plans of war, ch. ii; French, The British way in warfare, 160–1.
67 Hamer, British army, 258.

4

The Conquest of the Boer Republics: December 1899 – September 1900

The appointment of Lord Roberts as commander-in-chief in South Africa represented the British Cabinet's last chance to retrieve the poor military situation and gain some credibility from a public deeply concerned about the handling of the war. This action on the part of ministers deemed hesitant and vacillating was well-received by a public grown highly critical, but the benefits were only temporary and were soon outweighed by the costs. In attempting to show that the empire was safe in their hands, ministers gave Roberts *carte blanche* and in effect renounced any influence over the forthcoming campaign. Indeed, Lansdowne was quite content to let Roberts pursue his own plan of action, the only criterion being he should meet with success. Lansdowne, however, did not have much choice. His position was particularly vulnerable owing to the criticism directed at the War Office. Thus, both he and the rest of the government were to find they had little room to manoeuvre in their dealings with the military and later found it very difficult to ensure that political requirements during the campaign were given full and objective consideration by Roberts.

Given the circumstances of his appointment, Roberts was presented with an unlikely chance to acquire fame and glory denied him since 1881, and it was an opportunity he grasped with both hands. While doubtless determined to save the honour of the empire, we can assume that personal calculation was also not far from Roberts's mind. He must have realised that a successfully conducted campaign would open the way for him to succeed Wolseley as C-in-C, and perhaps effect the reform of the British army. Whatever moved Roberts at that time, and revenge for the death of his son cannot be discounted either, in the conduct of his operations, Roberts did not let the government down, for between January and September 1900 he completed the rout of the Boer armies and the conquest of the Boer republics. And to this end he ensured military considerations were given the utmost priority, despite the politicians pleas to the contrary.

Milner's priorities

The British government was not alone in finding Roberts unwilling or unable to consider political requirements. Milner too desired that his opinions be given due weight by the military and was irritated by Roberts continually putting the army's needs first. Milner discovered he could expect little support from the government which he found was more concerned with the campaign, the international situation and British public opinion. However, such considerations were not at first apparent to Milner who, initially, had his own ideas as to what the priorities of the British army should be. By January 1900 his immediate concerns centred on the vulnerability of Cape Colony. Buller, by taking the bulk of his army to Natal, had denuded the Cape of troops, leaving the area exposed to a Boer attack and a possible rebellion by disaffected Afrikaners. Both in fact had occurred, although the advance of OFS commandos had stalled owing to their own inertia. As a result, the rebellion was confined to areas under Boer occupation, but the possibility of it spreading could not be discounted. When General Gatacre was defeated at Stormberg on 10 December 1899, Milner became seriously alarmed about the military situation. He expected the Boers to advance any moment and increase the extent of the rebellion.

Ending the conflict in Cape Colony was Milner's immediate priority, and to that end he interfered in matters that were not his responsibility. He forwarded his own views when not called for, and stated how tasks ought to be accomplished. Milner showed his complete distrust of the military because their priorities did not match his own. He frequently interpreted differences between his views and those of the soldiers as evidence that the latter misunderstood the nature of Cape politics and society. He himself felt no respect for the current Afrikaner Bond government and questioned their loyalty. Nor did he trust the Afrikaner population generally, even those who had not joined the rebellion: to Milner they were all irredeemable. In such circumstances, he felt the actions of military men, uninformed by political insight, were potentially dangerous and guidance was therefore essential.

Milner's views were influenced significantly by his own recent experience. He had already been frustrated and angered by Butler's intransigence, by his apparent inability to see what for Milner was the obvious truth of the situation. In working with Butler, Milner had experienced the difficulty of dealing with a military mind totally distanced from his own and his own inability to do anything about it. In the short time he liaised with Buller, he had again faced military intransigence, although not on the same scale as that displayed by Butler. Buller had failed to see that the main priority was Cape Colony, which was virtually defenceless and rebellious. Milner's frustration was evident when he summarised events for Chamberlain and sought to justify his own predilection for interfering in military decisions. Milner was exasperated by the conduct of military operations, although he explained he had not interfered in any matters that were purely military. But he then asked, 'What is purely military in this country? Every military movement is so dependent upon political conditions and forecasts, that there can be no sound strategy without taking these into account. And also I am compelled to warn, suggest, remind – to worry, in fact, the soldiers in 100 ways . . . without as much result as might be hoped.'[1] By thus denying any demarcation between military and civil requirements in Cape Colony, Milner attempted to justify his past interference and that of the future.

Perhaps Milner's frustration was exacerbated by the fact that his titular title of commander-in-chief no longer applied while the country was at war.[2] In some cases it might be justifiable for civilian authorities to question military decisions; but there was a fine line between what might be considered proper questioning and blatant interference. Milner's actions verged on the latter, causing annoyance to the military and disquiet in the British government. The British authorities were particularly vulnerable at that time to criticisms of political interference and poor judgement. A recently published Blue Book[3] containing the correspondence between White and Hely-Hutchinson on the disposition of troops in Natal at the outbreak of war, revealed how the political authorities had interfered and limited White's options. The British government could not afford to be tarnished by a similar indictment. As a result Chamberlain rebuked Milner for his apparent interference. He explained:

> that in my view it is the duty of the Governors of the Cape and Natal to inform the military authorities of the political situation, but that the entire responsibility for military operations rests with the latter, and they must disregard the political question if the exigencies of the military situation require it. I do not want them to say that they were pressed to take a particular course which their own judgment rejected. The question has arisen in regard to the retention of Glencoe and Ladysmith, but it may arise in other forms if we are not careful.[4]

But as Milner, who was insensitive to these criticisms, endeavoured to place his own mark on military operations, he began to discover how difficult it was to cajole the soldiers, and how earlier civil–military difficulties had restricted his own room for manoeuvre.

With regard to future strategy, Milner had definite ideas that he was eager to impart to Lord Roberts. He wanted to see a large force deployed in Cape Colony, to defend it from the Boers and to deter rebellious Afrikaners. Outside the areas occupied by the Boers, the Afrikaners had proved reluctant to join the rebellion and it was clear that only a disaster of the greatest magnitude would provide the spark for a general uprising, but Milner remained apprehensive. Initially, he had felt that the fall of Kimberley would provide that spark.[5] As Kimberley had held out, Milner's fears abated until the defeats

---

1 Milner to Chamberlain, 27 Dec. 1899, JC 10/9/76.
2 See regulations nos 11, 11a in W. E. Mercer and A. E. Collins, *The Colonial Office list*, London 1899, 354–5.
3 Parliamentary papers (1900), lvi, Cd. 44, 'Correspondence relating to the defence of Natal', 22–6.
4 Chamberlain to Milner, 20 Jan. 1900, in *Milner papers*, ii. 58.
5 Milner to Selborne, 18 Oct. 1899, ibid. 24.

of 'black week': then he explained to Chamberlain, 'The opportunity is golden, the incitement incessant.'[6] Again, the rebellion Milner feared so much did not materialise, yet even with the arrival of Roberts and Kitchener, his anxiety persisted.

Although Milner was pleased that Roberts and Kitchener had arrived and had begun to take control of matters, he nevertheless considered he could not remain silent on issues upon which he felt deeply. As he told Selborne:

> there are political considerations which have a direct military value. For instance I have bothered, and shall continue to bother, every General, to prevent at almost any cost, the further spread of invasion in the Colony. Why? Because the Colonial Boer is the enemy's *only Reserve*. They have got their last man and boy in the field. Let them at once get *into the heart* of the Colony, even with a mere handful of men and a flag, and they tap that Reserve, and get certainly 10,000, and perhaps, even 15–20,000 *excellent recruits*.

Milner felt that a few troops stationed near what he termed 'points of entry' would be enough to deprive the Boers of this strategic reserve. 'But that is not Politics, though it looks like it. It is Military Arithmetic.'[7] Milner's somewhat self-contradictory note revealed the extent of his agitation and frustration. The day after Roberts's arrival in Cape Town, Milner was already sending him advice about the current situation in Cape Colony, and of the necessity of keeping the Afrikaners quiet. This advice ranged from arming loyalists, to removing arms and ammunition from certain districts, and to buying up all horses and fodder.[8]

Roberts, however, seemed to have no qualms about the security of Cape Colony. He was prepared to allay Milner's fears to some extent by sending the Sixth Division to unsettled areas, but as he told Lansdowne, the hesitation and reluctance, or inability, of the Boers to follow up their victories had lessened the seriousness of the situation in the Colony.[9] In any case, Roberts had already decided on the strategy he would pursue, having planned his operations on the voyage to South Africa with Kitchener and his chief intelligence officer, the noted historian, Colonel Henderson. It was decided that the main advance would take place along the western railway and not along the central lines from Port Elizabeth and East London. By so doing, Roberts could relieve Kimberley and, by abandoning the railway, invade the OFS from an area the Boers had thought safe owing to the British army's normal reliance on a fixed supply line.[10] But this strategy also meant that few troops would be spared for the defence of Cape Colony.

6 Milner to Chamberlain, 27 Dec. 1899, JC 10/9/76.
7 Milner to Chamberlain, 17, 31 Jan. 1900, JC 13/1/2, 7; to Selborne, 31 Jan. 1900, in *Crisis of British power*, 100.
8 Milner to Roberts, 11 Jan. 1900, Roberts papers (RP), PRO, WO 105/19/T38/3.
9 Roberts to Lansdowne, 12 Jan. 1900, WO 105/31/fos 10–14.
10 Roberts had considered this strategy as early as 1897 when he discussed the matter with

Milner was plainly aware of this and felt Roberts had forgotten the danger of rebellion. He believed that once Roberts's army had moved north there would be an uprising along the lines of communication. He added, 'The danger in the Colony is absolutely ubiquitous. There is no part of it, in which the Dutch population are not rebels at heart, and would not rise against us if they saw a chance.' He then suggested that Roberts should leave behind a mounted force which could quickly stamp out the first signs of rebellion.[11]

Roberts reply was immediate, and perhaps showed that he was anticipating such a response. It also showed that Roberts would not tolerate any interference from Milner: his priority, he explained, was to defeat the Boer forces in the field. No doubt Roberts was aware of the criticism levelled at the government and knew he had to obtain quick results. Just as importantly, the military situation had to be remedied for its own sake. The besieged towns were suffering and Cape Colony was ripe for revolt; but Roberts believed these difficulties could only be eased by a succession of battlefield victories. Also, the army itself needed these victories to restore its own self-esteem:

> A serious rising in the Cape Colony is a problematical danger, while the fall of Kimberley and Ladysmith, which is inevitable unless these places can be relieved at an early date, would produce a far reaching effect not only on the inhabitants of South Africa, but on the prestige of the British Army and on the prospects of the war.[12]

Roberts felt he had to take the risk because, as he explained to Lansdowne, 'the only chance of bringing the war to successful conclusion is to carry it into the enemy's country'.[13]

Chamberlain was disappointed by Milner's obvious disregard of earlier advice. He noted on the receipt of this correspondence that Milner was intruding in an area for which he was not responsible, and began to think Milner would need a strong hint in order to stop his interfering.[14] What began to emerge was a divergence of opinion between the civil authorities in London and South Africa. Chamberlain was conscious of the need for Roberts to allay the criticism directed at the government; not only was the government in need of encouragement, so too was the British public. Milner's parochial and, as Roberts pointed out, problematical concerns clearly paled before the needs of the British government and people. Milner, it seemed, remained unconscious of Chamberlain's difficulties.

Milner, however, appeared vindicated by a rebellion at Prieska, in western Cape Colony, following the appearance of a Boer commando, which forced

Henry Wilson and other officers: B. Collier, *Brasshat: a biography of Field-Marshal Sir Henry Wilson*, London 1961, 43.
[11] Milner to Roberts, 4 Feb. 1900, CO 48/545/fos 480–6.
[12] Roberts to Milner, 5 Feb. 1900, CO 48/545/fos 487–91.
[13] Roberts to Lansdowne, 5–6 Feb. 1900, RP 7101/23/110/1/fos 356–60.
[14] CO Minutes, 2 Mar. 1900, CO 48/545/fo. 475.

Roberts to send a small force under Colonel Adye to deal with the problem. Nevertheless, Roberts told Milner, somewhat exasperatedly, that the eastern and midland railways were more important to his operations than chasing rebels, implying that he would not give the Prieska rebellion much consideration.[15] Almost simultaneously both officials appealed to their respective superiors in London, no doubt preparing the ground should the situation develop into a trial of strength. Whereas Milner called for more troops to be sent to South Africa, which in itself was an oblique way of saying Roberts was not doing much to alleviate the crisis, Roberts was more direct. He made it clear to Lansdowne that Milner was making a nuisance of himself. Although he said he was doing everything to meet Milner's wishes, 'I feel that the one thing which will put an end to the war is to advance in strength in the Orange Free State, and that everything must be sacrificed to that end.'[16]

For the moment, with the battle of Paardeberg underway, neither Chamberlain nor Lansdowne reacted, but Milner's anxiety continued to get the better of him. A series of letters between 4 and 7 March showed how the rebellion in the west was affecting his peace of mind. He ignored the fact that by then the battle of Paardeberg had been won. Such was his preoccupation with events in Cape Colony that he urged Forestier-Walker to send troops to the Prieska district, without, at first, reference to Roberts. Milner had convinced himself Roberts could not move north until the rebellion had been crushed. Roberts refused to share Milner's anxiety as his operations in the OFS were proceeding apace. But a setback on 6 March, when Colonel Adye was defeated at Houwater, only exacerbated Milner's tension. This time he urged Roberts to allow Forestier-Walker complete latitude in sending extra troops to the area.[17] His frustration was evident. He felt everything had been hurried for the sake of Kimberley and Ladysmith, and that 500 men encamped at Prieska beforehand would have deterred rebellion.[18] Chamberlain, however, remained unsympathetic. He was not impressed by Milner's constant anxiety and was concerned lest his actions should become general knowledge in Britain. 'I have warned Sir A. Milner', he noted, '& he must take sole responsibility of intervention when it does not seem to be called for from the Civil Power.'[19] In the end Roberts let Kitchener oversee operations, which had the happy result of deflecting Milner's interference at Kitchener, by which time anyway the Boers had left the area and were moving north.[20]

For the time being Cape Colony remained quiet. Roberts's successful advance through the OFS had deprived potential rebels of an important

15 Roberts to Milner, 21 Feb. 1900, WO 105/34/8.
16 Milner to Chamberlain, 22 Feb. 1900, CO 48/545/fo. 640; Roberts to Lansdowne, 22 Feb. 1900, RP 7101/23/110/2/150.
17 Milner to Roberts, 4, 7 Mar. 1900 and Roberts to Milner, 5 Mar. 1900, CO 48/545/fos 792–5.
18 Milner to Chamberlain, 8 Mar. 1900, in Milner papers, ii. 67.
19 CO Minutes, 29 Mar. 1900, CO 48/545/fo. 790.
20 Milner to Kitchener and Kitchener to Milner, 9, 10 Mar. 1900, CO 48/545/fos 909–12.

pre-condition for active rebellion – a Boer commando. His strategy had worked, removing much of the justification for Milner's fears of a disastrous uprising in the weakly defended areas outside the main British advance.

In his early dealings with Roberts in 1900, Milner had thus found that his views had little power to affect the military situation. Roberts had been appointed under extraordinary circumstances, not to help Milner but to retrieve a war going badly wrong and to get the British government out of a dangerous political predicament. Milner had great difficulty in getting his opinions accepted by the military; but it seemed he could not accept he was no longer the paramount official in South Africa. His priorities did not match those of Lord Roberts, nor those of his superiors in London. Milner's attempts to persuade the British authorities that the problem in Cape Colony was a political as much as a military one failed. In the end, Roberts's victories provided a welcome tonic to both the British government and people, which enhanced his authority in South Africa and his popularity.[21] Milner was marginalised: all he could hope for was that Roberts would finish the war quickly and allow him to put into practice the ideas that he had been formulating ever since the beginning of the war, if not before.

The end of the Orange Free State

Roberts's advance into the OFS and the capture of Bloemfontein on 13 March meant the war would be waged in the Boer republics. From then on, his army made a steady advance into enemy territory, conquering the OFS (it was annexed on 24 May 1900) and then invading the Transvaal. Unable to face the British in open warfare, the Boers continued the conflict by launching guerilla attacks on railways and telegraph lines; the longer they persisted in this style of warfare the more adept at it they became. What also became apparent was the inability of the British forces to stop Boer raids, which led to increasing frustration on their part. It also encouraged suspicions that the war might last longer than anticipated. As the nature of the war deteriorated the relationship between Milner and Roberts soured. Milner found great difficulty in accepting the methods chosen by Roberts to settle the OFS, which merely reinforced his already low opinion of the military.

During his campaign Roberts had two main priorities. First, to ensure his lines of communication were secure in order to facilitate the advance north; and secondly, to occupy the leading centres of the OFS as this would be the most visible sign of British success. The post-war settlement was not his concern; that was for the politicians to sort out. His task, therefore, was to defeat the Boer field-armies and demonstrate the fact that the Boer republics had

---

[21] Brodrick wrote that 'Still everyone even the least initiated have felt the change to Roberts, who will return the greatest British Hero of the century since Wellington': Brodrick to Violet Cecil, 16 Mar. 1900, VMP VM35/C176/72.

been absorbed by the British empire. Roberts understood that the administration of conquered territory could not be undertaken by the military alone, except perhaps while operations lasted. On 15 March he issued a proclamation which offered lenient terms to OFS Boers who laid down their arms and went back to their farms having signed an oath not to participate in the war again. This proclamation supplemented one made just as Roberts entered the OFS, which declared that the British had no quarrel with the people, only their government. As far as Roberts was concerned the OFS had lost the war and should now surrender; leniency was to be his method of facilitating this.

Leniency, however, did not have the desired effect. Although many Boers chose to surrender, substantial numbers did not. And as the British were unable to protect those who returned to their farms, those still on commando easily induced them to renew the fight. Meanwhile, the Boers increased the scale of their attacks on the British lines which affected the British war effort noticeably. On 31 March and 4 April isolated British forces were defeated or forced to surrender at Sannah's Post and Reddersburg. Milner felt anxious that nothing was being done to discourage or prevent those who had taken the oath from rejoining their comrades. For once, Roberts was not annoyed by Milner's interference as he admitted: 'I am delighted to find . . . that your views and mine are in accord.' Roberts had in fact begun to inflict harsh penalties on oath breakers, sentencing one offender to one year's imprisonment and confiscating his property. He had also taken up Milner's suggestion about dividing the country into military districts, in which a governor would disarm the Boers and remove their horses. He hoped the governors would be able to ascertain who were 'for and against us' and hoped that the country would settle down.[22]

As an extra measure, Roberts advocated the early annexation of the OFS, which would allow him to set a date after which Boers still on commando would lose their property. He felt that many would return home once it was clear President Steyn would not be allowed to return. Roberts reiterated the point again five days later stating that the OFS Boers longed for peace and would accept defeat when assured the British would not leave the country.[23] He was too optimistic and it is difficult to know how he arrived at the view that the OFS Boers were desperate for peace. Undoubtedly Roberts was concerned about the condition of his army,[24] and in particular its inability to police the whole country owing to numerical weakness. If his forces were split simply to protect the Boers who had surrendered then his chances of

---

[22] Roberts to Milner, 30 Apr. 1900, MP IV/A/175/fos 20–1.

[23] Roberts to Milner, 4, 9 May 1900, WO 105/34/C1470, C1532.

[24] At Bloemfontein the army was decimated by typhoid. The poor medical arrangements caused a scandal in Britain and it was only Roberts's huge popularity and importance that prevented his censure in parliament: Pakenham, *Boer war*, 381–3, and M. S. Stone, 'The Victorian army: health, hospitals and social conditions as encountered by British troops during the South African war, 1899–1902', unpubl PhD diss. London 1993, 113–26.

invading the Transvaal would be slim. Roberts's prime concern was to occupy the Boer republics, and to bring the war to an end in a conventional way, which meant he was ready to resort to expedients that might facilitate a speedy conclusion to the war in the OFS without denuding his army of men.

In this respect Roberts shared the same view as Milner, the only difference being that Milner wanted to see signs of a permanent settlement, and not something that appeared hasty and ill-thought-out. This was evident in May when he made plain his concern about Roberts's tactic of letting surrendered Boers go back to their farms, and argued it was ill-conceived. Milner felt that only those who lived in areas under the complete control of the British army should be allowed to return home. Otherwise, those living outside those areas should be sent to heavily guarded camps and only allowed back once the country had been truly pacified. Furthermore, Milner advocated warning those surrendering and who lived in unsecured districts, that they would be placed in custody until the military authorities thought it safe for them to return. Milner was anxious lest the Boers should claim breach of faith when surrendering under the proclamation of 15 March and that they had not been given any warning.[25]

Milner was becoming very pessimistic about the end of the war and felt it would not finish early: 'The present trend of events seem rather to point to a prolonged guerilla warfare in the outlying districts.'[26] His discouragement, however, was not shared by Roberts to the same degree. Roberts was clearly aware that the military situation was unfavourable, but felt his ideas should be given a chance. He was, therefore, unsure about sending surrendered Boers to camps; by so doing he felt the British would merely confirm Steyn's and the Transvaalers' views, as they were telling the OFS Boers that anyone who surrendered would be sent out of the country as prisoners. While Roberts assured Milner that everything would be done to deprive the Boers of arms and horses, he added that those who surrendered knew the risks, and knew also that the British could do little to reduce them. As it was, those who surrendered and lived outside the zone of occupation would not be allowed to return until the country had been cleared. Up to that point some 400 men had surrendered and Roberts felt the present policy was worth persevering with.[27]

Milner was dismayed that Roberts believed Boer professions of war-weariness: 'In most cases all it means is that they want a rest and look at their families & property.' He hoped that names of those returning were being

---

[25] Roberts to Milner, 14 May 1900 and Milner to Roberts, 14 May 1900, CO 417/290/fos 35–8. Colonel Brabant suggested that surrendered Boers be sent to the Cape for safe keeping; Milner agreed in principle but wanted these Boers kept in secure areas in the OFS, to emphasise British protection. In August 1900, the British authorities seriously contemplated the use of concentration camps: Spies, *Methods of barbarism*, 47, 147–53.

[26] Milner's diary of events, 10 May 1900, CO 417/290/fos 83–4.

[27] Roberts to Milner, 15 May 1900, WO 105/34/C1622.

collected and swift punishment meted out to those who broke their oath.[28] Milner though remained unconvinced: in his view, too many surrendered Boers were falling prey to the commandos, whilst the motives of those who surrendered remained questionable. But while Roberts claimed to have obtained results, albeit of a limited nature, Milner could only remain on the sidelines without being able to influence the course of events. This was a try-ing time for him. Roberts's policy was not a clear demonstration of British power, and nothing was being done to make the British occupation a reality. British forces were too few to be seen everywhere, and where they were seen they were too weak to offer any real protection: the country was not being settled in either a permanent or systematic manner. All Milner could hope was that oath breakers would be punished severely, and their punishments well publicised. It was with some misgivings, therefore, that he received Roberts's assurances that everything was being done to disarm the Boers, that they were tired of the war, and that announcements of annexation and other proclamations would be enough to induce the Boers to surrender.[29]

On 24 May 1900 the OFS was formally annexed and four days later became known officially as the Orange River Colony (ORC). If Roberts hoped the Boers would consider the war to be over, then he was mistaken: the proclamation was ignored. On 1 June, therefore, a further proclamation was issued which stated that citizens of the former OFS still fighting would be treated as rebels and punished accordingly if they had not surrendered within two weeks. This measure revealed that British efforts to end the guerilla war were becoming desperate. On 31 May a battalion of the Imperial Yeomanry was captured by the Boers at Lindley; on 7 June De Wet's forces overwhelmed three garrisons in succession (at Rhenoster river, Roodewal and Vredefort). These disasters were symptomatic of the problems facing the British. At Lindley a British force had occupied the town but had insufficient men to garrison it, and had left it empty after marching on. The Imperial Yeomanry had then marched in thinking the main force still there, only to find an over-whelming force of Boers had got there first. The need for troops was so great that various towns were evacuated at times to provide them; places such as Smithfield, Wepener and Rouxville were all abandoned despite having been considered important earlier.[30] The basic tactics used against the Boers hardly changed during Roberts's command. Columns of troops, overladen with transport and supplies, would attempt to pursue the more mobile Boer com-mandos. They would march into a town, march out again only for the Boers to reappear soon after. Sometimes small garrisons would be left, but they often proved unable to withstand a determined Boer attack, as the actions at Roodewal and Vredefort demonstrated. Roberts never had enough men to provide for the columns, his field army and for permanent garrisons. As a

28 Milner to Roberts, 17 May 1900, CO 417/290/fo. 213.
29 Roberts to Milner, 19, 23 May 1900, WO 105/34/C1715, C1779.
30 *Official history*, iii. 105–6, 115–16, 470–1.

result it proved almost impossible to protect those who had surrendered. The situation was so desperate that some of the generals began to fall out amongst themselves.

The military governor of Bloemfontein, General Pretyman, was in dispute with General Kelly-Kenny, over who was responsible for the pacification and general administration of the occupied areas. Pretyman, who dealt with the civil side of the occupation and whose subordinates were the civilian district commissioners, was in communication with both Milner and Roberts. Consequently he kept Milner informed about the problems he faced in dealing with the 'military' Kelly-Kenny, who was directly responsible to Roberts, and the trouble caused by Kelly-Kenny's officers who clashed incessantly with the district commissioners over the administration of the occupied areas.

Milner was aware that the military authorities appeared to be acting high-handedly, as he had already received complaints about their conduct; evidently, officers were seizing stock without due reason, or purchased stock with 'chits' which were impossible to redeem promptly.[31] Surprisingly perhaps, Pretyman confirmed that Milner's enquiries were true. Officers were seizing stock without care or attention: 'I must, however, tell you that I have been greatly handicapped by the unnecessary interference of certain general officers in my administration of the more settled districts.' Pretyman did not elaborate, but explained he was writing to Roberts about 'chits', so they could be redeemed quickly, and would not honour those presented by speculators.[32]

For Milner, all this was plain evidence that the military were incapable of sustaining a coherent and systematic administration. If the soldiers were falling out amongst themselves within the limited areas they had apparently pacified, what hope was there that they could succeed in bringing the rest of the region under military control, and if the situation in the ORC was to be the standard by which Lord Roberts and his officers operated then the prospects of a swift pacification of the Transvaal looked bleak. Milner had plans for the Transvaal and he was unprepared to stand idly by while the military went chasing after Boers, without achieving any results.

On to Komati Poort

On 27 May 1900 Roberts's army crossed the river Vaal and began the invasion of the Transvaal. In response the Boers attacked Roberts's lengthening supply lines, garrisons and railway and telegraph communications. These attacks did nothing to harmonise the relationship between Milner and Roberts. Nor did they improve Roberts's relations with London. The reputation

31 Milner to Pretyman, 20 June 1900, in *Milner papers*, ii. 133–4.
32 Pretyman to Milner, 26 June 1900, MP IV/A/173/fos 17a–19. For the acrimonious correspondence between Pretyman and Kelly-Kenny, and Roberts reprimand of Pretyman see RP 7101/23/57/fos 24–51, 7101/23/111/3/989.

of the British government had been saved by Roberts's victories, although not enough to shake off all criticism. Moreover, events elsewhere in the world presaged a possible clash with other European powers, and reawoke critics who became concerned at the over-extension of Britain's military resources, most of which were in South Africa. This combination of foreign and imperial crises also began to undermine Cabinet cohesion, as certain departmental heads pressed for a greater consideration of their interests. Consequently, as the war in South Africa dragged on, so the government became more anxious.

A notable effect of the various crises was the drawing together of Milner and the British government following their differences over Milner's interference with Roberts's strategy. Yet both had different reasons for this convergence. Milner wanted a change in tactics to defeat the Boers and a change in strategy to permit the effective administration of the conquered areas. On the other hand, the government wanted to see immediate results to save money and to divert resources to other crises. Each then had their own particular reasons for wanting the war to finish quickly. Both however found great difficulty in trying to impose their interests in the face of military exigencies. While Milner's and the government's concerns appeared similar, they were not close enough to ensure a collective approach against the military conduct of the war. As a result they were unable to influence Roberts when they felt the war was going badly.

At first Lansdowne had acquiesced in Roberts's attempt to treat the Boers leniently. However, as this policy had not succeeded in abating the guerilla war, Lansdowne told Roberts that 'experience has shown that your confidence has been grossly abused & you will be supported if you insist on thorough going measures for disarming the suspect part of the population, and if you inflict stern retribution where unfair advantage has been taken of your clemency'.[33] Lansdowne, and no doubt the government, were anxious about the lack of results. After all, Roberts's army had been in the ORC for about three months and had effectively defeated the Boer army. By 6 June 1900 both Johannesburg and Pretoria had fallen (31 May and 5 June respectively) and ministers sensed that the war might soon be over; in fact some of them were already discussing the possibility of troop withdrawals. Lansdowne, however, felt it was too early to begin taking troops from South Africa, or to stop sending drafts there either. As he told Salisbury, 'Until we can form an estimate of the amount of opposition still to be encountered, it would . . . be unwise to relax the pressure.'[34]

The fact that the campaign had still to be concluded in its conventional form assisted Roberts in his dealings with the civil authorities. He believed Boer opposition was insubstantial. The armies of the former republics now appeared to be operating separately, and these were inconsiderable in

33 Lansdowne to Roberts, 19 May 1900, RP 7101/23/34/fo. 373.
34 Lansdowne to Salisbury, 6 Jun. 1900, Salisbury correspondence, fos 556–7.

number. The war in the Transvaal, like that in the ORC, was now turning into a guerilla war, but Roberts was confident it would not last long in that form. He admitted the commandos were a nuisance, threatening railways and telegraph lines, but believed he had been right to advance on Pretoria and would be 'greatly disappointed if our being here does not result in the war being soon brought to a conclusion'.[35]

Looking at the problem from a conventional military point of view, Roberts, like many others, believed that the capture of the visible symbols of Boer nationhood would be enough to terminate the war. Roberts was not alone in thinking the Boers prized their towns and particularly the goldfields. For example, in June 1899 Major Altham had stated that the Boer was no longer a simple nomad:

> The wealth in the land has excited him; the taint of corruption has reached him; his hopes and desires for favours in the shape of railways, personal loans, or good bargains are concentrated in the official offices at Pretoria or the markets of Johannesburg, and not a few of the old Boers are taking up a permanent residence in Pretoria to watch over their own interests on the spot, leaving their sons to take care of the farms.[36]

There were good reasons, therefore, for Roberts to capture key population centres. Unfortunately for British perceptions, the Boers did not share the same view and abandoned their towns without a struggle. Even so, Roberts could still reasonably hope that the capture of the towns would weaken Boer morale to such an extent that they would offer terms. To expect this however revealed Roberts's inability to comprehend the enemy he was fighting.

Yet he still had no real reason to suppose the guerilla war might be protracted. In any case, Roberts could not admit it would be, or that it would cause undue difficulty. He obviously had confidence in his own ability and, perhaps more importantly, had a reputation to maintain as well. Moreover, it must be remembered that even after the fall of Pretoria, General Botha had kept the Transvaal army in being, and despite its numerical weakness it still represented the military power of the Transvaal. As this army remained astride the last railway link with the outside world it could still hope that some form of help might arrive. Until the Boers had been completely cut off from the outside world, Roberts still had room for optimism because once Botha's forces were defeated, the Boers might finally recognise the hopelessness of their cause and surrender. For all Roberts knew, the existence of Botha's army might have been the one factor that kept the guerilla bands operating; once they knew of its defeat then they too might finally see that all was lost. Thus it was for these reasons that Roberts kept a bold front when corresponding with the government, and until the defeat of Botha's army the

[35] Roberts to Lansdowne, 7 June 1900, RP 7101/23/110/3/538.
[36] Memo. by Altham, 3 June 1899, WO 32/7844/079/8501.

government could at least appreciate why Roberts could not comply with their wishes.

It was not long before Roberts's confident tones became more gloomy. He began to realise that his forces could not defeat the guerillas and march to the Mozambique frontier at the same time. This became more apparent after Lansdowne telegraphed Roberts on 22 June. Lansdowne revealed that the international crisis arising from the Boxer Rebellion in China was causing the Cabinet great anxiety. He still believed it was too early to begin reducing the army in South Africa; but felt Roberts should keep the matter under consideration, especially when peace was assured.[37] Roberts, however, did not think any troops could be spared until September; the Boers were active against the lines of communication and it was taking time to get counter-measures, in the form of mounted columns, ready and active. Meanwhile, the Boers were destroying bridges and culverts at will.[38] This last communication was shown to the Cabinet, which confirmed they were now taking a greater interest in the day-to-day conduct of the campaign. Whether Roberts was aware of this is uncertain, but he seemed to have regretted his less than cheerful note of 24 June because four days later he was more optimistic, writing, 'beyond cutting the telegraph wire and destroying a culvert here and there, I doubt their being able to do us much harm'. He did acknowledge, however, that British difficulties elsewhere were giving fresh impetus to the Boer military effort.[39]

Roberts obviously realised there was no advantage in being pessimistic about the guerilla war; after all he had accused Buller of undue pessimism. Roberts had to be careful to ensure he presented a balanced version of events to the government. If he admitted he could not stop the guerilla war, or minimise its effects, then he would seem to have failed. Conversely, he could not present too rosy a picture otherwise the government might insist on taking some of his troops, when he was barely able to fight the guerillas and the conventional war. As it was, Roberts appeared to have succeeded in this balancing act because the government did not insist he make a definite statement on the condition of the campaign.

Before Roberts could embark on the final campaign, however, he had to build up his supplies and rest his men. Not surprisingly, the attacks on his communications began to affect adversely the speed with which this could be achieved. In response, Roberts sanctioned a more draconian approach towards the commandos, and those who aided and abetted them. This change in tactics reflected the failure of the policy of leniency, and the fact that the commando raids were becoming more than just a nuisance. As a result, on 16 and 19 June 1900 Roberts acknowledged this failure with the issue of two proclamations aimed against the guerillas. The main clauses

37 Lansdowne to Roberts, 22 June 1900, WO 105/30/fo. 318.
38 Roberts to Lansdowne, 24 June 1900, CAB 37/54/144.
39 Roberts to Lansdowne, 28 June 1900, RP 7101/23/110/3/606.

stated that property in the vicinity of a Boer raid was liable to be destroyed as it was deemed to have harboured the culprits, and that civilians would be used as hostages on trains in order to prevent the destruction of the railway. The latter clause was soon dropped after provoking an outcry in Britain and amongst Roberts's own staff; George Fiddes, his political secretary, argued that it was an inducement to the Boers to blow up those who had capitulated, that it upset those who had surrendered in good faith, and that it shamed the army.[40] Nevertheless, Roberts was not deflected from destroying property and informed General Clery, 'I am not in favour of lessening the punishment laid down for any damage done to our railway and telegraph lines. Unless the people generally are made to suffer for the misdeeds of those in arms against us the war will never end.'[41] Roberts told Lansdowne he was no longer treating the Boers leniently. In the Transvaal particularly the guerilla war was more pronounced and he was using 'much more severe measures than formerly. The people are beginning to understand this now, and the raids on the railway, cutting the telegraph wire, etc., are not nearly so frequent as they were'.[42] Yet Roberts was becoming sensitive to criticisms of his campaign, particularly regarding the length of time his forces had spent in Pretoria, arguing the delay was caused by his having to direct numerous minor operations. In fact his comments to Lansdowne on 18 August showed how discouraged he was becoming. He now blamed the guerilla war for delaying operations and conceded that he was wasting too many soldiers in fruitless secondary operations. No doubt it was with some relief that he told Lansdowne he was about to resume his march, and 'I trust they [operations] will have successful, if not final, result.'[43]

Roberts's advance on Komati Poort was effectively the last stage of the conventional war. Much was hoped from the success of this enterprise, not least the total capitulation of the Boers. Although China continued to trouble the government, Lansdowne told Salisbury, 'The South African news is good, and I hope we may soon hear of proposals for peace.'[44] On 1 September Roberts formally annexed the Transvaal. This was followed by a proclamation on 13 September which called on the Boers to surrender. On 25 September Roberts's forces occupied Komati Poort, and the Boers were cut off from the outside world.

From the remorseless march of the British army, few doubted that the war would be over once Komati Poort had been reached, and the only bone of contention outstanding concerned the seriousness of the guerilla war. Roberts informed Lansdowne and Milner on 2 September that, as the attacks on

[40] Fiddes to Roberts, 23 July 1900, WO 105/25/Index no. 66/fos 18–27; Spies, *Methods of barbarism*, 103–9.
[41] Roberts to Clery, 17 Sept. 1900, RP 7101/23/111/8/2371.
[42] Roberts to Lansdowne, 16 Aug. 1900, RP 7101/23/110/3/767.
[43] Roberts to Lansdowne, 18 Aug. 1900, RP 7101/23/110/3/782.
[44] Lansdowne to Salisbury, 31 Aug. 1900, Salisbury correspondence, fos 585–6.

his communications continued and as the Boer general, Christian De Wet, had publicly stated his intention to attack British outposts at every opportunity, sterner measures were required. In June Roberts had sent families of combatants who were residing in Johannesburg and Pretoria to Botha's forces, as he believed they should not be supplied at British expense. He further informed Botha that any farm near the scene of a Boer attack would be destroyed and those within a ten-mile radius would be cleared of stock and supplies. Moreover all remaining families who had not been removed would be sent to Botha's headquarters.[45] Roberts was becoming increasingly irritated by the resistance of the Boers. In fact, throughout August and into September, British units had carried out a policy of devastation in the countryside and especially against buildings in and around the railways. Indeed, farm burning began to be carried out with what Spies calls 'a casual ruthlessness'; and Roberts later told Botha he would send Boer families out on the veldt 'regardless of whether they were able to support themselves or not'.[46]

Lansdowne certainly supported a stringent policy at this time. The government clearly believed the Boers were finished and it was only a matter of time before they surrendered. He informed Roberts of government backing and told him to do everything and anything to bring the war to an end because the government was seriously concerned about events outside South Africa. Although the Boxer rebellion had been crushed in June, the crisis in China continued, owing to the Russian seizure of territory in Manchuria. Lansdowne explained that 'At the moment we are [spread] all over the face of the Earth, & the knowledge that we have so much on our hands weakens us diplomatically.' Six days later, he told him that severity had the support of the 'man in the street', especially after Roberts had tried to be lenient; it was time to abandon 'kid gloves' and resort to sterner measures. 'This is what you have done & the new departure has been welcomed.'[47]

In the letter of 13 September Lansdowne revealed the other major factor which disturbed the Cabinet – the cost of the war. Lansdowne himself was under constant pressure from the Treasury; in fact since the occupation of Pretoria the Treasury had continually demanded that the army in South Africa be reduced. All Lansdowne could do was argue that Roberts's measures would soon have the desired effect of ending Boer resistance. Hicks Beach was not placated by Lansdowne's assurances and repeatedly called for a reduction in troop numbers; he even wanted Salisbury to intervene directly and order Roberts to tailor his strategy towards lessening costs and troops. By showing the Cabinet the earlier correspondence, Lansdowne managed to allay their concerns for the time being.[48] Although Hicks Beach was not the

---

45 Roberts to Lansdowne and Milner, 2 Sept. 1900, WO 105/27/670/3/fo. 4.
46 Spies, *Methods of barbarism*, 124, 135.
47 Lansdowne to Roberts, 7, 13 Sept. 1900, RP 7101/23/34/fos 405, 406.
48 Yakutiel, 'Treasury control', 124–5, 130–3.

most popular member of the Cabinet his views regarding the cost of the war were duly noted. Ministers were aware that costs had risen dramatically since the first estimates had been produced almost a year before. Yet they faced a dilemma in trying to redress this problem. First they had to be careful not to alienate the electorate by increasing the tax burden, particularly on those sections of society from which they drew their support. Secondly, they could not impress this point too forcefully on Roberts otherwise they might have a public dispute with the country's favourite general. It was difficult for the government to know just how much pressure to apply; for the time being it had to be in the form of gentle persuasion because the war appeared to be coming to an end.

Indeed, everything was being prepared for the war to be terminated. Roberts reported from near Komati Poort that now, 'the settlement of the country will be more a civil than a military duty'. He explained that Baden-Powell was organising a police force and that, hopefully, by October, he could start sending troops home.[49] A week later, he modified his predictions and stated that few regulars could be spared, but intimated that the various volunteer regiments – British and colonial – would be disbanded first. This was favourably acknowledged by Lansdowne who was pleased the volunteers would go first as they were the most expensive troops in the army.[50] For the moment, relations between the British government and Roberts were cordial. Ministers had no need to apply unnecessary pressure because the war seemed to be over, and Roberts was proving responsive to their fears.

Milner's hopes of a rapid end to the war, like those of the government, were raised by Roberts's advance on Komati Poort. The apparent inevitability of a successful conclusion to the campaign allowed him to devote more time to consideration of the future. As virtually all the major population centres had been taken by the British, he told Chamberlain that it was time the occupied areas were properly pacified. Milner was not concerned whether Botha's forces escaped into the northern regions of the Transvaal as these areas were bad for horses and lacked supplies. He did not want to see British troops and resources wasted against these men because it would not help in pacifying the captured territories. Any further advances would only expose more lines of communication to attack.[51]

Two weeks later, as Roberts's final objective was in sight, Milner reiterated his views on the military situation more explicitly. He was particularly annoyed at the tactics being used by the army. He could not see the use of troops occupying a town one moment and then being withdrawn the next to go chasing Boers, only to give those Boers the luxury of recapturing the town. Throughout the South African winter months, especially between July and

---

[49] Roberts to Lansdowne, 16 Sept. 1900, RP 7101/23/110/4/865.
[50] Roberts to Lansdowne, 25 Sept. 1900, CAB 37/53/70; Lansdowne to Roberts, 12 Oct. 1900, RP 7101/23/34/fo. 416.
[51] Milner to Chamberlain, 5 Sept. 1900, CO 417/293/fos 682–3.

August, troops had been plundered from garrisons to assist in what became known as the first De Wet Hunt. These operations, however, were not the only ones being conducted: in the western Transvaal, General De La Rey was active, obliging the British to divert forces to hunt his commando. Milner felt that chasing Boers the length and breadth of the old republics was both slow and wasteful; instead he advocated

> the occupation, with a fixed resolve not to be turned out or to withdraw, of some commanding position in every district, which will form a base of supplies, and a rallying point for our friends or the neutrals who may require protection, and our firm retention of which will convince the people that we have come to stay. This is, in my opinion, a point of supreme importance.

The main advantage of this method would be that British troops could operate from numerous supply bases and not be hindered by having to take transport with them. Milner felt the commandos would soon be discouraged as they would be unable to penetrate the strongpoints, or evade the columns operating between them. Milner added that the protraction of the war prevented the restarting of industry, by which he meant the goldfields. While industry lay idle, the refugees from Johannesburg, who had fled to the Cape and Natal, were becoming destitute. In short, the guerilla war was not only impoverishing the countryside, it was ruining industry and the people who worked it.[52]

The latter part of Milner's lengthy communication was particularly important because he laid special emphasis on the speedy rehabilitation of the Transvaal and its economy. While the army seemed incapable of settling the countryside, Milner's annoyance became more discernible. Thus, by the time Roberts's forces had taken Komati Poort, Milner and the British government had converged after the breach earlier in the year. This convergence had been steady since the occupation of the ORC, and by the end of September Milner and the British government were once again united in wishing to see a rapid end to substantial, regular military operations. Although the interests of Milner and the government overlapped, their different priorities kept them apart. Thus, despite the united front shown by the politicians in both London and South Africa, they were unable to use it to ensure Roberts took notice of their views.

---

[52] Milner to Chamberlain 19 Sept. 1900, CO 417/294/fos 146–50.

5

Police and Refugees:
May – December 1900

From May 1900, alongside the problems in the ORC, Milner and Roberts also disagreed on how to proceed in the Transvaal. For Milner it was important that the new colony be pacified as quickly as possible to facilitate his plans for the rebuilding of South Africa. He wanted to see the mining industry restarted promptly, so as to provide the financial resources for reconstruction. The best method of achieving this, as far as Milner was concerned, was a short period of military government immediately followed by a substantial term of 'autocratic' civilian control. To do this, to clear the 'Augean stable' that was the Transvaal, also meant that Milner relinquished his post as governor of Cape Colony to become governor of the Transvaal; he still kept his position as high commissioner. Milner felt that his idea of a new British South Africa could only be created from the Transvaal itself – the centre as he called it. He thought Cape Colony was beyond redemption: 'But if we make the T.V [Transvaal] what it ought to be, the Colony will matter less, and in the long run, with the heart sound, the whole body will be saved, especially as Orange River is, I believe, easily saveable.'[1] For Milner, therefore, the reconstruction of the Transvaal was of the utmost importance. The success of his venture would make or break the British empire in South Africa. Consequently, civil–military relations were soured further by two problems, both linked and both dependent on the resolution of the other before one could be fully resolved. These were the fate of the Uitlander refugees in Cape Colony and Natal, and the establishment of a paramilitary police force to provide the means for the transition from military to civilian policing.

Returning to normal

As early as 10 May 1900 Milner contacted Roberts over the fate of the Transvaal and was plainly pushing for the establishment of civil administration and the formation of a new police force, one which would not only police Johannesburg but eventually the country districts too. Until all this was done, Milner acknowledged that the refugees could not be allowed back and was plainly aware the single line railway would not be capable of supplying

---

[1] Milner to Chamberlain, 30 May 1900, in *Milner papers*, ii. 142–6.

the army and a growing civilian population.[2] For the time being Roberts was in agreement with Milner: these ideas were, as Roberts stated, 'general principles', but as the campaign unfolded and the guerilla war took root further agreement became more problematic.[3]

On 1 June 1900 Milner began to consider ideas about sending Uitlanders back to Johannesburg. He was prompted to do so by the Chamber of Mines which wanted 580 staff members (drawn from a total of 12,541 employees) to be given permission to return to the city. Despite his earlier pronouncements to the contrary, Milner now favoured this idea. In Cape Colony the refugee problem was acute: many were destitute and protesting about their conditions, while the British government was unwilling to supply public money for their relief. Moreover, refugees in Britain were about to return owing to Roberts's victories. In any case, Milner was eager to see industry restarted: he explained to Roberts that by allowing these representatives back into Johannesburg, 'we shall satisfy industry, strengthen our hands in refusing miscellaneous inrush and prepare the way for prompt resumption of business whenever a larger population can be admitted'.[4] It seems Milner's eagerness and enthusiasm got the better of him. He gave no thought to the problems Roberts either faced or might have to face in the future. No consideration, for example, was given to the problem of supplying these people, and none to the pressure that might be exerted by others wishing to return. Milner's somewhat bland assurances that to allow a few back would be enough to reassure those left behind was based on nothing but conjecture. He ignored the possibility that the opposite effect might happen, the few becoming an avalanche of humanity, which the authorities would be hard pressed to stop. While Roberts agreed in principle with Milner's suggestion he made no firm promises and merely said he hoped to fix a date sooner rather than later.[5]

Roberts's evasive reply, however, did nothing to lessen the pressure on Milner to prepare a timetable for the return of the refugees. The Standard Bank, for example, was anxious to know what coin was left in their branches in Johannesburg and Pretoria. As they were the army's bankers, Milner felt some of their men ought to return. At the same time the mines, the banks, insurance companies and various other organisations, agitated for permission to return. Indeed the avalanche Milner had not suspected had begun to develop; he even stated that the first batch to return should contain representatives from all these institutions, which would number about 1,000. In just over two weeks, the 580 suggested by the Chamber of Mines had nearly doubled; by endorsing their suggestion, Milner had pulled the first stone of the avalanche.[6]

2 Milner to Roberts, 10 May 1900, MP IV/A/175/fos 68–70.
3 Roberts to Milner, 16 May 1900, MP IV/A/175/fos 28–30.
4 Milner to Roberts, 1 June 1900, CO 417/290/fos 781–2.
5 Roberts to Milner, 5 June 1900, CO 417/290/fo. 786.
6 Milner to Roberts, 7, 17 June 1900, CO 417/290/fos 102, 109.

Unfortunately for Milner, Roberts was unable to meet his requests, blaming the insufficiency of engines and the lack of supplies. As a sop, he was prepared to allow twenty persons to come north.[7] In fact, the supply situation was serious. A few days later Roberts telegraphed Milner requesting that the prohibition on trading with the enemy be lifted. Furthermore, Lt-Colonel Girouard, the director of railways, had informed Kitchener that allowing mining officials to return would provoke trouble in the irregular regiments drawn from Johannesburg. Girouard had heard that Milner wanted 350 employees to return but knew that former mine managers serving with the Johannesburg regiments would resent newcomers arriving at the mines and doing their old jobs.[8]

Milner was aware of this problem. If he was hoping that pressure from the refugees would make Roberts relent, then he was wrong. Milner asked Roberts if only those granted permits might be allowed to return, a suggestion which Roberts dismissed because 'at present there are military reasons against it. I would be very glad if you would undertake the granting of passes when the Military situation admits of civilians coming up'.[9]

Roberts was hinting that the situation was far from satisfactory. How unsatisfactory Milner soon discovered. He had, in collaboration with leading Uitlanders, been compiling a list of those most suitable for an early return. In this way he could send north any number Roberts decided to allow in. It must have been a great disappointment, therefore, for him to learn of the fate of the twenty representatives Roberts had allowed to return to Johannesburg. First, they were detained at Bloemfontein, and secondly were told by Girouard that they could only stay for a month. Milner considered this stipulation preposterous. To treat the representatives of the mining industry in such a way was absurd, especially as 'they have been most reasonable and helpful throughout and can be of immense use in the future'.[10]

Roberts, however, was experiencing troubles of his own. The day after receiving Milner's complaint, he told him that news of the twenty representatives had been received badly by members of the various Uitlander regiments, who felt their jobs would be lost. This was the reason for the delay. Members of the Railway Pioneers and Imperial Light Horse (ILH) had threatened to resign if the refugees arrived in Johannesburg and, as Roberts explained, some troops from De Montmorency's Scouts had actually done so. Roberts did not want others to follow their example and create a shortage of troops he could ill afford. Now beginning to lose patience with the Uitlander

7   Roberts to Milner, 26 June 1900, CO 417/291/fo. 328.
8   Roberts to Milner, 1 July 1900, RP 7101/23/111/3/835; Girouard to Kitchener, nd, WO 105/34/pol. sec. file. Milner rescinded the proclamation forbidding trade with the enemy on 2 or 3 July: Milner to Roberts, 2 July 1900, CO 417/292/fos 527–8.
9   Milner to Roberts, 1 July 1900 and Roberts to Milner, 2 July 1900, CO 417/292/fos 201–2.
10 Milner to Roberts, 5 July 1900, MP IV/A/175/fos 98–9, and CO 417/292/fo. 203.

soldiers themselves he threatened that if any resigned they would be sent back to their place of enlistment and not be allowed to return to Johannesburg. As most had enlisted in Cape Colony or Natal this was quite a threat.[11]

The opposition of the Uitlander regiments was proving irksome to Milner. He already had enough trouble persuading the high command to resume work on the mines; what he did not need was trouble from a quarter that, to him, had no reason to be troublesome.[12] Annoyingly for Milner, Roberts chose to give his own needs priority, and told Milner he would now allow the representatives only ten days in Johannesburg. Irritated by Roberts's lack of co-operation, Milner sent the field-marshal messages from the Chamber of Mines which promised to hold open the jobs of those on active service, alongside protestations that the Uitlander soldiers could have thought their employers so inconsiderate.[13] Milner, though, was caught in a quandary. He recognised it would take months before a sufficient number of refugees could return and restart industry. He admitted as much to Chamberlain, which begs the question why did he continue to harass the military? Presumably he still wanted to keep the issue alive, so that all returns would occur as soon as possible; furthermore, he was unable to remain idle, and the representatives of the Uitlanders refused to let him do so. And to add to his frustrations the military situation continued to worry him, particularly after outposts around Pretoria were attacked, costing the British several hundred men and two guns.[14]

The refugee problem

On 21 July 1900 Roberts began his march on Komati Poort. Milner's hopes of a quick end to the war may have got the better of him, because nine days later he sent a long note to the field-marshal outlining the difficulties he faced. The 'impatience of the exiles' troubled him greatly, as did the attitude of the irregulars who had incensed the refugees. Perhaps Milner felt this note would be a last plea to Roberts. He tried to explain that by allowing some representatives back in order to restart industry, the irregulars would benefit once they were disbanded. But recognising how matters were decided in South Africa, he added that it was up to Roberts to judge and that he would back him whatever decision was made.[15]

Unable to escape Milner's pleas even when away campaigning, Roberts replied rather testily: 'There is not the least use in the exiles worrying themselves about Johannesburg, no one will be allowed to return until peace is

11 Roberts to Milner, 6 July 1900, RP 7101/23/111/3/898; to Mackenzie, 4 July 1900, RP 7101/23/111/3/877.
12 Milner to Roberts, 9 July 1900, CO 417/292/fos 205.
13 Milner to Roberts and Roberts to Milner, 9 July 1900, CO 417/292/fos 206, 208.
14 Milner to Chamberlain, 11, 18 July 1900, CO 417/292/fos 191–3, 427.
15 Milner to Roberts, 30 July 1900, RP 7101/23/45/fo. 37.

made.'[16] This uncompromising statement revealed Roberts's own impatience with events. Probably he believed his march would end in final victory and that the refugees could be put off until then – when he had either left South Africa or was in the process of leaving. But as his march proceeded so refugee impatience grew, forcing Milner to continue pestering him to resolve the crisis. Not unnaturally expectations amongst the refugees had begun to rise again as the end of the war was in sight, and the further the campaign progressed the greater the anticipation. Thus, throughout August and up to the capture of Komati Poort on 25 September, the refugee problem continued to plague civil–military relations. It was not surprising it should do so considering how many refugees were destitute. Milner explained that the refugees knew that 'notorious anti-British traders' were operating in Johannesburg and resented it. (Doubtless a consequence of allowing trading with the enemy.) He recommended, therefore, that twenty representatives of the commercial interest be allowed to return, just as those of the mining companies had earlier. To this Roberts agreed, but only for a week.[17] Nevertheless, the anticipated conclusion of the war created a climate which generated much tension between Milner and Roberts. More than anything this tension led to the development of false hopes and a failure to appreciate the direction the war was taking.

Roberts was increasingly irritated by the growing impatience of the refugees, and the criticism from both the British and South African publics. In having to defend himself he admitted that the guerilla war was far more dangerous than first thought.[18] Milner's criticism of the army, however, was now becoming more specialised. The inability of the army to get the refugees back to Johannesburg made him think about the present course of the war. He was convinced the army was not doing an efficient job, and he was losing confidence in Roberts. He was prepared to admit that the process of subjugation would be slow, but emphasised that the essential point was to make some effort at establishing civil administration; which of course included industry and commerce. 'If we can confine resistance to a definite area – even a wide one – sufficiently removed from the centres of industry, it will die of itself.' Milner was perturbed at the thought of Roberts having to conduct several minor campaigns, which left him no time to consider establishing a civilian presence in the conquered territories.[19] Consideration of the refugee problem and his own overwhelming desire to begin the reconstruction of South Africa meant Milner was ready, once again, to interfere in a politically dangerous area – military strategy. He was no longer content with trying to hustle

[16] Roberts to Milner, 10 Aug. 1900, MP IV/A/175/fos 52–6.
[17] Milner to Fiddes and Roberts, 8, 16 Aug. 1900; Fiddes to Milner, 14 Aug. 1900, CO 417/293/fos 459, 460, 474; Roberts to Kitchener, 29 Aug. 1900, RP 7101/23/111/7/1956.
[18] Roberts to Milner, 18 Aug. 1900, WO 105/34/C3685. Lansdowne was sent the same note.
[19] Milner to Chamberlain, 22 Aug. 1900, JC 13/1/56.

Roberts along, merely to ensure he did not forget important details which might get lost in the minutiae of military technicalities.

Having appealed to London, Milner tried to impress on Roberts that his policy of leniency had failed and that able-bodied Boers should now be detained in camps. By so doing they would be kept away from the commandos, and any inclination to rejoin their former comrades would be reduced. Keeping them in South Africa, moreover, would limit any fear they might have of being sent abroad. As for the refugees, Milner merely reiterated that destitution was rife.[20]

Milner's concerns, however, appeared to cut little ice with Roberts. He had his hands full trying to conduct his campaign, the guerilla war and the deteriorating supply problem in the Transvaal. Roberts telegraphed Milner offering little hope to the refugees, and stated, rather sarcastically, 'It might perhaps satisfy some people who are eager to return to Johannesburg if they were told there is a meat famine there, and that horses have now to be eaten by the few civil residents in the place.'[21] Such was the seriousness of the supply problem that Roberts had to go begging to the Natal authorities for railway engines and had to promise Natal due consideration in the trade to supply the Rand with food. Indeed, on 29 August, Roberts even ordered Kitchener to plunder other lines of rolling-stock in order to supply his army marching on Komati Poort.[22]

The impending conclusion of the war was indeed raising British hopes everywhere. Milner's appeal to London had seemed to work because Chamberlain replied by expressing his frustration about the delay in establishing civil administration. He was also disappointed that a military police force had not yet been formed, and agreed that business should be restarted on the Rand. He felt that thousands of 'Englishmen' back on the Rand, suitably armed, would have a disquieting effect on the Boers. Chamberlain hoped that Roberts's imminent success would, in conjunction with the establishment of a police force, mean that he could start sending regular troops home.[23] Milner had obviously struck a chord when he had written to Chamberlain on 22 August, although not as deeply as he might have hoped. The government was still reluctant to press Roberts as the results of his campaign had yet to be known. For the Cabinet, their anticipated peace dividend did not match Milner's sufficiently enough to warrant a direct questioning of Roberts's conduct; nor was it the time to do so as optimism was running high. The thought of

20 Milner to Roberts, 23 Aug. 1900, RP 7101/23/45/fo. 38.
21 Roberts to Milner, 23 Aug. 1900, WO 105/34/C3811. Roberts explained this more subtly in a letter to Milner, in which he agreed with Milner's suggestion about the internment of Boer prisoners. He also agreed that leniency had failed and that it was time for harsher measures: Roberts to Milner 3 Sept. 1900, MP IV/A/175/fos 58–61.
22 Roberts to Hely-Hutchinson, 30 Aug., 9 Sept. 1900, RP 7101/23/111/7/1974, 1957; to Kitchener, 29 Aug. 1900, RP 7101/23/111/7/2198. Roberts calculated he would require 4 trains of 13 trucks each every day from Pretoria.
23 Chamberlain to Milner, 10 Sept. 1900, JC 13/1/68.

reduced costs and the ability to reassert British interests throughout the world more forcibly was enough for ministers.

In any case, Milner had little to complain about. On 13 September he had sent another imploring note to Roberts about the destitution of the refugees. This time he asked Roberts to be more forthcoming about setting a date when they could return.[24] Having returned to Pretoria early, with his army in sight of Komati Poort, Roberts clearly felt more confident about the turn of events. Consequently, he was able to inform Milner that supply trains for civilians would be sent once a week and, therefore, he could permit a select few to return. For the first time he gave Milner a date – 10 October – when the first Uitlanders could return to Johannesburg.[25]

By so doing, Roberts raised expectations, which were boosted by his announcement that with enough trains, some 3,000 refugees could be moved north every week. The only proviso was that veterans, men who had served in the Uitlander regiments, and particularly those who had been wounded or were sick ought to be given precedence.[26] Indeed, Roberts was extremely conscious of the need to placate the Uitlander volunteers, especially after the problems he had encountered earlier. He told General Buller and General Hildyard on 4 October that they were to discharge 10 per cent of their irregulars so they could reach Johannesburg before the refugees from the Cape and Natal.[27] As the war seemed over, the various volunteer corps were clamouring for their release. Although Roberts could save the British government money by discharging the volunteers – these were paid 5s. a day and were the most expensive men in the British army – he would create problems for himself. The loss of some of the finest mounted troops would create a shortage at a time when he needed all the forces he could muster. Roberts could not stop the return of the British units; the Dominion soldiers he could keep a little longer; but for those who lived in South Africa it was a different matter. He could insist that these remained on active service as the war had still not subsided. Roberts wanted Milner to assure Colonel Wools-Sampson, commander of the ILH, that his men would be given preferential treatment when applying for jobs in the newly forming police or elsewhere, principally to keep the regiment together.[28] In fact over the next three or four days, Roberts despatched a host of telegrams endeavouring to keep the Uitlander regiments in the field with a promise of preferential treatment.

Two telegrams to Milner on 10 October revealed Roberts's concern. First, he wanted only fit and loyally disposed men to return to Johannesburg, after having agreed to serve in a volunteer unit or the town guard. Second, he wanted Milner to intercede with Wools-Sampson for him, by utilising the

---

24 Milner to Roberts, 13 Sept. 1900, RP 7101/23/45/fo. 41.
25 Roberts to Milner, 22 Sept. 1900, WO 105/34/C4863.
26 Roberts to Milner, 28 Sept. 1900, WO 105/34/C5055.
27 Roberts to Buller and Hildyard, 4 Oct. 1900, RP 7101/23/111/9/2776, 2777.
28 Roberts to Milner, 9 Oct. 1900, RP 7101/23/111/9/2846.

services of Percy FitzPatrick, a leading representative of the Uitlanders, as a mediator.[29] Roberts was sensitive to the demands of the British government for the release of troops, but he had none to spare. He had to be honest and admit the Boers were causing trouble and that he needed all the troops he could muster.[30] Disbanding the volunteers would be a retrograde step and deprive his forces of good quality soldiers. Roberts was in such an awkward position that he was forced to make strenuous appeals to the Chamber of Mines, asking that the volunteers be given preferential treatment so as to prevent any trouble when the refugees arrived home.[31]

Although Roberts's relations with the volunteers had been improved his supply problems had not. On 9 October railway repair parties were attacked causing more disruption, and four days later Roberts was forced to tell the leading civil and military officials in South Africa – Milner, Hely-Hutchinson, Girouard, Forestier-Walker and Major-General Murray [the GOC, Lines of Communication in Natal] – that the departure of the refugees had been postponed.[32]

A want of system

For Milner the blow must have been tremendous; once more he was faced with a crisis which he could do little to alleviate without the co-operation of the army. The extent of his anger can be discerned by the fact that in a meeting with Roberts, he told the field-marshal that he should leave South Africa and let Kitchener take over. Although Milner told Roberts to go politely and did not offend him, it is clear he had ceased to believe that Roberts could finish the war.[33] Indeed, Milner began to cultivate Kitchener and attempted to bring him round to his way of thinking, particularly over the refugee crisis. Milner had travelled north, had discussed the situation with Roberts in Pretoria, and then spoken to Kitchener in Johannesburg. Afterwards, he explained to Kitchener that it was imperative, both for military and political reasons, that the refugees be allowed back. Militarily, if thousands did return they could provide a reservoir of potential volunteers for the army. Moreover they would be useful in catching spies and counteracting their activities. Politically, if disgruntled refugees remained in Cape Colony and became even more disenchanted, they might encourage rebellious Afrikaners to take advantage of the discontent. Milner was worried about the 6–7,000 Boer prisoners kept in the Western provinces amongst a sympathetic population. He also tried to assure Kitchener that the problem with the irregulars would

---

29 Roberts to Milner, 10 Oct. 1900, WO 105/34/C5434, and RP 7101/23/111/9/2854.
30 Roberts to Lansdowne, 11 Oct. 1900, RP 7101/23/110/4/970.
31 Roberts to Chamber of Mines, 11 Oct. 1900, RP 7101/23/111/9/2871.
32 Roberts to Milner and others, 13 Oct. 1900, CO 417/295/fo. 238.
33 Roberts to Lansdowne, 22 Oct. 1900, WO 105/33/fo. 296.

disappear once they were properly informed about the extent of the crisis and thought they would not cause trouble as a result. He explained, 'I have fenced with their growing impatience for [four] months, not altogether unsuccessfully; but I am getting to the end of my tether.' As a token of the army's commitment to the refugees, Milner wished for 6,000 tons of supplies to be sent to Johannesburg ready for their return; he felt it would dissipate their anger.[34]

Milner was clearly perturbed by the worsening situation, not only for the refugees but for himself also. Everything seemed to be going wrong: the refugees and irregulars were totally disenchanted, and the army were doing little to get the Rand operational again. Milner appealed once more to Chamberlain, appraising him of the discontent amongst the irregulars and the near 'mutinous' state of the refugees. The latter group were so incensed they had begun to fall prey to radical agitators who blamed the capitalists for the delay and the fact that Roberts was under 'capitalistic influences'. Milner was exasperated by what he felt was an unnecessary situation, caused by the wilful obstinacy of the irregulars to see that the return of the refugees was in their own interests, and that the high command had kept them in the field too long. Milner felt that Roberts should release the irregulars immediately in the hope of getting many to join the paramilitary police.[35] Milner's troubles were now getting out of hand; the army, in attempting to alleviate their own problems, were making his even worse.

For Roberts his problems stemmed from the fact that the irregulars, both South African and Dominion, were clamouring for their release. It seemed the Boers were aware of this and had stepped up their activities as a result. Roberts refused to grant any more discharges until fresh South African units had been raised: as he told Lansdowne, 'I mention all this in order that you may understand why troops cannot be sent home.'[36] Roberts, in fact, was running out of ideas: he could only offer Milner a scheme of public relief to get poor, surrendered Boers working, possibly on railway construction, and thus prevent them from going back on commando.[37] Kitchener, though, offered more immediate hope. Milner was informed that if refugees joined the new irregular regiments 'they would no doubt considerably accelerate their own return, and that of their fellow refugees'. Milner approved of this, and wanted it mentioned to the Uitlander committees.[38]

Milner was more in tune with Kitchener than he was with Roberts. Kitchener had apparently given a more substantial assurance that as long as the Uitlanders were prepared to help the army, the army would help them. At least it was more than Roberts's bland statements about relief work and a step

[34] Milner to Kitchener, 25 Oct. 1900, CO 417/295/fos 368–70.
[35] Milner to Chamberlain, 28 Oct. 1900, JC 13/1/78.
[36] Roberts to Lansdowne, 28 Oct. 1900, WO 105/33/fo. 299.
[37] Roberts to Milner, 31 Oct. 1900, RP 7101/23/111/9/3154.
[38] Walrond to Milner, 31 Oct. 1900, and Milner to Walrond, 1 Nov. 1900, CO 417/295/fos 372–3, 378.

in the right direction. This must have added to Milner's belief that Kitchener was the one to do business with and not Roberts. Milner had now clearly tired of Roberts; and although his opinion of the high command overall was not great, he must have felt that Kitchener would provide some impetus to the refugee problem and be more receptive to his ideas. He thus felt able to despatch a long letter to him on 31 October. Without mentioning Roberts by name, it is plain Milner was criticising him. 'It is quite evident', he wrote, 'that what is the matter now is not so much anything the Boers do as our own choppings & changings & want of system.' Milner, in the hope of gaining support, if not in the present then in the future, was, it seems, attempting to convert Kitchener to his way of thinking; or, at least point out the fallacies of Roberts's methods: 'if by concentrating our efforts we could absolutely subjugate certain definite areas and screen the people in them, in *their usual occupations*, from molestation from without, we should dishearten the enemy & encourage the waverers to come to us. Every step in that direction will make the next step easier'. It was this reasoning which prompted Milner to continue to demand the return of the refugees. In order to placate the irregulars, Milner wanted them to be released, because he believed that within a month of their return, alongside 20,000 refugees, the army would get enough recruits to form an Uitlander corps which could garrison the Rand and the outlying districts.[39] Milner had reiterated at greater length what he told Kitchener on 25 October. But in this last letter he had disclosed his intense frustration at the lack of progress in Johannesburg. The point here, and it must have galled Milner, was that he had to spell it out, in no uncertain terms, to the high command, and keep hammering the point home. However, Milner's preaching to Kitchener was not to the converted; if anything it was to the heretic.

Milner was continually looking ahead, trying to make preparations for a peaceful South Africa. The army, however, had more immediate problems, which they thought more important and better understood. This was the question of troop numbers and the amount they would lose if the irregular corps resigned *en masse* on the arrival of the first refugees. Percy FitzPatrick had arrived in Johannesburg to mediate between the irregulars and the army, following Roberts's suggestion of 10 October. His mission, therefore, was of vital importance, not only to engender good relations between the high command and the irregulars, but also to remove one prominent impediment blocking the return of the refugees. Moreover, FitzPatrick also carried the interests of the mine-owners who, no doubt, were eager to see a return to partial, if not full, production.

The problem in dealing with the irregulars was that the army regarded them as indispensable, and they knew this. The generals had made this plain because they had promised disbandment on numerous occasions, and then failed to deliver at the last moment. The final straw had come in October

---

[39] Milner to Kitchener, 31 Oct. 1900, Kitchener papers (KP), PRO 30/57/17/S7.

when the irregulars were marched to Pretoria for demobilisation and then told their services were still required. This caused a storm of protest, obliging the army to discharge some to quieten the rest. However, the irregulars were then informed that preferential treatment would only be given to those men still in the field when the war was over. FitzPatrick's visit to see both Roberts and Kitchener had succeeded. Roberts willingly accepted FitzPatrick's idea of creating a reserve of discharged irregulars, to be recalled if and when necessary. Kitchener, reluctant at first, eventually agreed to FitzPatrick's suggestion that discharged volunteers be given a free travel warrant to see Johannesburg's desperate situation; once seen, FitzPatrick argued, they would return to their units and say no more about going home before anyone else, and persuade the others to cease their agitation.[40]

Although this accommodation with the irregulars had removed a major obstacle to the return of the refugees, other problems surfaced which confounded a solution to the problem. On 5 November 1900 Roberts told Milner that the reason which prevented the refugees moving north was the precarious food situation. Roberts explained that owing to the continual attacks on the railway, the food requirements of the army were not being met and that they were drawing on scarce reserves. He added that once enough food had been brought in, and a substantial reserve stock accumulated, he would consider allowing the refugees to return home.[41] Roberts was not making excuses. Girouard confirmed how bad the situation was and how difficult it was to supply the army let alone an increased civilian population.[42] In fact, Roberts's problems were monumental, and by mid November, his telegrams began to take on an air of desperation. On 16 November he told Forestier-Walker that supplies and remounts only should be given precedence on the railways.[43] That same day, owing to a lack of supplies coming from Natal, only thirty trucks in the last three days, representations were made to Hely-Hutchinson to increase the flow.[44] Roberts summarised the position for Milner's benefit: 'I am most anxious to get them all back as I believe the political effect would be excellent. I would be very glad also to see you take office at Pretoria, but at present we barely get sufficient supplies for the daily use of the troops, and to increase the number of people to feed would be a danger instead of a strength.'[45] So great were the problems, that Roberts refused, at first, to allow sixty-six managers and engineers to return after they had been

[40] FitzPatrick to Beit, 7 Nov. 1900, in *FitzPatrick: South African politician: selected papers 1886–1906*, ed. A. H. Duminy and W. R. Guest, Johannesburg 1976, 281–9. For correspondence appraising Milner of FitzPatrick's mission see CO 417/295/fos 380–1, 391–2, 502–3.
[41] Roberts to Milner, 5 Nov. 1900, WO 105/34/C6049.
[42] Milner's diary of events, 15 Nov. 1900, CO 417/295/fos 690–1.
[43] Roberts to Forestier-Walker, 16 Nov 1900, RP 7101/23/111/10/3386; A. H. Page, 'The supply services of the British army in the South African war 1899–1902', unpubl. DPhil diss. Oxford 1976, 84–119.
[44] Roberts to Hely-Hutchinson, 16 Nov. 1900, RP 7101/23/111/10/3385.
[45] Roberts to Milner, 16 Nov 1900, WO 105/34/C6367.

given permits by Milner. Roberts thought this would raise the hopes of the refugees unduly; he also felt that there was no room on trains given over to the task of bringing in supplies. Milner disagreed and practically demanded these representatives be allowed to return. It would, in his opinion, give the mining companies equal representation on the Rand, as each would have employees guarding their property. More important, it would demonstrate to those left behind that something was being done to facilitate their return, even though, as Milner pointed out, the Uitlanders had realised their move north had been postponed indefinitely.[46] More likely, it was Milner who now accepted that the move had been postponed. As far as the army was concerned the problem of the refugees had been shelved. Consequently, Milner lost what little faith he still had in Roberts's ability and was by now totally disillusioned by his failure to get to grips with the guerilla war, and the pacification of the country; as he told Chamberlain 'We are making but little progress, though I believe military policy is gradually settling down on sounder lines. Personally, I think this process will be facilitated by Lord Roberts's return home.'[47]

Arresting the Boers

By mid September 1900 Roberts's main priority was to leave South Africa. He first asked to be relieved on 17 September and had left the occupation of Komati Poort to his subordinates.[48] On receiving this request, the Cabinet quickly nominated Roberts to succeed Wolseley on his retirement, and were thus able to settle two pressing problems: to remove Roberts from South Africa, and to ensure Wolseley was replaced.[49] Roberts arrived back in Pretoria on 21 September to await Lansdowne's reply, which came eight days later, acceding to Roberts's request and confirming him as Wolseley's successor. Roberts was convinced that operations were now of a 'police nature' and as far as he was concerned his task was over. Despite the fact that he and Milner agreed that only police operations were necessary, even this failed to settle the differences between the two officials.

If only police operations were required, it was essential that a para-military police force be established. This type of organisation was prevalent throughout the empire and played a vital role in maintaining peace and order. More often than not it was the colonial policeman who 'stood at the cutting edge of

46 Roberts to Milner, 20 Nov. 1900, WO 105/34/C6496; Milner to Kitchener, 17 Nov. 1900, CO 417/295/fo. 747; to Roberts, 21 Nov. 1900, CO 417/295/fos 750–1.
47 Milner to Chamberlain, 14 Nov. 1900, JC 13/1/91.
48 On 2 June Roberts told Milner that he wanted to see a civilian governor installed in the Transvaal, 'and that I may be allowed to leave South Africa as soon as necessity no longer exists for actual military operations': Roberts to Milner, 2 June 1900, MP IV/A/175/fos 36–41.
49 James, *Lord Roberts*, 342–3.

colonial rule'.[50] The foremost colonial police force was the Royal Irish Constabulary, which seems to have been the precedent upon which virtually all other forces were based, although recent work suggests that no colonial force was modelled exactly on the same lines as that in Ireland.[51] For Roberts, the likely paradigm appears to have been that provided by the operations in Burma between 1886 and 1890. There, the army happily gave way to a military police force which eventually pacified the disturbed areas, occasionally using methods that Roberts later utilised in South Africa, such as deportation of civilians and the burning of villages. The official in charge of the 'pacification' called it the 'vigorous administration of civil government' and used the army only when he felt the police were unable to cope on their own.[52] As far as Roberts was concerned this sort of action was now required against the Boers.

A South African police force was considered as early as July. The guerilla tactics of the Boers appeared to be more banditry than regular military operations at the time, and less of a threat. Eventually, as the Boers increased the scope of their activities, and the measure of their success, Milner considered the need to establish a police force more urgent. He asked Roberts for Baden-Powell's services to create and command such a force. Milner proposed to recruit a special mounted force from 'good men' in the yeomanry and irregular corps. He needed about 5,000 men and wanted them ready as soon as possible, in order that they could take over settled districts and let the army do its own work. Roberts agreed to these proposals, but mentioned that 10,000 men be recruited instead.[53]

Having gained Roberts's acceptance of the idea, Milner informed Chamberlain on 12 September. Chamberlain's initial response was to express concern about Treasury attitudes, especially as the Transvaal was supposed to bear its own financial burdens.[54] Roberts told Lansdowne that he was arranging with Milner for a police force to be established. Although Roberts did not make the point explicitly, Lansdowne must have gathered that the formation of a police force would facilitate the reduction of the army – and costs – in South Africa.[55] The cost of a police force concerned the War Office greatly.

[50] David M. Anderson and David Killingray, 'Consent, coercion and colonial control: policing the empire, 1830–1940', in their Policing the empire: government, authority and control, 1830–1940, Manchester 1991, 1–15 at p. 2.

[51] Richard Hawkins, 'The "Irish model" and the empire: a case for reassessment', in ibid. ch. ii. For relations between the army and the RIC see Elizabeth Muenger, The British military dilemma in Ireland: occupation politics, 1886–1914, Kansas 1991, ch. iv.

[52] Sir Charles Crosthwaite, The pacification of Burma, London 1912, 15, 72–3, 105–6. See also Dorothy Woodman, The making of Burma, London 1962, 338; George Bruce, The Burma wars 1824–1886, London 1973, 160–1; Maung Htin Aung, A history of Burma, New York 1967, 267.

[53] Milner to Roberts and Roberts to Milner, 10, 11 Sept. 1900, CO 417/294/fos 605–7.

[54] Milner to Chamberlain, 12 Sept. 1900, and CO Minutes, 14 Sept. 1900, CO 417/293/fos 893–4.

[55] Roberts to Lansdowne, 16 Sept. 1900, RP 7101/23/110/4/865.

Fleetwood-Wilson, the under-secretary of state, wrote to his counterpart in the Colonial Office, Frederick Graham, on 19 September, that it was presumed the cost of the police would not come from the Army Estimates. The Colonial Office felt, however, that the War Office had no choice but to pay while the two new colonies were under military administration, and eventually told Milner to proceed on this understanding.[56] As both departments seemed to accept the situation it is most likely they did not believe military administration would last for very long.

On 24 September Milner told Chamberlain of Baden-Powell's scheme and eagerly endorsed its main points: first, that it would enable large numbers of troops to be sent home; and second, that it would enable British settlers to remain in the country and be compatible with any scheme of state assistance for settlement on the land. Evidently Baden-Powell wanted 6,000 men and 200 officers, who would be paid 5s. a day. That same day Milner told Chamberlain that he, as high commissioner, should command the police otherwise he would be unable to control costs, its organisation and personnel. As for the army, 'I shall have no difficulty whatsoever about it with the military provided that they understand my position.'[57] Milner obviously feared the army would take and use the police to chase commandos, something he was determined to prevent.

However, Milner did have problems with the military. Roberts informed him that 10,000 men should be recruited as it would be easier to reduce a force than increase it if necessary. With only 6,000 men, the police would have to rely on imperial help and this might be withdrawn if Britain became involved in a war elsewhere. Moreover, Roberts wanted the police to have an extra 2s. because the cost of living in South Africa was expensive.[58] Obviously, Milner had ignored Roberts's earlier recommendation about the size of the police force, perhaps regarding it as a suggestion rather than a point of principle. Milner immediately informed Chamberlain and included his own reply to the field-marshal, which pointed out the difficult financial position of the new colonies. As it was, Milner expected a large garrison would be left for some time in South Africa, thus negating the need to raise extra police officers. In any case he emphasised that the new colonies could not afford a large police force, and he did not want to alienate the loyalist population immediately. Cost was a factor which Milner seemed keen to stress, perhaps because ministers were susceptible to this sort of reasoning: an extra 2s. a day would cost more than £200,000 a year, and if paid out initially could not be withdrawn easily if it was found necessary to do so.[59] Milner was clearly anxious: he was trying to obtain the return of the refugees, and also attempting to

56 Fleetwood-Wilson to Graham, 19 Sept. 1900; CO Minutes, 21–3 Sept. 1900; Chamberlain to Milner, 25 Sept. 1900, CO 417/307/fos 103–6.
57 Milner to Chamberlain, 24 Sept. 1900, CO 417/294/fos 210, 221.
58 Roberts to Milner, 5 Oct. 1900, WO 105/34/C5299.
59 Milner to Chamberlain, 6 Oct. 1900, CO 417/294/fos 495–7.

obviate the need for extra police and thus lessen the costs of his new colony. But, perhaps more than anything, he was trying to ensure that his police did not become a mere adjunct of the army. If they were used to chase Boers, they could not begin the process of reconstruction. If Roberts's suggestion was accepted then the need for the refugees to return might not be so pressing.

This disagreement between Milner and Roberts prompted much discussion amongst Colonial Office officials. Most, in fact, favoured the larger number but were aware how much this would cost; consequently, Chamberlain told the War Office that as Milner regarded a force of 6,000 men as the basic establishment, and Roberts felt an extra 4,000 men were necessary 'to cope with the existing state of affairs' then the additional number ought to be met by the Army Vote for the garrison in South Africa.[60] Apart from this intervention, the Colonial Office remained quiet during the ensuing row between Roberts and Milner, and the War Office was left to act as mediator. This was due, it seems, to the fact that on 22 October Chamberlain had stipulated in the proclamation of inauguration that the South African Constabulary (SAC) might occasionally 'discharge military duties'.[61] From then on the SAC were virtually regarded as part of the army which therefore reduced the Colonial Office's influence over its affairs.

Roberts's desire to see the police force begin operations at maximum capacity can be attributed to two factors. First, to reinforce the impression that the war was indeed over and police work would be sufficient to finish off the commandos; second, to relieve the pressure being exerted from London for the return of troops and a reduction in costs. The latter point was perhaps the most pressing at the time. Parliament had been dissolved on 25 September for a general election and at the time the campaign was at its height, but the government had not gone into it with much confidence. Lord Salisbury, in particular, showed little faith in the electorate especially as no government had been returned for nearly fifty years, and his pessimism affected other ministers.[62] Within the Cabinet there were already signs of strain owing to the situation in South Africa. The apparent ending of the war had naturally raised expectations, especially those of Hicks Beach. He expected to see troop numbers being reduced, but nothing appeared to have been done, and he warned Salisbury that Britain's financial position 'is becoming very grave'. Hicks Beach had even analysed the military situation and felt that a large garrison was maintained in Cape Colony unnecessarily; he also felt that troops on the lines of communication were not required, 'now that there is no army in the field against us . . . For all I know, there may be a similar useless force in Natal.' Hicks Beach considered that money was being wasted for no apparent reason.[63] Understandably, the Cabinet would have liked to have seen costs

---

60 CO Minutes, 9–16 Oct. 1900, and CO to WO, c. 16 Oct. 1900, CO 417/294/fos 490–3.
61 T. Jeal, *Baden-Powell*, London 1989, 332.
62 Marsh, *Discipline of popular government*, 302–3.
63 Hicks Beach to Salisbury, 1 Oct. 1900, Salisbury correspondence, fos 222–3.

being reduced, in order to offer something concrete to the voters. As a result, Lansdowne again asked Roberts for his views about the future garrison of South Africa, to which Roberts replied once more that until the police force was operational it was impossible for troops to leave South Africa. As a riposte to Hicks Beach, Roberts also explained that the garrison in Cape Colony numbered 20,000 men and both he and Milner wanted that part of South Africa well garrisoned. No explanation was offered but the deterrence of rebels and the guarding of prisoners were clearly of prime concern. In an attempt to mollify the Cabinet, Lansdowne presented this correspondence on 15 October, to show that both he and Roberts were aware of the situation.[64]

In order to defend himself, Roberts explained to Lansdowne that Milner's plans regarding the police were inadequate. He believed strongly that only police work was required and wanted the imperial authorities to provide a grant in aid to the new colonies if they could not afford the extra men. Lansdowne agreed to this and informed the Colonial Office accordingly.[65]

While these ideas were being considered, Milner, for some reason, believed Roberts had agreed to see the numbers of the SAC limited to 6,000 men. Why he should think this is not clear. It may have been due to a lack of communication on the issue between the two men. Indeed, most of October was taken up by correspondence on the refugees, so Milner may have reached the erroneous conclusion that Roberts had not decided to pursue the matter further. He was concerned anyway that the SAC would never be able to recruit more than 6,000 men owing to present circumstances. He did not elaborate, but probably meant that owing to the guerilla war, and the fact the irregulars were not being disbanded, there would barely be enough recruits.[66]

Later, Milner expressed his views on the police more forcibly. By the end of October his hopes had been dashed. No progress had been made on any major problem, and he felt, mistakenly, that only on numbers had any headway been made. Milner explained that the British would look foolish if they recruited too many men; they would look doubly foolish if they paid them too much money. He was convinced that 5s. a day would be enough to recruit 6,000 men and more if necessary. Furthermore, if the new colonies had to pay for the extra men, on top of what they were paying already, then this meant they would contribute less in reparations. For Milner a strong police force was ideal for the strategy he advocated. Here he launched another attack on the 'scouring policy' still being pursued by Roberts. By using the SAC to patrol

---

[64] This included Lansdowne to Roberts, 9 Oct. 1900, and Roberts to Lansdowne, 10 Oct 1900, CAB 37/53/70. Hicks Beach was so concerned about the rate of expenditure that he felt he ought to consider his own future in the government: Hicks Beach to Salisbury, 15 Oct. 1900, Salisbury correspondence, fo. 226.

[65] Roberts to Lansdowne, 10 Oct. 1900, WO 105/32/1322; WO to CO, 25 Oct. 1900, CO 417/307/fo. 244.

[66] Milner to Chamberlain, 22 Oct. 1900, CO 417/295/fo. 26.

between strong-points, Milner felt it would be possible 'to substitute within that area the policy of protection for that of reprisal'. Similarly, this meant an end to the wholesale destruction of farms and a return to farm-burning as a definite punishment. Indiscriminate destruction now appalled Milner as wasteful and designed to increase the numbers of those in arms against the British.[67] This was a plain indictment of Roberts's system – or lack of it. Milner had now launched an attack on the field-marshal and was attempting to enlist the aid of the British government to press home his offensive.

Roberts departs

On 7 November the Colonial Office informed the War Office that Milner believed Roberts had agreed to keep SAC numbers at 6,000 for a certain period.[68] This news must have surprised Brodrick, the new secretary of state for war, who had replaced Lansdowne following the general election in October. He had been bullying the Cabinet and particularly Hicks Beach into acquiescing to Roberts's demands, and had appealed to Salisbury for his unreserved backing. Brodrick was concerned about the severe measures Roberts was using in the new colonies. He preferred to see farm-burning as an exemplary punishment and may have been less than impressed by Roberts's assertion that when railway or telegraph lines had been destroyed, 'the district within a ten mile radius is cleared of supplies'.[69]

Brodrick's concern about the tactics being employed in the new colonies was not engendered solely by the situation in South Africa. He was more interested in pursuing his schemes to reform the War Office and the army in the Cabinet. This was the main reason why he had enlisted Salisbury's help. Brodrick, therefore, wanted to see some progress made in South Africa, and from Milner's reports he concluded nothing substantial was being done.

In his first major communication with Brodrick, Milner attacked both Roberts and Kitchener. It seemed Kitchener's unresponsive attitude to Milner's suggestions of 31 October had convinced him that he was not to be trusted. Milner explained to Brodrick that Roberts had done all he could and was tired out, whereas Kitchener was stale. Accordingly, the time had come, as he had said often in the past, for the subjugation of the country: 'The fatal error is not to hold District A & make sure of it before you go on to District B. I mean the fatal error *latterly*, not at first, when you *had* to rush. The consequence is we have a big army campaigning away in the front & the enemy

---

[67] Milner to Chamberlain, 28 Oct. 1900, JC 13/1/78.
[68] CO to WO, 7 Nov. 1900; CO Minutes, 26 Nov. 1900, CO 417/307/fos 247–8, 417–18.
[69] Brodrick to Roberts, 7 Nov. 1900, WO 105/30/fo. 182, and Roberts to Brodrick, 8 Nov. 1900, WO 105/32/1480; Brodrick to Salisbury, 28 Oct. 1900, Salisbury correspondence, fos 140–3.

swarming in the country behind it.'[70] For Milner this might have been his last chance to influence the future conduct of the war, hence his direct attack on the generals. Perhaps for the first time Milner actually found the Cabinet receptive to his ideas. Indeed, the Cabinet had become apprehensive about the methods employed by Roberts. Salisbury told the queen that the Law Officers doubted whether his tactic of destroying farms within a ten-mile radius of a Boer attack on railway or telegraph lines was within the laws of war. Chamberlain preferred to see individuals punished not property as this was arbitrary and affected the innocent. Consequently, Brodrick was obliged to ask Roberts to explain his methods and suggested that it might be possible to proclaim districts which had been effectively occupied by the British.[71]

The effect of Milner's attack had seemingly instilled in Brodrick a determination to get Roberts out of South Africa and into his new job in Britain, and to get the largest number of SAC in the field. Thus once Brodrick heard from the Colonial Office that Roberts had agreed to the lower figure, he became greatly concerned. The guerilla war would be prolonged, invite civil–military disputes, and upset the accord he had reached with Hicks Beach. On contacting Roberts on 9 November, Brodrick found that he agreed to no such thing.[72] Roberts's motives for adhering to his viewpoint are not hard to fathom. He was acutely aware of the need to reduce troop numbers and, therefore, expenditure. More police, who were also considered better against the Boers, meant the release of more troops. Moreover, once the police were operational, and on a grand scale, Roberts could state the war – the conventional war – was over. He could then leave South Africa sooner rather than later.

In Cabinet, Brodrick and Hicks Beach had agreed that if 10,000 SAC were recruited they could relieve 25,000 infantry. The Cabinet agreed, therefore, to pay for the extra 4,000 men if the new colonies could not cope with the added costs. The savings anticipated by this measure would be more than enough to settle payment for the extra men. Roberts was asked if this was a reasonable assumption and promptly replied it was. He also told Milner of this, saying he had agreed to it because 'The [settlement] of the Transvaal and the ORC depends much more on police than military arrangements. This was my experience in Burmah & I hope you will agree with me.'[73] Also, in answer to Brodrick's enquiries of 23 November, Roberts told him that officers had taken advantage of the latitude given them in order to combat the commandos. But it was up to them to make full enquiries before ordering the

70 Milner to Brodrick, 5 Nov. 1900, SJB PRO 30/67/6.
71 Salisbury to the queen, 23 Nov. 1900, CAB 41/25/50; Brodrick to Roberts, 23 Nov. 1900, CAB 37/55/234; Chamberlain to Milner, 25 Nov. 1900, JC 13/1/92A.
72 Brodrick to Roberts, 9 Nov. 1900, CO 417/307/fo. 421; Roberts to Brodrick, 13 Nov. 1900, WO 105/32/1517.
73 Brodrick to Roberts, 23 Nov. 1900, CAB 37/55/234(4); Roberts to Brodrick, 24, 26 Nov. 1900, WO 105/32/1600, 1609; Roberts to Milner, 24 Nov. 1900, CO 417/296/fo. 89.

destruction of property. He added, 'but as it is essentially police work I anticipate that when our police force is established we shall find the necessity of
burning houses less and less'.[74] Roberts was obviously saying the army could
not be blamed because it was undertaking a task it was not trained to do.
Therefore, it was up to the politicians to hurry the creation of the SAC,
release the army from its onerous work, and thus lessen the damage done to
property. It was nothing to do with Roberts and he could do nothing more.

Milner did not have much choice in the matter once the government had
convinced themselves of the benefits of having a large SAC. As the government was willing to pick up the bill, Milner could not argue, but felt the extra
police might not be found, especially as Kitchener was finding it difficult to
release irregulars owing to the paucity of troops.[75] Milner's main worry, of
course, was that as the government had accepted Roberts's advice, they had
in fact endorsed the use of the police in a military capacity, as replacements
for troops. The only victory gained by Milner was that Roberts could now
leave South Africa. The future, however, remained uncertain: Kitchener was
still an unknown quantity and the war seemed far from over.

For his part, Roberts had been able to relieve the pressure on himself and
Kitchener for troop reductions because of the government's desire to see a
large police force, and because of his protestations that the guerilla war was
police work. The politicians now hoped that troop reductions would become
a reality once the police force was fully operational; after all, Roberts had
assured them 10,000 policemen were worth 25,000 infantry. Hopes and
expectations had been raised once more. The SAC united most politicians in
the belief that it was the panacea for ending the war.[76]

In the end Milner was glad to see Roberts go, as were many others, soldiers
included.[77] The guerilla war had defeated Roberts's talents and his experience
in Burma did not help in South African conditions. But the fact that his campaigns had changed the face of the war was well remembered. He returned to
Britain the greatest hero since Wellington and no politician could stand up
to that sort of reputation. In South Africa, nothing had changed except personnel. Milner still had to deal with a leading military figure. The only hope
was that the guerilla war might be finished quickly.

[74] Roberts to Brodrick, 26 Nov. 1900, WO 105/32/1614.
[75] Milner to Roberts, 26 Nov. 1900, CO 417/296/fo. 90.
[76] For more on the SAC after the war see Albert Grundlingh, ' "Protectors and friends of
the people"? the South African Constabulary in the Transvaal and Orange River Colony,
1900–08', in Anderson and Killingray, Policing the empire, ch. x.
[77] Many thought Roberts was worn out, or not severe enough; some thought Kitchener
would be severe: Brian Gardner, Allenby, London 1965, 42; G. J. De Groot, Douglas Haig
1861–1928, London 1988, 84–6.

6

Battling for Supremacy:
December 1900 – July 1901

In October 1900, Captain R. J. Marker told his sister that while Roberts was in command the war would not end, 'but I think Kitchener should succeed him & be given a free hand [then] it will be over in a very short time'.[1] Thus when Kitchener succeeded Roberts on 29 November 1900, expectations were raised that a significant change in the direction of the war would occur. Whereas Roberts's conduct had been perceived as too 'gentlemanly', Kitchener was expected to end the war with the same ruthless efficiency which had characterised his conquest of the Sudan. However, as both he and Milner held differing views regarding the prosecution of the war, this triggered a long-running dispute which further shifted the balance of civil–military relations in Britain and South Africa.

Kitchener wanted an all-out effort to defeat the Boers, to ensure his army received all necessary resources and to give civil reconstruction a low priority. Milner wanted to marginalise the war, to downgrade the military effort and give precedence to the reformation of the Transvaal. Underlying these differences was something more fundamental: the character of the future South Africa. An integral part of both Kitchener's and Milner's strategies was the treatment of the Boer leaders. For Kitchener, the future peace of South Africa could only be assured by a military victory, followed by negotiations, after which he expected the Boer leaders to settle down as citizens of the empire. Otherwise, he felt there would always be a discontented, rebellious element within Boer society. Milner wanted to undermine their authority and exclude them from political matters. He hoped to form a new leadership comprised of those willing to settle under British rule. Furthermore, in dealing with Kitchener, Milner was no longer willing to suffer military intransigence without a fight. Thus, the dispute between the two officials, to which both the British government and Lord Roberts were party, highlighted the dilemma facing the British authorities as a whole. From it two persistent major questions arose: what was the nature of the war in the region? And how was it to be fought? Eventually, in attempting to answer these questions, the British authorities, both civil and military, were forced to consider who should exercise supreme control in South Africa: Milner or Kitchener.

The British government became extremely anxious about the continuing

---

[1] Marker to his sister, 5 Oct. 1900, National Army Museum, Marker papers, 6803–4/4/7.

war. Spiralling costs and the need to consider domestic and foreign issues found ministers unable to decide on a policy in South Africa. They feared antagonising public opinion if they spent more money on the war, or did not provide enough. Should they crush the Boers or should they negotiate? And, most important, how far should the government allow Kitchener to exercise military authority without consideration of costs and imperial policy? More-over, disputes between ministers threatened Cabinet cohesion. The two new service ministers, Brodrick and Selborne, who was now first lord of the Admi-ralty, were both keen to increase expenditure, whilst the Chancellor was determined to cut back.[2] Thus, with army reform and naval expansion both on the political agenda, combined with the near impossibility of Kitchener's task, the British government was faced with a major political headache.

The military problem

In December 1900 the Boers opened a new phase in the war. Following the occupation of Komati Poort, the Boer leadership had met at Pietersburg in northern Transvaal to decide future strategy. There they resolved to continue the guerilla war and, significantly, to invade Cape Colony, which they did on 16 December and where they believed substantial support awaited. The pur-suit of this strategy ensured the war continued unabated, deflating British expectations in the process and forcing both the politicians and generals to search for new ways to end the war.

Already, on 24 November, Brodrick had told Kitchener that the govern-ment harboured serious doubts about the conduct of operations. The army in South Africa numbered 230,000 men, and Brodrick believed they faced only 8,000 Boers. He wondered whether British strength was being wasted trying to pacify the whole country and protect the cleared areas.[3] His remark, 'It has been suggested to us', revealed that he was forwarding Milner's views which he had received earlier, perhaps testing Kitchener's reactions to them. Even so, the difficulties before the British government were real enough, and this despatch was clearly intended to hurry Kitchener's preparations, and to implement his plans. Brodrick stated that the war had already cost £80m., at £2½m. a month; a further £15m. was required to prosecute the war until March. Troops were stale, there were hardly any regulars left in Britain; and the volunteers and militia had been embodied far too long. It was a bleak pic-ture, but Brodrick hoped Kitchener had something planned; he also hoped that Kitchener and Milner would work together amicably, and begin starting work on the Rand.

Milner's views had had some effect on ministerial attitudes. From Brodrick's despatch it seems that ministers, having removed Roberts, were

---

2 Yakutiel, 'Treasury control', 138.
3 Brodrick to Kitchener, 24 Nov. 1900, KP PRO 30/57/22/Y4.

now determined to maintain some control over events in South Africa. Not long afterwards, in early December, Brodrick questioned Kitchener on the extent of farm-burning and hoped such a punishment was inflicted only in extreme cases. Kitchener confirmed this was so and that he had issued orders to that effect.[4] Thus, from the outset, the government had practically accepted Milner's ideas, which provided guidelines for Kitchener to operate in. Brodrick's despatches, however, were instructions and suggestions, not orders: it was too early to question Kitchener's leadership. Moreover, while accepting that the military conduct of the war had not been a total success, ministers were conscious of the lessons learnt as a result of political interference earlier in the war.

Kitchener appeared co-operative. He had issued instructions making farm-burning a last resort, and, as yet, had not formed any clear conviction about dealing with the commandos. That his job was going to prove difficult was confirmed by events a few days later. On 13 December General Clements's force was defeated at Nooitgedacht. It showed that talk of reducing troops was too premature. Through the medium of Lord Roberts, Kitchener wrote back saying he wanted fresh troops; his forces were overstretched holding what they had and defending the railway lines at the same time.[5] The vitality and vigour of the Boer forces increased fears in London and South Africa, and Kitchener was able to use this as a reason for obtaining more troops. It was not to be the only time a Boer victory would scupper ministerial attempts to get Kitchener to reduce his forces. Consequently, Brodrick promised to do everything in his power to provide the manpower Kitchener required, although he did question the nature of Kitchener's dispositions, and wondered whether these might be contracted to spare troops. 'We cannot help it if the Boers overrun some places which we cannot defend, but the outlook will be serious if these attacks continue to be successful.'[6]

The invasion of Cape Colony, coupled with Clements's defeat, shattered any lingering complacency amongst soldiers and politicians alike. Kitchener realised that the invasion would overstrain his already stretched manpower resources. In replying to Brodrick's note of 24 November, he used the opportunity to express his opinions. First, he objected to the withdrawal of troops from areas already occupied as this would give the Boers the opportunity to 'put up their flag and start a sort of government again'. Second, he estimated Boer numbers at 20,000, a figure greater than that supposed by the government. (It is probable Brodrick used Milner's figures.) Thirdly, as a measure against the Boer supply lines, Kitchener said he intended to take the women

---

[4] Brodrick to Kitchener, 4, 6 Dec. 1900 and Kitchener to Brodrick, 5 Dec. 1900, CO 417/307/fos 581–2.
[5] Kitchener to Roberts, 14 Dec. 1900, RP 7101/23/33/fo. 6.
[6] Brodrick to Kitchener, 15 Dec. 1900, KP PRO 30/57/22/Y8.

off the farms and laager them near the railway, thus encouraging burghers to join them there in relative safety.[7]

For the British government, the situation was alarming but not serious, although differences of opinion began to surface as ministers reviewed the crisis. Salisbury promised Brodrick that Kitchener would have the men he wanted, even if the Treasury resisted. His solution, however, was draconian, although it presaged the nature of the war to come; he told Brodrick, 'You will not conquer these people until you have starved them out.' Hicks Beach said the worst aspect of the situation was the lethargic response of the Cape government, especially as the invaders were so few in number. Chamberlain felt the invasion to be serious, and deemed it necessary for more mounted troops to be sent to South Africa. As he told Brodrick: 'If you want money or men from the Cabinet you ought to have both at once. A shilling saved now means pounds lost hereafter.' However, Chamberlain wanted to make sure that the need to restart the mines should not be lost in the general uproar over the Cape. Brodrick told Roberts that Kitchener's request for extra troops and the obvious need for them meant trouble with Hicks Beach, who was still calling for reductions.[8] Thus, ministers began to take sides, although the motives for doing so were disparate. For instance, Chamberlain's chief reason for backing Kitchener was to ensure the mining industry was restarted, as a sort of *quid pro quo*. Brodrick was a friend and admirer of Kitchener, and regarded him as a future asset in his plans to reform the army.[9] Brodrick was therefore determined to support him as part of his struggle against Treasury intransigence. Hicks Beach simply did not want to sanction an increase in men and resources when, to him, the nature of the war did not appear serious enough. Even so, Brodrick and the Cabinet were not averse to Kitchener's scheme to send delegates from the Burgher Peace Committee to commandos in the field, in an attempt to induce them to surrender.[10] Furthermore, Brodrick reminded Kitchener that the Cabinet wanted to see the Rand restarted, although, he added, after Kitchener had 'dealt with the present raid', an indication perhaps of the Cabinet's anxiety regarding the progress of the invasion.[11]

By the end of 1900 the extent of the Boer offensive and the stamina of their forces were becoming apparent. Everywhere the Boers were on the attack and gaining victories. On 26 December they had attacked the gold-fields at the South Rand mine. On 4 January 1901 Kitchener's Bodyguard was defeated at Kronspruit. Six days later, as an example of Boer resolution,

---

7 Kitchener to Brodrick, 20 Dec. 1900, KP PRO 30/57/22/Y9.
8 Salisbury to Brodrick, 19 Dec. 1900, SJB PRO 30/67/6; Hicks Beach to Chamberlain, 23 Dec. 1900, JC 11/18/1; Chamberlain to Brodrick, 21 Dec. 1900, JC 11/8/5; Brodrick to Roberts, 20 Dec. 1900, RP 7101/23/13/fo. 12.
9 Royle, *Kitchener enigma*, 149–50.
10 Kitchener to Brodrick 27 Dec. 1900, and Brodrick to Kitchener, 28 Dec. 1900, CO 291/32/fo. 373.
11 Brodrick to Kitchener, 28 Dec. 1900, KP PRO 30/57/22/Y10.

Morgendaal, a delegate from the Burgher Peace Committee, was murdered in De Wet's laager. In Cape Colony, the commandos had re-ignited the rebellion, forcing the British authorities, by 17 January, to declare almost the whole colony under martial law.

After an anxious period, both Milner and Kitchener highlighted the unsatisfactory situation to their superiors in London, but stressed it was not disastrous. Milner felt the Cape government was taking the invasion seriously and beginning to show some energy in formulating counter-measures. He also believed that stale troops needed replacing. Kitchener felt the invaders had not inflicted great damage and that the situation was under control. Kitchener, like Milner, hoped the peace committee would succeed, but added an opinion which was significant for future developments: 'my view is that if we could only hit hard, and at the same time leave the door open we might get the Boers to give up but I am not sanguine of success'.[12]

Yet for the British government, the continuing disturbances in Cape Colony and elsewhere undermined any reassurance offered by Milner or Kitchener. Brodrick was extremely anxious. On 10 January he told Salisbury that he expected a further demand for troops from Kitchener. Although some 2,000 fresh troops were being sent out the need for more drafts was urgent, and he explained to Chamberlain about the difficulties his department faced; he would have to use the SAC as reinforcements, and implied the SAC would have to be placed under military command. Otherwise, if he gave the go-ahead for various agents to recruit for the yeomanry it would 'give the final *coup de grace* to your Police'. And, so that the gravity of the situation was not lost on Chamberlain, he added 'The business presses and we have no more cavalry to send – only 3 Line Regts left in England & no mounted infantry.'[13]

A further problem for Brodrick was the attitude of Hicks Beach, who could not understand why fresh troops were required when too many of those in South Africa were spread out doing nothing. The uneasy alliance secured with Hicks Beach in November, regarding the SAC and troop withdrawals, was breaking apart.[14]

Moreover, Milner's uneasy relationship with Kitchener was under severe strain. Milner's latent contempt for the ability of British generals was reawakened following the success of the Boer offensive. Although he realised Kitchener was not receptive to his way of thinking, he was, for the moment, prepared to give him the benefit of the doubt. He knew nothing of Kitchener's plans, but said he was prepared to wait; and despite nothing being done to restart the mines, Milner hoped Kitchener's scheme to recruit a Rand

---

12 Milner to Chamberlain, 3 Jan. 1901, JC 13/1/108; Kitchener to Roberts, 4 Jan. 1901, RP 7101/23/33/fo. 9.
13 Brodrick to Salisbury, 10 Jan. 1901, Salisbury papers, fos 164–5; to Chamberlain, c. 10 and 10 Jan. 1901, JC 11/8/6, 9.
14 Hicks Beach to Brodrick, 16 Jan. 1901, SJB PRO 30/67/7.

defence corps might presage something more substantial.[15] Unhappily for Milner his patience was eroded throughout January and February, as news from elsewhere seemed to confirm the inadequacy of military administration. General Pretyman continued to be a valuable source of information, and apparently justified Milner's suspicions that Kitchener's plans either lacked substance, or were ineffectual. Pretyman explained about the evacuation of important towns in the ORC, such as Jagersfontein and Smithfield. Evidently, Kitchener wanted garrisons removed to provide troops for field operations, which meant 'that our attempt to build up a fabric of civil government in the districts has come to a stand still, very little can now be done far from the line of railway'.[16] Furthermore, the loyalists residing in these towns had been evacuated alongside the troops and were now resident in refugee camps; it was these people who suffered most, not the Boer sympathisers or commandos.[17]

Milner's own disenchantment was palpable. His first reply to Pretyman summed up his own frustration:

> Of course, as long as our authority in the new Colonies is restricted to the lines of the railway and a few big towns my appointment as Administrator is more or less a farce. Military considerations are still absolutely supreme. I am therefore not attempting to do anything but allowing things to go on for the present on their old lines.[18]

Milner, however, was unable to sit back and let the military do as they pleased. On 29 January he sent Chamberlain an extract from a letter written by General Ridley, the commander of the SAC, to his private secretary, Osmond Walrond. Ridley's letter seemed to endorse the ideas which Milner had vainly espoused to generals and politicians alike. Ridley explained his strategy at Bloemfontein, where he was forming concentric rings of police posts around the town. Interestingly, he announced he had used thirty-five burghers in action against the Boers. This last point was used by Milner as evidence to support his own ideas: 'The bulk of the population want to stop, but they must *have something to lean on*. Our wandering columns do not give them that.' Milner was confident that the SAC would be valuable for this sort of work, and hoped they would not be taken by the military.[19] In December Chamberlain had asked for Milner's opinions so that they might be published.[20] By the time he received this request, Milner's patience with the

---

[15] Milner to Chamberlain, 17 Jan. 1901, JC 13/1/118. Kitchener told Brodrick that it would be some time before the mines were restarted, especially after the recent attack on the South Rand mine: Kitchener to Brodrick, 4 Jan. 1901, KP PRO 30/57/22/Y13.

[16] Pretyman to Milner, 2 Jan. 1901, MP IV/A/173/fos 138–9.

[17] Pretyman to Milner, 13, 29 Jan. 1901, MP IV/A/173/fos 128–31, 133–6.

[18] Milner to Pretyman, 7 Jan. 1901, MP IV/A/173/fo. 142.

[19] Milner to Chamberlain, 29 Jan. 1901, and Ridley to Walrond, 19 Jan. 1901, MP IV/A/173/fos 123–7.

[20] Chamberlain to Milner, 22 Dec. 1900, in *Milner papers*, ii. 180–1.

military had worn thin. Consequently, on 6 February 1901, he vented his anger and frustration, and stated that the last six months had been a period of retrogression, referring to the outbreak of guerilla war, and the new rebellion in Cape Colony. This was due to Roberts's flawed strategy, and, as a result, the concentration on the guerilla war meant that the loyalists were being ignored.[21] Milner was determined to use the chance of publicity to acquire the strength of loyalist opinion, and thus secure a counterweight against military obduracy.

The continuing guerilla war did have one effect at this time; it hardened the resolve of the government. Thus Brodrick informed Kitchener that 'We realise to the full the difficulties which you have to meet, will give you every support in our power, with full confidence that things will be better before long.'[22] All the Cabinet could do was to hope that the military difficulties would be temporary, and that an injection of more troops would enable Kitchener to end the guerilla menace. For the moment, at least, ministers felt they had no choice but to back Kitchener, and resolved to meet all his requirements.[23] Chamberlain, therefore, could offer Milner little concrete reassurance. He could only hope that Kitchener might meet with a military success against De Wet or Botha, and that some start might be made to get Johannesburg working again. Chamberlain confirmed that the Cabinet had agreed to recruit and send 30,000 reinforcements to Kitchener. Perhaps to justify the Cabinet's decision and appease Milner, Chamberlain somewhat exaggerated the problems faced by the government. Ministers, he wrote, had to hope some progress was made, otherwise 'public dissatisfaction may become serious and threaten the existence of the Government in spite of its enormous majority'.[24]

The war news remained discouraging. On 10 February De Wet entered Cape Colony, having evaded all attempts to capture him. Kitchener explained that the country was too big and not every point could be watched.[25] Milner's assertion to Pretyman, that he would not interfere in military business, was ignored as the continual bad news provoked him to urge Kitchener to begin work at the mines. Milner realised that, for the moment, he could not ask Kitchener to alter his military strategy; but the resumption of work in Johannesburg was, to Milner, both a weapon against the Boers and a linch-pin of his future plans. Therefore, a start would be a positive move at a time when the news was anything but encouraging.[26]

21 Milner to Chamberlain, 6 Feb. 1901, ibid. 193–202.
22 Brodrick to Kitchener, 2 Feb. 1901, KP PRO 30/57/22/Y20.
23 Salisbury to the king, 4 Feb. 1901, CAB 41/26/2.
24 Chamberlain to Milner, 7 Feb. 1901, JC 13/1/121.
25 Kitchener to Milner, 12 Feb. 1901, MP IV/A/175/fo. 159.
26 Milner to Kitchener, 18 Feb. 1901, MP IV/A/175/fos 160–2.

Peace feelers

The continued resistance of the Boers baffled the British authorities. The British army had conquered the Boer republics and apparently the Boers had lost the war, yet still they remained defiant. One response to Boer pugnacity had been to devote more financial and manpower resources to the war effort. A second response undertaken by the government was the consideration of peace proposals. In fact, the prospect of peace was explored by British officials throughout the period from December 1900 to February 1901. Chamberlain's speech in parliament on 7 December 1900 indicated the British government's interest. Chamberlain spoke about the future settlement of South Africa, and stated that the Boers would only get self-government after a period of direct rule, and after they had demonstrated their loyalty.[27] Afterwards, Chamberlain requested that Milner respond to the speech as a gesture towards the British public, and to demonstrate the conciliatory policy of the British authorities. Again Milner used the opportunity to air his views, to impress upon public opinion that the commandos were ruthless and desperate, and that the best policy was the one he had advocated throughout 1900. He felt the best time to approach the Boers would be after the establishment of protected areas. He believed it was too early to make offers, because Chamberlain's speech had been viewed as a sign of weakness by Afrikaner newspapers:

> From the political point of view I think there is only one thing which can hasten the submission of the Boers generally, and that is the spectacle of one or more fairly extensive districts so strongly held against raiders that we can promise any people willing to settle down in them efficient protection.

Furthermore, he hoped to see and encourage surrendered Boers to take up arms in defence of these protected areas, and Milner felt such men existed who from 'disgust at the continuance of the present aimless and ruinous resistance would stand by us'.[28] In all, he attempted to bolster his position in relation to the generals, and to air his views before a wider and, perhaps, more influential audience.

The Boers made no response to Chamberlain's speech (they usually had access to information through an unofficial 'grapevine' between the British and Botha's headquarters), but this did not stop him pursuing the issue and he made sure Milner did not forget the need to promote ideas about peace. Although Chamberlain felt that the Boers' unresponsive attitude was due to their ignorance of his speech, he wanted to show critics that the government was being reasonable, and that the main impediment to peace was the irreconcilable attitude of the Boers. Chamberlain was conscious of the need to placate the loyalists, but he did not want their obstinacy to be a barrier to

---

[27] *Hansard*, 4th ser. lxxxviii, 7 Dec. 1900, 261–3.
[28] Milner to Chamberlain, 11 Dec. 1900, CO 417/296/fos 429–30.

peace: 'we have to keep in mind the fact that the Dutch must in the long run live side by side with the English, and that the best settlement would be one which left them fairly satisfied with their condition'.[29] Already, the British government was moving away from the concept of 'unconditional surrender', which had dominated their thinking during 1900. They had realised, no doubt, that the Boers might react positively to a more reasonable attitude.

Kitchener had also been active in trying to promote peace. He told Brodrick he had been utilising the Burgher Peace Committee, and in January he had managed to secure the services of ex-President Pretorius to see Botha. Kitchener explained that he envisaged the Boers asking for certain conditions before they surrendered, so he suggested that the Boers be told that the native laws of the OFS would be maintained to allay their fears about the place of natives in post-war South Africa. Secondly, he felt that compensation for damage to private property could be arranged, especially if the mines paid for it, and believed £1m. would suffice. Thirdly, Kitchener knew the Boers might ask for an amnesty for rebels; he offered no opinion himself and just asked 'Will this be allowed?' Kitchener believed the Boers would want some guarantee that they would not be ruled by capitalists and would have some form of self-government; he explained, 'They are I believe absurdly afraid of getting into the hands of certain Jews, *who no doubt wield great influence in this country.*'

Kitchener also realised the Boer leadership was divided, that De Wet and Steyn were more fanatical than Botha. But this division, rather than providing an advantage which the British could exploit, tended to make the peace process more difficult: none of them, it seemed, wanted to be the first to surrender. Kitchener was not sanguine about the success of any peace overtures; he did not give any reasons but the current Boer offensive must have demonstrated the fact that they were not ready to give in – yet. For the present he was more hopeful that his own military operations would force the Boer leadership to the negotiating table.[30] This despatch clearly reflected his own opinions and revealed an inclination towards leniency. Whereas Milner hoped to exclude the influence of men such as Botha, De La Rey, De Wet and Steyn, from the peace and reconciliation process, Kitchener expected these men, or some of them at least, to be part of that procedure.

Evidence of this development in Kitchener's outlook came on 22 February when he informed Brodrick that some progress had been made: Botha had agreed to meet him. Kitchener's initial reaction was to think that his military operations had convinced the Boers that resistance was futile. In his apparent euphoria over the prospect of peace, he warned the government what was expected of them: 'I think a personal meeting may end the war if we are prepared not to be too hard on the Boers. . . . It will be good policy for the future

29 Chamberlain to Milner, 22 Dec. 1900, JC 13/1/105.
30 Kitchener to Brodrick, 25 Jan. 1901, KP PRO 30/57/22/Y18.

of this country to treat them fairly well. I hope I may be allowed to do away with anything humiliating to them in the surrender if it comes off.'[31]

On 28 February 1901 Kitchener met Botha to discuss terms. Kitchener's instructions had been considered by the Cabinet and sent to him and Milner the day before. As Salisbury told the king, the two officials were required not to 'commit themselves in respect to specific proposals in detail until the precise terms in which those conditions were to be couched were submitted to Your Majesty's Government'.[32] Kitchener reported the gist of the talks to Brodrick and outlined the terms Botha wanted. Such matters as representative government; financial assistance; amnesty for rebels; and the franchise for blacks were discussed, with Kitchener promising that every consideration would be given to Botha's demands.[33] Kitchener was optimistic about the outcome, and clearly felt the terms wanted by Botha were reasonable. As he told Roberts, 'If the Govt. wish to end the war I do not see any great difficulty in doing so but I think it will go on for some time if the points raised by Botha cannot be answered.'[34]

However, difficulties had already developed. Brodrick wrote to Kitchener on 1 March, replying to his note of 25 January, and at the same time incorporating the government's views about the talks. Virtually every proposal Kitchener had forwarded was challenged. For example, no money could be promised to the Boers otherwise the colonial governments would demand more; loyalists would not like rebels being granted an amnesty; and although the fear regarding rule by capitalists was acknowledged, the men who generated the wealth could not be excluded from government.[35] The outlook was not promising for Kitchener.

Milner met Kitchener at Bloemfontein on either 1 or 2 March. Milner had just left Cape Colony to take up his post as governor of the Transvaal and met Kitchener half-way. He did so again, as it were, when discussing the talks, except on the point of amnesty which he later told Chamberlain was not 'a point which His Majesty's Government can afford to concede. I think it would have a deplorable effect in Cape Colony and Natal . . . to obtain peace by such a concession'.[36] Milner had no faith in the negotiations and would have avoided them if possible, but at that stage he had no choice: the negotiations had taken place and the peace process was underway. Milner knew he could not openly sabotage the process. He believed public opinion favoured peace; he knew the government was concerned about costs; and Kitchener had told him that elements of the army could not be trusted. It seemed

31 Kitchener to Brodrick, 22 Feb. 1901, KP PRO 30/57/22/Y26. Kitchener also wanted to know 'how far I may have a free hand in discussing such points': to Brodrick, 22 Feb. 1901, CAB 37/56/27.
32 Salisbury to the king, 27 Feb. 1901, CAB 41/26/3.
33 Kitchener to Brodrick, 1 Mar. 1901, CAB 37/57/34.
34 Kitchener to Roberts, 28 Feb. 1901, RP 7101/23/33/fo. 17.
35 Brodrick to Kitchener, 1 Mar. 1901, KP PRO 30/57/22/Y28.
36 Milner to Chamberlain, 3 Mar. 1901, CAB 37/57/34.

Kitchener had lost faith in the reliability of several units. Some of the militia regiments had not proved capable or willing to fight their way out of precarious situations, as some of the actions in December and January had demonstrated. No doubt, with the poor standard of troops arriving in South Africa, Kitchener expected much the same to happen again. Thus Milner realised that all he could do was to ensure, or insist, that no desperate concessions were granted to the Boers.[37]

On 6 March Chamberlain telegraphed the government's instructions to Milner. Basically, ministers endorsed Milner's views regarding the amnesty for rebels, and would not concede this point. On one other point, the government differed with both Milner and Kitchener. Ministers insisted that financial assistance should take the form of loans. Furthermore, Chamberlain added a section on the native question which Kitchener thought was unnecessary. The government insisted that blacks and coloureds be treated the same as those in Cape Colony, with the civil rights they enjoyed.[38]

Kitchener thought the government's attitude incomprehensible. After receiving the terms and communicating them to Botha, he complained to Brodrick and Roberts. He deprecated the attitude of the Colonial Office, for not agreeing to assist the Boers financially, and for adding the extra clause about the civil rights of blacks and coloureds. As he told Roberts, 'I am much surprised the Cabinet were not more keen on getting peace as the expenditure on the war must be terrible.'[39]

Colonel Rawlinson, recently arrived at Kitchener's headquarters, was similarly scathing. He also wrote to Roberts and echoed Kitchener's own words: 'It seems rather ridiculous to prolong this enormous expenditure in men and money simply for the sake of sending a few hundred men to prison.'[40] Perhaps the point to be emphasised here is not Kitchener's own view of the talks, but the prevailing view at headquarters. It seems to be indicative of a wider outlook, one based on the idea that the politicians were prolonging the war unnecessarily.

On 16 March 1901 Botha refused to accept the British terms. No reason was given: all Botha said was that he did not 'feel disposed to recommend [that] the terms of the said letter shall [have] the earnest consideration of my government'.[41] Both Milner and Chamberlain were relieved; as Milner explained to Violet Cecil, 'I hope we shall take warning and avoid such rotten ground in the future.'[42]

---

37 Milner to Violet Cecil, 2, 8 Mar. 1901, in *Milner papers*, ii. 211–15.

38 Chamberlain to Milner, 6 Mar. 1901, CAB 37/57/34; Brodrick to Kitchener, 22 Mar. 1901, KP PRO 30/57/22/Y32.

39 Kitchener to Brodrick, 7 Mar. 1901, KP PRO 30/57/22/Y30; to Roberts, 8 Mar. 1901, RP 7101/23/33/fo. 18.

40 Rawlinson to Roberts, 23 Mar. 1901, RP 7101/23/61/fo. 19.

41 Kitchener to Brodrick, 16 Mar. 1901, CAB 37/57/34.

42 Milner to Violet Cecil, 22 Mar. 1901, in *Milner papers*, ii. 215; Chamberlain to Brodrick, 18 Mar. 1901, JC 11/8/17.

Some historians have focused on how Kitchener blamed Milner for the talks breaking down, believing that Milner's resistance to the idea of amnesty was the root cause of the failure.[43] Kitchener called Milner vindictive and was unable to fathom the reasoning behind the decision not to grant an amnesty.[44] However, Milner's vetting of Kitchener's proposals was not instrumental in guiding the response of the British government. Brodrick's despatch of 1 March showed that ministers already harboured grave doubts about the terms.

Milner was not the only one whom Kitchener blamed. After further consideration, he further vented his anger, first on Botha, describing him as a 'pettifogging attorney', and then on those in Britain who had denounced the terms. It must be remembered that Kitchener's ideas had been germinating since the beginning of the year, if not before. He believed that even if the Boers accepted unconditional surrender, the only way for a lasting peace would be to follow the terms he had advocated 'that is . . . if you really want to live in peace and security with them and be able to give them self-government later. The strain on the Empire will be very great if we are to have our Alsace 6,000 miles away instead of next door as Germany has'.[45] Much of this despatch contained, like that of 22 March mentioned above, Kitchener's ideas borne out of frustration and disappointment; hence the extremity of some of his outbursts. According to some historians this is indicative of Kitchener's lack of foresight and reveals his true objective: merely to gain the quickest settlement possible, so that he could assume the Indian command.[46] This view takes little notice of the fact that Kitchener was concerned about the future of South Africa and saw beyond the mere need to make peace. It is true he wanted a quick settlement, but only if he felt it would last and be seen by future generations as his achievement. Viewed in this light his extreme opinions do have some purpose. If the British authorities were not willing to treat with the Boers then the only way to ensure lasting peace would be to resort to drastic measures, such as the deportation of the bulk of the population. Kitchener also raised more cogent points. For example, he felt a policy of divide and rule might suffice to keep South Africa quiet. He wanted to exploit the bitter feeling between surrendered Boers and those still on commando. In effect, Kitchener told the British authorities that the only way to defeat the Boers, without negotiating, was to employ severe measures to complement the work already being done, such as farm-burning

[43] Pakenham, Boer war, 499–500; Magnus, Kitchener, 224–5; J. L. Garvin and J. Amery, The life of Joseph Chamberlain, London 1932–69, iv. 31–2.

[44] Kitchener to Brodrick, 22 Mar. 1901, KP PRO 30/57/22/Y33–6; to Roberts, 22 Mar. 1901, RP 7101/23/33/fo. 20.

[45] Kitchener to Brodrick, 19, 26 Apr. 1901, KP PRO 30/57/22/Y44–5, 48.

[46] G. H. Le May, British supremacy in South Africa 1899–1907, Oxford 1965, 127; Pakenham, Boer war, 561; Amery, Life of Joseph Chamberlain, iv. 55; Leo Amery, My political life, London 1953, i. 165; D. A. Denoon, A grand illusion: the failure of imperial policy in the Transvaal Colony during the period of reconstruction 1900–1905, London 1973, 23.

and the 'concentration' of civilians. Kitchener had warned ministers that without generous terms the war would be hard, unedifying and bitter.

Brodrick told Kitchener that he had informed the Cabinet of his views. Ministers, however, were adamant that 'the extreme limit of concession has been reached'. Further offers would only imply that the government was weakening.[47] Moreover, Roberts informed Kitchener that he had agreed with Chamberlain. It is not clear how far Roberts's opinions influenced either Brodrick's or the Cabinet's views. Brodrick was probably aware of them and might have used them during Cabinet discussions. Roberts never respected the Boers as much as other officers; after all, his son had been killed by them. He never understood why they prolonged the war, and tended to label them the same way he regarded any other colonial enemy, such as the dacoits of Burma. Roberts expected the Boers to be governed like any other conquered people, and to accept their fate; he never regarded them as potential fellow-citizens who might later join in imperial decision-making. In this respect, he was out of touch with Kitchener.[48] As it was, ministers had already made up their minds, and did not need Roberts to make a decision for them.

Milner offers a policy

What has also not been emphasised is the development of Milner's own opinions after the talks.[49] Realising that Kitchener was beyond redemption, and was a danger to his plans, Milner abandoned his policy of restraint and now sought to press his ideas on the British government. The failure of the talks opened the way for him to assert his own views and to do so in the knowledge that the British government was politically and financially pressed, and inclined to look for another way forward.

Difficulties arose when Milner pressed Kitchener to alleviate some problems in the ORC. On 9 March the deputy-administrator in Bloemfontein, Major Goold-Adams, complained to Milner that the army antagonised those Boers who were prepared to settle down under British rule. Evidently columns were depriving farmers of their stock, whilst the animals on farms within reach of the commandos were being left, because they were too far from the protected areas.[50] Consequently, Milner informed Kitchener, and reiterated the need to protect those who might be encouraged to take up arms

---

47 Brodrick to Kitchener, 20 Apr. 1901, KP PRO 30/57/22/Y47.
48 Roberts to Kitchener, 19 Apr. 1901, KP PRO 30/57/20/O18.
49 Only Royle has mentioned this aspect, although briefly and I believe incorrectly. Royle says Milner suspected Kitchener of attempting 'to make a hasty and ill-advised peace to further his own career'. This view is too elementary, and does not consider Kitchener's wider perspective: Royle, *Kitchener enigma*, 183.
50 Goold-Adams to Milner, 9 Mar. 1901, MP IV/A/175/fo. 174.

against the commandos.[51] Although this irritated Kitchener, Milner pressed the point and informed him that the SAC were now being brought in to widen the protected areas, thus making accommodation of all the livestock more practicable.[52] However the use of the SAC further undermined the deteriorating relationship between Milner and Kitchener.

On 15 April Kitchener, clearly exasperated, addressed a memorandum to Milner regarding the role of the SAC. This had been prompted by an earlier discussion between them, particularly over the work the SAC were to do around Bloemfontein. From that meeting, Milner thought he had gained Kitchener's agreement to concentrate the SAC in order to secure certain areas from Boer encroachments.[53] But Kitchener complained that the SAC were not being utilised properly, and that too few were being used outside military garrisons. Kitchener explained that the SAC were part of the rein-forcements sent by the government earlier in the year, and so far they had achieved very little; also, valuable officers had been removed from the army to train them. His concluding remarks added a controversial element to his letter: he wanted Milner to tell Baden-Powell that for the duration of the war 'the distribution of the SAC, and the manner in which they carry out their military duties, both officers and men, are points on which he should receive instructions from the Commander-in-Chief, in order to practically carry out the scheme of their employment agreed upon between us'.[54] Unsurprisingly, Milner did not agree with Kitchener's remarks. In relaying the news to Chamberlain, Milner explained that apart from feeling too much was expected of the SAC too soon, he was anxious about Kitchener's concluding paragraph. He agreed that the SAC should come under Kitchener's orders, but only if they were used as constabulary, 'not as just so many more mounted troops'. Milner, of course, regarded the SAC as a guarantee that some effort would be made to establish protected areas, and that these areas would remain protected. Milner wanted to use the SAC to convey a sense of perma-nence to those Boers who wanted to settle down. Without the SAC, it was clear Milner did not envisage his protected areas lasting.[55]

Fortunately for Milner the Colonial Office endorsed his views and asked the War Office to intervene and heed his advice.[56] Once again, Milner found that Kitchener, by coveting control of the SAC, could not be trusted. By the end of April Milner had accumulated a great deal of evidence which

---

[51] Milner to Kitchener, 20 Mar. 1901, MP IV/A/175/fos 175–6; to Fiddes, 30 Mar. 1901, in *Milner papers*, ii. 240.
[52] Kitchener to Milner, 20 Mar. 1901, and Milner to Kitchener, 29 Mar. 1901, MP IV/A/175/fos 177, 179–82.
[53] Milner to Chamberlain, 12 Apr. 1901, CO 879/73/650/126.
[54] Memo. by Kitchener, 15 Apr. 1901, CO 879/73/650/130.
[55] Milner to Chamberlain, 19 Apr. 1901, ibid. Evidently, Baden-Powell complained to Milner that he had received no help from the military, who often took his horses and sup-plied his needs last: Jeal, *Baden-Powell*, 330–42.
[56] CO to WO, 22 May 1901, CO 879/73/650/134.

suggested that the time was ripe for him to make a personal intervention. On the one hand, Kitchener's military strategy was not working; the Boers were as active as ever, and the sweeping operations appeared to cause more trouble than they suppressed. Milner's correspondence had failed to convince the British government that an alternative strategy existed. On the other hand, news from his friends painted a bleak picture concerning the popularity of the British government. Milner had already heard from Chamberlain how hostile public opinion was to the ministry, and that a dramatic change of ministerial personnel was in the offing. From his friends and correspondents Milner learnt that the government was indeed losing the confidence of both the public and the Unionist party.[57] From all this negative correspondence, Milner perhaps gained the impression that he had to act against Kitchener sooner rather than later, before some crisis brought down the government. At his own request, he asked Chamberlain for leave to visit London not only for a rest, but to discuss the situation: 'If I could get four or five fundamental points settled, it would immensely facilitate my, and I venture to think, your task.'[58] Thus Milner's concerns about Kitchener's attitude towards the Boers, his intentions towards the SAC, and the apparent weakness of the government converged to induce him to return to London and present his case in person. On 8 May 1901 he left South Africa.

Milner had judged the opportunity carefully. Ministers were unhappy about the course of the war, and events elsewhere were becoming alarming. On 13 March the Cabinet had met unexpectedly to discuss Russian encroachments in China, and to consider a Japanese request to know how Britain would stand if Japan went to war with Russia.[59] Hely-Hutchinson, now governor of Cape Colony, reported that the military situation in the Cape remained discouraging.[60] Hicks Beach continued to complain about the financial situation and wanted Milner to defer the establishment of civil administration in the Transvaal until after his return to South Africa, as a cost cutting exercise.[61] Although Kitchener was eager to discuss and enumerate his military successes, he remained pessimistic when reviewing the long-term prospects, saying only that the war would last a long time.[62] The sense of unease prevailing within the Cabinet was highlighted by Brodrick in two despatches to Kitchener. At first, on 18 May, Brodrick explained that ministers hoped Kitchener might concentrate on driving out Boer forces from Cape

57 Godley to Milner, 27 Mar. 1901, and Camperdown to Milner, 29 Mar. 1901. Camperdown complained about Salisbury's nepotism and felt he should go: MP IV/B/214/fos 14–15, 135.

58 Milner to Chamberlain, 29 Mar. 1901, in *Milner papers*, ii. 245.

59 Salisbury to the king, 13 Mar. 1901, CAB 41/26/5.

60 Hely-Hutchinson to Chamberlain, 27 Mar. 1901, JC 11/17/6.

61 Hicks Beach to Chamberlain, 10 Apr. 1901, JC 11/18/5. Hicks Beach wondered why Milner wanted a rest by returning to Britain: 'It looks as if he and Kitchener are not agreeing, unless his nerve is gone.'

62 Kitchener to Brodrick; to Roberts, 9 May 1901, CAB 37/57/54.

Colony and the ORC, and then 'localising' the war to the Transvaal, after which Boer resistance might be claimed to be mere brigandage. A week later, in more forthright tones, Brodrick told Kitchener that ministers were now pressing for the return of troops. They wanted Kitchener to answer four questions: first, when might it be possible to reduce the area of operations? Second, what troops could be withdrawn once this was done? Third, if Kitchener was asked to return 100,000 men suddenly, how much territory could be held with the remainder? And fourth, did Kitchener still believe that amnesty was the only reason why the Boers rejected the government's terms?[63]

While ministers awaited Kitchener's answers, Milner arrived in London on 24 May and held talks with Chamberlain over three days between 31 May and 2 June. The results of these discussions were set down in a memorandum which was circulated to members of the Cabinet. Basically, the memorandum reiterated all that Milner had said over the past year. However, in addition, Milner now argued that if Kitchener's recent offensive had failed to defeat the enemy, even with the help of the South African winter, then a new plan ought to be devised, based on the establishment of secure areas from which fast-moving, unencumbered columns could pursue the commandos into the inhospitable regions of the old republics, where they would either waste away or surrender.[64]

Before the Cabinet made a decision, however, ministers had to await the arrival of Kitchener's answers to the questions posed by Brodrick on 25 May. Although these reached London in a piecemeal fashion they all bore one overall impression: Kitchener could not guarantee success or comply with ministerial wishes. He told both Roberts and Brodrick that he could not reduce troops as he felt this would encourage the Boer leaders, and could not spare the troops anyway because of extensive operations underway in Cape Colony.[65] These remarks probably caused some concern, if not outright disappointment. After all, ministers had provided Kitchener with an extra 30,000 men since February, the bulk of whom had arrived in South Africa. Consequently, ministerial attitudes began to harden. Kitchener received an intimation of this on 15 June, when Brodrick informed him of the War Office decision regarding the use of the SAC. Brodrick said that as far as dispositions and the strength of garrisons were concerned, Kitchener held the authority. But, with the concurrence of Milner and Roberts, Brodrick stated that the government did not want to see the SAC used as part of flying columns: 'The aim and duty of the Constabulary. . .should be to achieve prolonged, continuous, and effective occupation of definite areas.'[66] On the same day Brodrick

63 Brodrick to Kitchener, 18, 25 May 1901, KP PRO 30/57/22/Y55, Y57.
64 'Conversations with Lord Milner', Memo. by Chamberlain, 31 May – 2 June 1901, JC 13/1/144. This was circulated to the Cabinet on 12 June
65 Kitchener to Roberts, 7 June 1901, RP 7101/23/33/fo. 31; to Brodrick, 7 June 1901, KP PRO 30/57/22/Y60.
66 Brodrick to Kitchener, 15 June 1901, CO 879/73/650/139.

explained to Salisbury the trouble he was having in reaching agreement with Hicks Beach over the cost of army reform, especially the need to obtain more recruits.[67] It is conceivable this dispute also had an influence on the Cabinet meeting of 21 June, which renewed discussions of Milner's suggestions, now that Kitchener's answers had arrived.[68]

Evidently Milner addressed the Cabinet himself and outlined his ideas further. His views on the concentration of forces around strategic points doubtless struck a chord with Salisbury and Hicks Beach who had aired similar opinions themselves. Moreover, Milner emphasised the need to restart the mining industry, a subject which ministers had discussed for some time. It appears, however, that again no concrete decision was made at this meeting. There seemed to be a reluctance to interfere, a legacy no doubt of the earlier problems arising from political interference. Kitchener was told that the government was prepared to face parliament and obtain more cash; that ministers were prepared to await the results of the winter operations in South Africa, although they wanted to see more progress made at Johannesburg. Furthermore, the idea of confiscating the property of those on commando, which was being pressed by Kitchener at the time, was rejected because it would not hurt men whose property had already been destroyed; nor would Cape Colony pass such legislation against rebels.[69] However, the Cabinet held back from a direct confrontation with Kitchener. Ministers were doubtless aware that both Milner and Kitchener agreed that Cape Colony should be cleared first, and were therefore happy to follow.[70]

Although the government had shown mounting concern about the situation in South Africa, they had still not pressed Kitchener very hard. Milner's frustration at this setback was clear; five days later he presented another memorandum to the Cabinet. This was more extensive than the last, and emphasised his belief both that the winter operations would not end the war, and that a new policy had to be considered. If the war was to drag on 'it would surely be of great compensation for our protracted efforts to have something to show on the other side. And especially if that something was indirectly, and in the long run, itself conducive to the termination of hostilities'. Yet again, Milner called for a complete resumption of the mining industry; the return of the refugees; and the development of protected areas. Kitchener's 'aggressive and destructive policy' had achieved all it could. For Milner this would not mean a change in strategy: 'It is rather the natural development due to the change of circumstances.' He acknowledged the process might be

67 Brodrick to Salisbury, 15 June 1901, Salisbury papers, fos 209–14.
68 Salisbury to the king, 21 June 1901, CAB 41/26/14.
69 Brodrick to Kitchener, 21 June 1901, KP PRO 30/57/22/Y64.
70 Brodrick to Roberts, 21 June 1901, RP 7101/23/13/fo. 68; Roberts to Kitchener, 21 June 1901, RP 7101/23/124/1/fo. 33.

slow, but believed it to be certain, and, importantly, thought it would reduce the rate of expenditure, if not the actual total.[71]

Milner offered the government something concrete: a policy. His memorandum was positive, whereas Kitchener offered little that was either constructive or practical. Kitchener continued to explain how difficult everything was; the country, the Boers; and the few opportunities there were to catch them. He could not see how he could reduce his troops given the protracted nature of the war.[72] In a long despatch to Brodrick, he explained that if the government wanted to end the war, they had either to deport the Boers to Fiji or Madagascar, or to renegotiate, making sure the Boers gave up their independence and then let them fight amongst themselves:

> The howls with which the terms were received in England and by the Cape loyalists have to my mind put off the termination of the war for a very long time, and made it almost impossible for Boer and Briton to settle down peaceably, so this course having failed, we are, as far as I can see forced into the more objectionable first course proposed.[73]

Kitchener's extreme views regarding the treatment of the Boers were expounded at great length in this despatch. He also referred to the bulk of the Boer population as 'uncivilized Africander savages with a thin white veneer'. Several historians who have commented on this despatch have ignored the fact that the Boer leaders were not included in this insult.[74] If anything, Kitchener admired the Boer leadership, particularly since his meeting with Botha, where the two had got on famously. Kitchener's views contained what might be termed an unpalatable truth: if the government wanted lasting peace it would have to be negotiated. This was a constant theme throughout Kitchener's tenure, but he had to bombard ministers with this advice before the message was received and fully accepted.

As it was, in the summer of 1901, British ministers either did not receive the message, or preferred to ignore it. The government's willingness to sponsor talks in South Africa had been demonstrated. To do so a second time, especially so soon, meant the talks would need to have a clear chance of success. The government could not afford to be seen either scuppering further talks, or achieving a settlement that treated the Boers too leniently. As Milner offered a policy that did not carry such a great element of risk, it is not surprising that the Cabinet shifted its position in his favour following a further meeting on 28 June.

Evidently, ministers were irritated by the lack of information from the military authorities, and after two hours of discussion it was decided to tell Roberts of ministerial concern. Ministers wanted an 'explanation of the plans

[71] Memo. by Milner, 26 June 1901, CAB 37/57/62.
[72] Kitchener to Roberts, 21, 28 June 1901, RP 7101/23/33/fos 33, 34.
[73] Kitchener to Brodrick, 21 June 1901, KP PRO 30/57/22/Y62.
[74] Magnus, *Kitchener*, 226–7; Pakenham, *Boer war*, 500.

by which it is hoped to bring the war to a conclusion, and their relation to the resources which are at our command'.[75] Brodrick communicated the Cabinet's decision to Kitchener the following day. Milner, it seemed, had gained everything he wanted. The mining industry was to be restarted on a larger scale, not in the limited fashion allowed by Kitchener; troops would be reduced after the South African winter; and military operations would be curtailed in favour of special columns formed to hunt down individual commandos.[76]

It was at this stage that Roberts began to play a more prominent part in the proceedings. The reasoning behind the Cabinet's decision to notify Roberts of the decisions made at the meeting of 28 June was to ensure that he communicated them to Kitchener. This of course was a way of making unpalatable news less so, in the expectation that Kitchener would take orders from a military superior rather than from politicians. Roberts explained to Kitchener that ministers were fearful the country would not tolerate any more heavy expenditure, especially when it became more widely known that the Boers numbered only 16–18,000 men. As the old republics had been thoroughly devastated the Cabinet thought it possible just to hold the railways and the principal towns, so that troop numbers could be reduced in September. Roberts also noted that he thought it essential that Cape Colony be cleared first.[77] Three days later Roberts again informed Kitchener of the Cabinet's ideas in a despatch that showed Milner's influence and also reflected the fact that 'Treasury control was starting to tell.'[78] Curiously, the tone of this letter is a lot harsher than the one before; this suggests that Roberts might have been obliged to be more explicit. Roberts emphasised that Kitchener's winter campaign, no matter how successful, was hardly likely to end the war. He expressly stated that the Rand was to be restarted and refugees returned, as well as the 'necessary number of natives'. It was assumed Kitchener would carry out this policy with about 140,000 men, leaving only 15,000 in the Cape; if the railway lines were not safe as a result the Delagoa Bay and Natal railways would be utilised even more: 'The operations now about to be undertaken are more of a police than military nature, as their success will depend on the thorough pacification of the more important and populous districts which it is now proposed to hold, and the gradual extension of these protected areas until they embrace the whole country.'[79]

Both Roberts and Brodrick had been obliged to put pressure on Kitchener, and as both supported his position this must have seemed distasteful. But both officials were well aware of the problems caused by the war, and realised other alternatives had to be considered. The reference made by Roberts that

75 Salisbury to the king, 28 June 1901, CAB 41/26/15.
76 Brodrick to Kitchener, 29 June 1901, KP PRO 30/57/22/Y68.
77 Roberts to Kitchener, 29 June 1901, RP 7101/23/122/1/fos 261–6.
78 Yakutiel, 'Treasury control', 186.
79 Roberts to Kitchener, 2 July 1901, RP 7101/23/124/1/fo. 50.

current operations were of a police nature revealed his ambivalence at the time. Was Roberts still convinced, it might be asked, that when he left South Africa the war was 'practically over'?

Strangely, Kitchener made no overt protest against the changes wished on him by Milner and the government. He claimed he was not surprised by the call to reduce forces, which he had already set in motion by the construction of blockhouses linked by barbed wire, which were intended to protect the railways. However, he said he had hoped to use the troops freed from defending the railway lines to garrison the blockhouses as they were extended across the countryside.[80] This failed to elicit any sympathy from the politicians. Ministers were enamoured of Chamberlain's idea to set up *corps d'élite* designed to hunt down the Boer leaders. Roberts too pushed this idea, probably because it was close to his vision of 'police action'.[81]

Whether Kitchener disliked the whole idea of reducing troops, or just baulked at being ordered by politicians, is unclear. It was probably a mixture of both, as Kitchener could not tolerate any interference in his campaigns. Certainly he remained unconvinced by the orders he had received. He thought his troops were incapable of being turned into *corps d'élite*; he said he had already been chasing the leaders and did not think the British could live off the land like Boers. He could not reduce troop numbers without surrendering some occupied territory, and was not prepared to lose his best troops; instead he would remove only yeomanry and militia.[82] The tone of Kitchener's remarks seems to have had an effect on both Roberts and Brodrick, and both tried to soothe his feelings; this can be seen in the notes they sent to him on 13 July. Brodrick hoped Kitchener did not think them 'nervous or nerveless' in London, and 'we are most grateful to you for responding to Lord Roberts' suggestions'. He explained that the recent correspondence did not mean the government had lost faith in him. Roberts said much the same adding, 'I at any rate, can appreciate the great difficulties with which you have to contend.'[83]

Kitchener was not deterred by assurances or instructions. Despite being told by Roberts that the government did not want him to surrender territory, and that the policy of developing protected areas should continue, he stated that the situation in Cape Colony would determine whether he could reduce troops or not. The best thing, according to Kitchener, was for the government to bring pressure on the Boers, by which he probably meant

---

[80] Kitchener to Brodrick, 5 July 1901, KP PRO 30/57/22/Y69; to Roberts, 5 July 1901, RP 7101/23/33/fo. 35.
[81] Roberts to Kitchener, 5, 6 July 1901, MP IV/A/175/fo. 395, and KP PRO 30/57/20/O28; Brodrick to Kitchener, 6 July 1901, KP PRO 30/57/22/Y70. Brodrick recommended the scheme because 'it would use up less of our men than the general sweeping process'.
[82] Kitchener to Roberts, 6, 10 July 1901, MP IV/A/175/fo. 396, and RP 7101/23/33/fo. 36.
[83] Brodrick and Roberts to Kitchener, 13 July 1901, KP PRO 30/57/22/Y73, and KP PRO 30/57/20/O30.

confiscation.[84] Brodrick did not prove receptive to Kitchener's suggestions. The question of special or severe measures was no longer possible, and he advised Kitchener to consider the *corps d'élite* scheme. Brodrick felt that if one leader was captured, the British might declare the war at an end, and the remaining Boers brigands.[85]

Although both Roberts and Brodrick sympathised with Kitchener and said they understood the problems he faced, neither could argue against the implementation of Milner's schemes. Milner could now enjoy his triumph over the military and look forward to the realisation of his personal plans and the reconstruction of the new South Africa.

[84] Roberts to Kitchener, 15 July 1901, RP 7101/23/124/1/fos 95–6; Kitchener to Roberts, 19 July 1901, RP 7101/23/33/fo. 38.
[85] Brodrick to Kitchener, 26 July 1901, KP PRO 30/57/22/Y76.

7

Kitchener's Victory: July 1901 – March 1902

By the end of July Milner had seemingly achieved the position of paramount official in South Africa, and could now look forward to the commencement of his plans. In a letter to Brodrick, written just before he left Britain, Milner's main concern was that in the meantime Kitchener would do something rash, although he felt able to express his pleasure in developments in the occupied areas which appeared to vindicate his views.[1] In all, Milner seemed content and one senses his eagerness to return, to take the job in hand and put the military in their place.

The Cabinet had now finally agreed on an all-encompassing strategy designed to end the war. Ministers had apparently committed themselves to Milner's policy and had shown a commendable degree of cohesion in so doing. Yet such unity was to be short-lived. In the face of escalating costs and pressing domestic issues Cabinet solidarity began to unravel.[2] Moreover, developments in South Africa did not help the government's position either. The Boers proved remarkably adept at inflicting small but spectacular defeats on British columns, and were still trying to provoke a widespread rebellion in Cape Colony. All this cast serious doubts on Milner's prognosis for the South African situation.

The major beneficiary of these developments was to be Kitchener. Although he paid lip-service to the Cabinet's wishes, he proved quite reluctant to begin reducing troops and altering his strategy. How far this was planned, was just sheer bloody-mindedness, or due to a concatenation of events is unknown. The effect however was to undermine Milner's earlier success. In part, this had much to do with the government's reluctance to over-ride the military 'expert', when Kitchener presented ministers with certain conclusions about the military situation. Basically, the government was made to realise that Cape Colony was the strategic hub of the war effort and before any alterations could be attempted elsewhere the war in the colony had to be ended first. Otherwise, all plans for the reconstruction of the Transvaal would be upset if the Boers were still able to disrupt supply lines. Milner, forever fearful about rebellion in the colony and aware of its prime importance to the future peace of South Africa, readily agreed. This was to be his

---

1   Milner to Brodrick, 12 July 1901, MP IV/A/175/45/fos 368–73.
2   Marsh, *Joseph Chamberlain*, 508–12.

Achilles' heel and it allowed Kitchener to reassert his own authority in South Africa. By the time this was made clear to the government, cohesion within the Cabinet had almost collapsed. Eventually, the British authorities were faced with a dilemma: should they sack Kitchener, as Milner came to believe, or should they endorse Kitchener's expensive and cumbersome strategy and maintain Cabinet cohesion? Ministers now recognised that although Milner offered a policy it was untried, while Kitchener's schemes had operated for over six months and were gradually producing results. In the latter part of 1901, the government lost its nerve and clung to the familiar and comforting voice of the 'expert'.

Severe measures

All this, however, was to come later and in amongst the discussions relating to changes in strategy and tactics was a debate centring on the need to complement military operations by introducing other severe measures, such as confiscation of property or banishment from South Africa. As such, this was to be Milner's last success and apparently reinforced his hopes for the future. Initially, Kitchener took up the idea following the Botha talks; Milner then also took an interest in such measures, in order to secure his position, both immediately and in the future.

On 5 April 1901 Kitchener first mooted the idea of confiscating the property of Boers still on commando. Kitchener felt it was time to introduce severe measures as the only way to induce the Boers to surrender quickly, without further recourse to protracted military operations. Milner endorsed the idea and recommended it to Chamberlain just before he left South Africa for his visit to Britain.[3] Milner's reasons for supporting this idea are not clear. At the time he probably felt much the same as Kitchener and wanted to see the war ended quickly; perhaps he mentioned it merely to see how the government stood on such an issue. Ministers were apparently unsure about using confiscation as a weapon. Milner's telegram was shown to the Intelligence Department to determine whether confiscation came under the rules of 'civilized warfare'. Two notes appended to the telegram were shown to the Cabinet on 13 June, and they provide an interesting military viewpoint. Apart from the legal arguments against the idea, it was considered that confiscation would create 'a class of white paupers'. But to restrict the scope of confiscation was not a sound idea either: 'To enforce confiscation in the case of particular men only, such for example as Louis Botha, would be unjust and would put against us in the future those leaders whose support is necessary to the peaceful settlement of the country.'[4]

---

[3] Kitchener to Roberts, 5 Apr. 1901, RP 7101/23/33/fo. 22; Milner to Chamberlain, 8 May 1901, CO 879/73/650/128.
[4] Notes by the Intelligence Division, c. 13 June 1901, CAB 37/57/58.

Whether Kitchener was informed of this opinion is uncertain, although he would have understood the sentiment. Whereas Milner might have favoured the tactic to deprive the Boer leadership of power and influence, it is likely Kitchener wanted to frighten the Boers into submission without actually proceeding with the punishment. With Roberts's backing, Kitchener pressed his case and attempted to convince the government that confiscation was a worthwhile expedient.[5] Ministers, however, were more inclined to promote what they considered legitimate methods to help shorten the war. Thus in areas where 'our occupation is so far effective', Kitchener was asked to consider the idea of taxing those farmers still on commando.[6] Kitchener was not so sanguine and replied there was no precedent in Boer legislation, which Chamberlain believed to have existed. Moreover, the idea of declaring zones to be fully occupied did not commend itself to Kitchener either: 'There is no district in which it could be said that our occupation is more effective than it is over practically the whole country.' Instead, Kitchener wanted the Boer leaders told their property would be confiscated if they did not surrender within a given time. Furthermore, Kitchener advocated the banishment of Boer prisoners and their families, and treating the commandos in the same manner. Now that the consideration of severe measures was on the agenda, Kitchener refused to let the matter drop, and feared the war might go on indefinitely if nothing was done. The unexpected harshness of banishing families from South Africa would, he felt, succeed in this way.[7]

By the end of June, as Kitchener continued to implore ministers, Milner had obtained what he had set out for and appeared to be no longer interested in endorsing severe measures. His opinion had shifted somewhat and he was against wholesale confiscation, although he now favoured its use in protected areas so that newcomers could be settled in the property and protected.[8]

Kitchener remained undeterred by the continual refusals to support his views. As the government now wanted him to clear Cape Colony as a matter of urgency, he argued that this could only be done in tandem with a policy of strong measures: 'I fear opinions at home are far too optimistic about matters out here, and if nothing is done we may still have very grave trouble.'[9] He was wasting his energy. Confiscation and banishment were ideas ministers were no longer willing to discuss. As Brodrick explained, severity had achieved very little: farm-burning had been promoted as likely to end the war and this had failed. With regard to banishment, this was dismissed. The British government was not prepared to keep 16,000 hostile Boers in camps on islands

5 Roberts to Kitchener, 7 June 1901, KP PRO 30/57/20/O26; Kitchener to Roberts, 14 June 1901, RP 7101/23/33/fo. 32.
6 Chamberlain to Kitchener, 18 June 1901, CO 879/73/650/140.
7 Kitchener to Chamberlain, 19 June 1901, KP PRO 30/57/19/U10; to Roberts, 21 June 1901, RP 7101/23/33/fo. 33; to Milner, 26 June 1901, MP IV/A/171/fo. 115.
8 Milner to Kitchener, c. 27–8 June 1901, MP IV/A/171/fo. 116; to Brodrick, 12 July 1901, MP IV/A/175/fos 368–73.
9 Kitchener to Brodrick, 14 July 1901, CAB 37/58/107.

such as St Helena; nor were they prepared to off-load the Boers elsewhere because they were 'not a marketable commodity in other lands'.[10]

On 25 July, after giving the matter some thought, Milner agreed something ought to be done to coerce the Boers after Kitchener's recent military operations, but was at a loss to decide on the best method. He still thought confiscation within the protected areas the best solution under the circumstances, but not banishment.[11] However, Milner had second thoughts because the day after he wrote to Kitchener he contacted Chamberlain about a modified form of banishment. Instead of mass deportations, Milner favoured banishing only the Boer leaders. This course, if adopted, would solve a problem for him by removing those whom he deemed his most implacable enemies; and, he said, it would be good policy to help Kitchener. 'His tendency to discouragement is, to my mind, one of the most serious features of the situation.'[12] Milner's support for a limited form of banishment, coupled with the perceived need to do something for Kitchener, obliged the government to acquiesce.[13] On 7 August a proclamation was published which threatened Boer commandants, field-cornets, and 'leaders of armed bands', with permanent banishment unless they surrendered by 15 September 1901. Furthermore, those Boers with families in the camps would be charged for their maintenance, the cost to be taken from property 'moveable and immoveable'.[14]

Milner felt he was in a strong position. His policy was to be implemented and he had bolstered it by obtaining a measure against the Boer leadership. His confidence must have been high as he contemplated the future, and it perhaps explains why he wrote to Roberts on 29 July 1901. Milner attempted to persuade Roberts that it was time to restructure the command in South Africa. He hoped to break up Kitchener's command into three separate ones, leaving one general officer who would arbitrate over any dispute. Milner did not think the war, 'if it can be called a war', had any unity, being a 'mass of scattered and petty operations' requiring 'several directing minds'. Milner's objective was to place himself in overall command, as the leading official in South Africa, and this step would ensure his policy was properly implemented by more pliable generals. For Milner civil considerations, such as the return of the refugees, and the resumption of industry, were equal to the need to defeat the enemy: 'Throughout the whole country civil and military

10 Kitchener to Brodrick, 19 July 1901, CO 48/568/fo. 618; Brodrick to Kitchener, 20 July 1901, KP PRO 30/57/22/Y75.
11 Milner to Kitchener, 25 July 1901, MP IV/A/175/fos 376–7.
12 Milner to Chamberlain, 26 July 1901, JC 13/1/166.
13 Chamberlain to Kitchener, 30, 31 July 1901, and Kitchener to Chamberlain, 2 Aug. 1901, CO 879/73/650/160–2. Kitchener felt banishment did not go far enough, as the Boers believed a change of government would reverse such measures: 'Confiscation is the only thing that will touch them': Kitchener to Roberts, 9 Aug. 1901, RP 7101/23/33/fo. 41.
14 Chamberlain to Kitchener, 5 Aug. 1901, in Parliamentary papers (1901), xlvii, Cd. 732, 'Correspondence relating to the prolongation of hostilities in South Africa', 6.

questions are clearly intertwined & constant . . . communication between the High Commissioner & the several Generals Commanding will be essential to a satisfactory result.'[15]

Roberts was not so sure; he now saw that Kitchener's position was under threat. He told Milner that his scheme might work when peace was proclaimed and martial law ended, but 'So long as columns have to take the field, it would, I am sure, be a mistake to make a change in the chief command.' Roberts felt there had to be one army commander with Milner in South Africa, and that ought to be Kitchener. Roberts still thought Kitchener would carry out the Cabinet's wishes regarding the change in strategy and hoped Milner would agree with the arrangement.[16] The attempt to sway Roberts had an unhappy result for Milner. At the time Roberts was at odds with the British government over army reform arguments and parliament's desire to try unsuccessful officers, something both Roberts and Kitchener were against.[17] Roberts was therefore in no mood to sympathise with the wishes of politicians and all Milner did was to add to his growing resentment.

August thus marked a turning point in civil–military relations. With Roberts becoming ever more hostile towards the government and Kitchener growing ever more recalcitrant, the political authorities found themselves facing soldiers who were again no longer willing to take political considerations at face value. Kitchener felt he had good military reasons for taking a negative attitude to the government's wishes. Since July and earlier, he had said the situation in Cape Colony needed to be resolved before any changes in strategy – and its corollary of troop reductions – could take place. He believed the war was proceeding satisfactorily, particularly in Cape Colony, and that major victories had been achieved. The success of the burgeoning blockhouse line reaffirmed his faith in the current system. The Boers were being drained and would eventually give in: there was no other way to deal with such an obstinate people.[18]

The obstructive tone of Kitchener's correspondence alarmed ministers in London, particularly Brodrick. He knew Kitchener was not happy with the terms of the banishment proclamation, and revealed his own concern by telling Chamberlain that he had asked Kitchener to explain his remarks regarding the need to clear Cape Colony.[19] Chamberlain, however, was not convinced by Kitchener's pronouncements, and ridiculed his suggestions and

---

[15] Milner to Roberts, 29 July 1901, RP 7101/23/45/fo. 49.

[16] Roberts to Milner, 4 Aug. 1901, RP 7101/23/122/1/fos 304–5. Roberts informed Kitchener of Milner's views: Roberts to Kitchener, 3 Aug. 1901, KP PRO 30/57/20/O32.

[17] For more on the dispute between Roberts and the government see L. J. Satre, 'St John Brodrick and army reform 1901–03', *Journal of British Studies* xv (1976), 117–39; Rhodri Williams, *Defending the empire: the Conservative party and British defence policy 1899–1915*, London 1991, ch. ii.

[18] Kitchener to Roberts, 17, 23 Aug. 1901, RP 7101/23/33/fos 42, 43; to Brodrick, 23 Aug. 1901, KP PRO 30/57/22/Y80.

[19] Brodrick to Chamberlain, 17 Aug. 1901, JC 11/8/39.

recent schemes. Chamberlain, in fact, remained wedded to his idea of using *corps d'élite*. Brodrick informed Kitchener of Chamberlain's views, but toned them down, clearly anxious to avoid a rift between the two, and conscious perhaps of his own difficulties with Roberts.[20] Brodrick also informed Milner of Kitchener's views, and added that the government was keen to get troop numbers reduced after 15 September, so as to save money and obviate the need to summon parliament for financial assistance. Brodrick, however, was reluctant to force Kitchener's acquiesence, or to bring home cavalry prematurely. He asked Milner, therefore, to see Kitchener and try to find a 'middle-course'.[21] But if he was after a modicum of help from Milner then he was mistaken to expect it over Cape Colony. Milner was not convinced the best way to make savings was to reduce troop numbers in Cape Colony, even though the situation was improving. He suggested instead that 'rubbish' should be disbanded (he did not elaborate but was probably referring to yeomanry and militia, of which Kitchener also complained), and that the Cape government should be pressed to contribute to costs by paying certain units currently financed by the imperial authorities.[22] Milner, of course, continually feared a widespread uprising in the Cape, brought about by a Boer military success. He readily understood Kitchener's fears regarding the safety of the colony, and this was his weak point. His support for Kitchener undermined his own case, as did his support for a banishment proclamation, as well as his own over-confidence in discussing military matters with Roberts. Not only had he ranged the army high command against his scheme, he had helped Kitchener to use the situation in Cape Colony as basis for rejecting his scheme altogether.

Milner's position crumbles

Although Kitchener and Roberts were becoming obstructive, Milner's position still remained strong. By the end of August he had persuaded the British government to implement his policies and to issue a proclamation of banishment against the Boer leaders. The main reason behind the Cabinet's acceptance of Milner's strategy was that it held out the hope of cuts in expenditure, and the likelihood of troop reductions. This, of course, was of paramount importance in furnishing reserves for both the defence of Britain and India. As Milner's ideas seemed to promise much, the Cabinet was impatient for some intimation from Kitchener that his strategy was working.

In early September Brodrick tried to impress on Kitchener the need for troop reductions and financial retrenchment. He told him he was anxious

---

[20] Chamberlain to Brodrick, 24 Aug. 1901, and Brodrick to Kitchener, 26 Aug. 1901, JC 11/8/41, 43.
[21] Brodrick to Milner, 27 Aug. 1901, MP IV/A/171/fo. 117.
[22] Milner to Brodrick, 31 Aug. 1901, ibid.

about the reduction of troops and was fearful of having to call parliament in December, which he felt would encourage the Boers. He suggested 15 September as a suitable occasion to announce reductions, proclaiming at the same time that the character of the war had changed. Then Kitchener might be able to reduce his army to 140,000 men without much comment being made about it.[23]

Milner, following Brodrick's request on 27 August, also spoke to Kitchener personally to emphasise these points, and reported back that although Kitchener was averse to troop reductions at present, the situation in the Transvaal and the ORC was better than he (Milner) had anticipated. Moreover, Kitchener was beginning to make effective cuts in costs, especially by reducing the most expensive troops in the army. Recruiting for local corps had been stopped, and he was busy reducing the number of yeomanry. 'Taking all things together', Milner continued

> expenditure in South Africa on pay and rations should now begin to show substantial & progressive diminution. . . . But I think it would be dangerous to press K. to reduce at this moment beyond what he is already doing except possibly in artillery, amount of wh. appears to me still excessive. If Cape Colony could be quieted much larger reductions would at once be possible.[24]

Kitchener, with a subtle reminder of the efficacy of his system, told Brodrick that his columns were achieving satisfactory progress, owing to the limited space within which the commandos operated. He was in the process of reducing some troops, but it was difficult to release too many, as there were more blockhouse lines to hold, and baggage trains to guard for the mobile columns. He promised he would reduce numbers as soon as it was possible.[25]

All in all, things did seem to be improving: on the military front two encouraging successes had been recorded, both against troublesome commandos in Cape Colony. On 5 September Lotter's force was routed and Lotter himself was captured by Scobell's column near Cradock; five days later Scheeper's commando was badly beaten by Crabbe at Laingsburg. However, despite the cheerful outlook forwarded by Milner and Kitchener, this was not a happy time for Brodrick, for he was soon at loggerheads with Hicks Beach. The chancellor was angered by the rising costs of the military estimates and embarked on a campaign to reduce the expenditure upon which Brodrick's reforms schemes depended.[26]

Chamberlain was caught in the middle of this bad feeling and was able to appreciate both sides of the argument. He sympathised with Brodrick, and realised that a dictatorial stance taken by the Treasury was likely to induce the resignation of both Brodrick and Roberts. But he himself had little

[23] Brodrick to Kitchener, 6, 13 Sept. 1901, KP PRO 30/57/22/Y84, and CAB 37/58/86.
[24] Milner to Brodrick, 11 Sept. 1901, MP IV/A/171/fos 119–24.
[25] Kitchener to Brodrick, 13, 14 Sept. 1901, KP PRO 30/57/22/Y85, and CAB 37/58/107.
[26] Yakutiel, 'Treasury control', 187–203.

sympathy for Kitchener. The despatches from Cape Colony continually told of the problems caused by the military administration of martial law; and as this was the time when Kitchener was doing his utmost to secure martial law in the Cape ports and antagonising the Cape ministry as a result, Chamberlain's patience with him had worn thin. Eventually, he was obliged to inform Brodrick that he also felt that Kitchener could manage in South Africa with 150,000 men.[27]

The problem as far as Brodrick was concerned was that Kitchener seemed to be doing his best to meet the Cabinet's demands. Added to Milner's rather sanguine report of his conversation with Kitchener, Brodrick reacted with undisguised contempt to the way Hicks Beach was trying to pressurise the military to make drastic reductions in South Africa, reductions which could possibly jeopardise future operations. Brodrick, it seemed, took the Chancellor's strictures personally, and took out his annoyance on Chamberlain.[28] On 18 September Brodrick, by now overstrained with events in Cape Colony and army reform at home, told Chamberlain: 'I am straining every nerve to decrease expenditure. But last week the return . . . from S. Africa showed men to feed 315,000, horses & mules 241,000. . . . I am doing all that a man here day after day can do, short of ordering troops home whom K. cannot spare.'[29] Brodrick himself was as convinced as Kitchener seemed to be regarding the efficacy of clearing the Cape Colony, before any reductions could be made; and, coupled with Kitchener's desire to be co-operative, Brodrick stuck firmly to the military point of view.

Roberts also backed Kitchener, and was only too ready to support him after the distasteful business in the summer, when he had been obliged to order him to implement Milner's ideas. His unreserved backing of Kitchener was due to a combination of factors. First, Roberts held Kitchener in high esteem after their successful time together in 1900; second, Roberts was now extremely irritated by the British government; third, he resented Milner's interference; and finally, as the sum of all these, professional solidarity ensured his support for a fellow officer. Unsurprisingly therefore, on 19 September, Roberts made his support for Kitchener apparent in a long memorandum to Brodrick, in which he outlined Kitchener's difficulties in the Cape. A copy was also sent to Kitchener, letting him know that he did have friends in high places.[30] Moreover, Roberts was prepared to take the argument further; on the following day, Brodrick received a letter that combined both pomposity and an indirect threat to members of the Cabinet:

---

[27] Chamberlain to Brodrick, 12, 17 Sept. 1901, JC 11/8/52, 54. See also Marsh, *Joseph Chamberlain*, 508–10.

[28] Brodrick was also under pressure from the king who said the only way forward was to 'allow Lord Kitchener an entirely free hand': S. Lee, *King Edward VII: a biography*, London 1927, ii. 79.

[29] Brodrick to Chamberlain, 18 Sept. 1901, JC 11/8/55.

[30] Roberts to Brodrick, 19 Sept. 1901, RP 7101/23/122/2/fos 134–6.

As regards any reduction of the force now in South Africa, we need not trouble ourselves. I consider that an impossibility until peace has been established throughout Cape Colony, and a reliable Police Force has been raised. . . . *The Times* of to-day takes the view, which I feel pretty sure is generally held throughout the country, and it is for us at the War Office to see that everything is done to keep the Army in South Africa in a thoroughly efficient state.[31]

Roberts was obviously full of his own self-importance, but his opinion could not be ignored and was, perhaps, nearer the truth than the politicians might have wished. Already Chamberlain had warned Hicks Beach that his demands might risk the resignation of both Brodrick and Roberts: 'We cannot fairly say to all the experts "cut down the army by so many millions" unless we have some broad idea of how the necessities of our defensive position can be met with the smaller sum.' Chamberlain also realised that the time was not ripe for cuts, and that the public and the party would not support reductions, 'against the advice of all the experts and merely to save taxation and pay off debt'.[32]

A few days later the military situation took a turn for the worse, and ironically bolstered Kitchener's position rather than undermining it. On 17 September Gough's force in Natal was ambushed by Botha, and Gough himself captured. On the same day in Cape Colony Smuts surprised a party of 17th Lancers and defeated them also. If this was not enough, De La Rey twice emerged from his lair in the Western Transvaal to attack Von Donop's forces at Kleinfontein, and Kekewich's column at Moedwil. The effect of these humiliations, far from blotting Kitchener's record, merely showed that it was far too early to start thinking of troop reductions while the Boers were still active and capable of administering such stinging defeats. A further irony was that in themselves these setbacks hardly affected the military situation at all: they were humiliating but they did not hold up the process of grinding down Boer resistance. British forces were still numerically superior and the blockhouse line was beginning to deny the Boers access to foodstuffs. But press reports tended to over-react when news of these minor engagements arrived in Britain, and exaggerated their value to the Boers. And, as Roberts's earlier note suggested, the government was sensitive to adverse press coverage, especially from those papers deemed sympathetic to the Unionist cause.

On 30 September Brodrick presented a memorandum to the Cabinet, in answer to the criticisms made recently by Hicks Beach and Roberts. He reiterated the now unshakeable 'opinion', that in order for the Cabinet's strategic recommendations to be carried out, it was necessary first to end the fighting

---

31 Roberts to Brodrick, 20 Sept. 1901, RP 7101/23/122/2/fos 149–50. *The Times* noted (20 Sept. 1901, 7) that, 'The public, with their plain common sense, grasp the truth, which seems to escape the custodians of the national purse, that to attempt to make war "on the cheap" is, in the long run, the costliest and the most inept of all follies.'
32 Chamberlain to Hicks Beach, 12 Sept. 1901, JC 11/18/10.

in Cape Colony, something even Milner agreed with. All efforts to increase mobility and destroy the commandos operating in Natal and the Cape were being made. 'The net result, however, of these proceedings is to make it impossible as well as impolitic to withdraw any body of troops, and Lord Kitchener makes it clear that he cannot part with any infantry.' Brodrick explained that Kitchener was doing all he could to make economies, as he himself was doing at home. Essentially, Brodrick pleaded for a relaxation of the pressure he and the military were under to make concessions for the political well-being of the party. In fact, he argued that reductions in expenditure and troop numbers would have the opposite effect, and alienate the party from the electorate. With the recent defeats as evidence for the military, Brodrick quieted criticism for the time being.[33]

Kitchener also became more blunt in his appreciation of the situation. He told Roberts on 15 October that it was impossible for him to follow the instructions of the government, and said that as the Boers showed no signs of reducing their operations he 'could well employ even more mounted troops that are efficient'. Brodrick laid this communication before the Cabinet, which reinforced the points he had made two weeks earlier and recommended that 'the supply of necessary troops to Lord Kitchener must not be slackened'.[34] Two days later, Kitchener stressed that although the Boer invasion of Natal had been a failure, 'they seem as fanatically disposed to continue the war as ever, and I fear it can only end by our catching all or almost all of them. It is hard work for our men and horses, and must take a considerable time. I think you ought to be prepared for this'. Kitchener was now distancing himself from the orders he had received in the summer; he was openly asking for more troops and arguing that it would take time to defeat the Boers. He even suggested that if Brodrick thought anyone else could do better, 'I hope you will not hesitate for a moment in replacing me. . . . You must remember that as we go on catching Boers, we weed them out, and the residue left in the field are generally their best men and therefore more difficult to deal with.'[35]

Kitchener was known to suffer bouts of depression and to sulk for days on end, but his recommendation that he should be sacked was never supposed to be taken seriously. In fact, it can be seen as a calculated gesture because it also served as a reminder that there really was no-one else who could replace him. This was emphasised when the government became concerned about Kitchener's health, thinking he might have been suffering from stress and strain. The only replacement qualified enough to oversee the whole of the South African military theatre was Roberts. He told Kitchener that the government had consulted him about a replacement should he need a rest and added, 'My hope is that you will be able to hold on and bring the war to a satisfactory

---

33 Memo. by Brodrick, 30 Sept. 1901, CAB 37/58/91.
34 Ibid. 16 Oct. 1901, CAB 37/58/99.
35 Kitchener to Brodrick, 18 Oct. 1901, KP PRO 30/57/22/Y95.

conclusion, but we cannot afford to lose your services, and whenever you think you have had enough don't hesitate to let us know.' He then volunteered his services as a replacement should Kitchener want to take up the offer of a rest.[36]

The effect of these words on Kitchener can only be guessed, but it may be assumed that while they offered comfort to a man suffering from periodic bouts of self-doubt, they may have also increased his sense of self-worth. It was now obvious that whatever the government might think of his methods, the only threat they could offer in the form of a replacement was Roberts, whose reputation had been somewhat tarnished by the onset of the guerilla war in 1900. Kitchener's reply to Roberts does not seem to indicate any concern about his own position, but more for the situation in South Africa. In fact, Kitchener's concerns relate only to those problems that beset any commander in such a war; the annoyance of the pin-prick defeats; press exaggeration; staleness of officers and men; and a desire for fresh troops.[37]

If Kitchener was untroubled by government anxiety and hardly feared for his position, he spared little thought for Milner's view either. In mid September, Kitchener spoke to Milner on the issue of the 'three commands' and told him that it was not in the best interests of the army. Triumphantly, he told Roberts that Milner had evidently agreed that 'it was quite a bad plan, and that you will hear nothing more about it from him'. Roberts reply was equally comforting, 'I think, as I believe I must have told you, Milner's idea of three separate commands [is] out of the question. It would inevitably result in his becoming the Commander-in-Chief in South Africa. You may depend upon such a proposal never being accepted here.'[38]

On 30 October one of Kitchener's best commanders, Colonel Benson, was killed and his column heavily defeated during operations in Natal. Kitchener was able to use this disaster finally to reject the government's strategy. Again, although the defeat was not one of prime military importance, Benson had been a very successful leader. This in itself tended to make the setback seem far worse than it was; Benson's death certainly shook Kitchener, but it gave him the excuse he needed to begin his own counter-attack on the Cabinet's demands for reductions. Kitchener rammed home the problem in a way the politicians would find hard to refute: he told them that some risks had to be run:

and if a column like Benson's, operating 20 miles outside our lines is not fairly safe it is a very serious matter and will require a large addition to our forces to carry on the war. . . . I am sending you a telegram on the subject of reinforcements, I have been in hope that the recent loss of prestige in Natal and shortness of everything, would cause the break-up of a large section at least of the

36 Roberts to Kitchener, 19 Oct. 1901, RP 7101/23/122/2/fos 209–10.
37 Kitchener to Roberts, [?] Nov. 1901, RP 7101/23/33/fo. 58.
38 Kitchener to Roberts, 13 Sept. 1901, RP 7101/23/33/fo. 46; Roberts to Kitchener, 27 Sept. 1901, KP PRO 30/57/20/O40.

enemy's forces. The recent activity of the Boers everywhere however, makes me reconsider the situation. As we drive them out of areas it takes more troops to keep them out, and I consider that more troops will hasten the end which we all so much long for.[39]

Kitchener's letter not only showed again how military defeat could be exploited to help his cause, it exacerbated tensions within the Cabinet. The consequence of Kitchener's reasoning was effectively to isolate Hicks Beach and his notions of expenditure cuts. Ministers were determined to maintain the Cabinet's effectiveness and cohesion by acquiescing to Kitchener's demands, and they agreed to despatch reinforcements.[40] It might be asked why the Cabinet did not order Kitchener to reduce his forces and adopt Milner's strategy, when it was obvious that other columns would be destroyed as a result of Kitchener's policy? The answer is probably that the Cabinet realised they might have risked Kitchener's resignation if such an order had been sent. And without a viable alternative they could not gamble on his meekly following their orders.

Sack Kitchener?

By the end of October Milner was heartily sick of the military's management of affairs in South Africa and his patience with Kitchener had reached breaking point. Kitchener had earlier told Brodrick that he and Milner were co-operating quite happily, opening more mines and bringing in more refugees to Johannesburg.[41] But this assumption revealed his lack of understanding in dealing with Milner.

Although no record of Milner's views has been found, it seems unlikely that he took kindly to Kitchener's rejection of his idea about the 'three commands'. For Milner, it was further evidence of Kitchener's intransigence and surely added to his growing frustration. Moreover, he must have been aware that Kitchener was now asking for reinforcements, which meant that he was not going to reduce his forces as a preliminary to setting up protected areas. And, to make matters worse, the situation in the concentration camps had deteriorated to an all-time low in October.[42] So when, on 31 October, having been prompted it seems by Benson's disaster, Chamberlain wrote on behalf of

39 Kitchener to Brodrick, 1 Nov. 1901, KP PRO 30/57/22/Y100.
40 Brodrick to Kitchener, 21 Oct. 1901; Kitchener to Brodrick, 23 Oct. 1901; Memo. by Brodrick, 25 Oct. 1901, CAB 37/58/107; Salisbury to the king, 29 Oct. 1901, 5 Nov. 1901, CAB 41/26/22, 23.
41 Kitchener to Brodrick, 11 Oct. 1901, KP PRO 30/57/22/Y94.
42 Le May, British supremacy, 109. By September there were over 110,000 inmates in the camps; in March there had been about 35,000, but there had not been an increase in the number of camps themselves. In April 395 deaths were recorded; in October 3,205. In Brandfort and Kroonstad camps the death rate exceeded 1,000 per annum: Spies, Methods of barbarism, 215–16.

the Cabinet to ask what exactly had happened in South Africa since Milner's visit in May and June, Milner was ready with his reply.

Chamberlain's telegram revealed an underlying impatience within the government for the way in which the war was being conducted. Milner was to tell them why protected areas had not been set up; why special columns had not been formed to go after specific Boer leaders such as Steyn and Botha; and why the condition of the camps had deteriorated so drastically, especially as this was causing comment in Britain, and becoming a serious political liability. He added, 'I know it is a delicate matter interfering with military discretion but you might discuss this question with Kitchener & in any case I desire fullest possible report & explanations from you.'[43]

Milner wasted no time in sending his reply and informing the Cabinet what exactly he thought of Kitchener. It shows more than anything the reality of the civil–military position in South Africa; Milner confessed that:

> I do not think that my opinions, frequently expressed have any weight with the C.in.Chief. . . . He has probably more than the ordinary soldier's contempt for the opinions of a civilian, &, though he is always perfectly friendly & ready to listen, I find discussion of these matters with him quite unprofitable & am indisposed to continue it . . . . It is impossible to *guide* a military dictator of very strong views & strong character.

Milner had virtually given up trying to influence Kitchener's decisions and was resigned to letting him get on with it. He acknowledged that Kitchener was not going to conduct the war according to his views, or anyone else's; the only way to ensure there was a change was to have Kitchener replaced, even though there was no guarantee that his replacement could do the job better. Milner believed, however, that the more amenable General Lyttelton, who commanded in Natal, would be prepared to see the occupied areas put to work and not view the whole issue as a military one: if Lyttelton was given explicit instructions, Milner was quite convinced he would carry them out to both his and the government's satisfaction. He added that he wanted control of the railways, in order to facilitate rapid reconstruction; at present he believed the railways were not working to their full capacity and were doing very little for the civilian population. And for good measure, Milner explained that Chamberlain's idea of using special mobile columns to catch specific Boer leaders had not been carried out according to plan; that is, the leaders themselves had not formed the specific target that Chamberlain wanted, only their commando had been the object of Kitchener's pursuers. In summing up, Milner was quite clear as to what was needed: 'Let us make up our minds that the Boers will fight on; let us beat them as hard as we can; but let us *simultaneously* go on with our own business.'[44]

Chamberlain showed this letter to many of his ministerial colleagues,

---

[43] Chamberlain to Milner, 31 Oct. 1901, JC 13/1/190.
[44] Milner to Chamberlain, 1 Nov. 1901, JC 13/1/191.

including the prime minister. Chamberlain was reluctant to endorse or criticise Milner's letter until he had discovered the views of other ministers, a recognition perhaps that a decision for or against Milner might change the course of the war.[45] The question before them was should civil authority be asserted or not. This probably explains the fact that those who recorded their opinions for Chamberlain were not unanimous. Those who favoured Milner's scheme were Selborne, Walter Long and Lord Ashbourne: those opposed to Milner's ideas were Lansdowne, Lord James of Hereford, R. W. Hanbury, Brodrick, Balfour of Burleigh, Lord George Hamilton and Aretas Akers-Douglas. The reasons for the division are revealing: the pro-Milner group believed Kitchener was exhausted and that a stage had been reached when it was quite safe to replace him with another officer. On the other hand, the opposing group felt that replacing Kitchener would be looked upon as a defeat, and that he was not as tired as his critics and Milner made out. Lord George Hamilton believed that the Buller affair would make the army unmanageable if Kitchener was removed;[46] but Akers-Douglas was, perhaps, more correct when he suggested that Kitchener was second only to Roberts in the confidence of the public, implying that the loss of public confidence in the government would be a disaster.

Lord Salisbury's opinion was the decisive element in settling the matter. He could not understand why Milner wanted Kitchener replaced, and stated that Milner was vague in his criticisms of Kitchener; nor had he explained fully why Lyttelton would do a better job:

> I do not see how we can move in this direction. No one will take our bare estimate (even if we all agree) as a ground for casting what must be a slight on a servant who has done and is doing valuable service, and reversing or changing the course of military policy, which has had a measure of success, in favour of an indefinite experiment for whose issue we have no sort of guarantee: and which will always have this objection adhering to it, that it is the judgment of laymen against the judgment of soldiers. We must know much more fully in detail what it is that Milner has asked *in vain* of K. before we make it a ground for superseding K. by a commander chosen by Milner.[47]

This was the real crux of the matter, not the possible effect of a combined Kitchener–Buller sacking on army morale.[48] Lord George Hamilton did not speak for the majority of the Cabinet when he said the Buller affair would make the army unmanageable; no other minister even mentioned Buller and

45 Ministerial comments. c. 15–16 Nov. 1901 JC 13/1/192–7.
46 In October, Buller had contravened army regulations by making a public speech about the aftermath of Colenso, and referred to documents which the government had withheld from the public. Consequently, Roberts and Brodrick had Buller sacked. However, many Liberals took up Buller's cause and he still remained immensely popular: Geoffrey Powell, *Buller: a scapegoat?: a life of General Sir Redvers Buller VC*, London 1994, 197–205.
47 Salisbury to Chamberlain, 26 Nov. 1901, JC 11/30/216.
48 Le May, *British supremacy*, 122–4.

Hamilton was not a weighty voice in the Cabinet. Sacking Kitchener at any time was fraught with danger. Even offering him an early appointment in India, in the hope of mollifying his feelings, would hardly have disguised the fact of his sacking from him or the general public. It might have provided a smokescreen to hide the truth from the public, but all smokescreens vanish fairly quickly: it would soon have become common knowledge that Kitchener and the politicians had fallen out. But, as Salisbury pointed out, the great imponderable was that there was no clear, hard evidence to suggest that the alternative approach would succeed. For a government already lambasted by the press, such a policy was too dangerous to contemplate. What if Milner's policy had backfired; what if the Boers did manage to disrupt the protected zones and made the business of reconstruction impossible? The government might then be left with the humiliating task of recalling Kitchener – that is if he wanted to go back to South Africa. If Lyttelton failed, who could replace him?

Milner's letter obliged the government to look hard at their position in relation to Kitchener; what they saw was not encouraging. Salisbury might use the Buller affair as one of his own reasons for not sacking Kitchener, but that episode was merely a convenient cover. He knew that to remove Kitchener against his will would have caused the break-up of his Cabinet, especially as there was no one of high renown (or of high public profile) to succeed him. The Buller episode hid the unpalatable truth that ministers were tied to Kitchener: if he sunk into oblivion, so would they. Moreover, Salisbury might have felt that Milner needed reining in, that he would acquire too much authority if Kitchener was sacked, and that the government would then have to play second fiddle to the high commissioner. Salisbury had already complained about Milner's predilection to push matters forward without due consideration for British interests elsewhere in 1899.[49] Now, to give Milner what amounted almost to complete control over the direction of the war, as well as the reconstruction of South Africa, seemed, on reflection perhaps, to accede to personal empire-building.

Chamberlain, reluctantly it seems, acknowledged the force of Salisbury's viewpoint – that nothing should be done to give the impression the government had lost faith in Kitchener – although he ventured the thought that it might look natural if he were transferred to India.[50] Salisbury's reasoning dashed any hopes that a way might be found to control Kitchener. Chamberlain ended his acknowledgement with the vain hope that it might be possible to relieve the military of control of the railways and supplies, but it was not expressed with any degree of conviction and fell far short of persuading Salisbury.

Milner had, moreover, weakened his own position by supporting Kitchener on certain issues. For example, he had already backed Kitchener on the

[49] See Porter, Origins, 247–8.
[50] Chamberlain to Salisbury, 26 Nov. 1901, Salisbury correspondence, fo. 203.

banishment question, despite the reluctance of ministers. Furthermore, in September, Milner asked Chamberlain for an extra proclamation to complement that of 7 August. He wanted to see a wider definition accorded to the term confiscation. He wanted to sell off the property of all burghers in the field to defray the costs of keeping civilians in the concentration camps. This was particularly aimed at the Boer leaders whose families were not in the camps, but in the towns, with the commandos, or absent in Europe. Chamberlain prevaricated, said it was against international law, and might be considered a breach of faith if a new penalty was established rather suddenly.[51] Again, in November, Milner intervened on behalf of Kitchener when he discouraged Chamberlain's 'special columns' idea, virtually contradicting his earlier pronouncements:

> I doubt whether, with the *single exception of Steyn* the capture of any leader, even Botha or De La Rey (tho' these two are far the most important) would have quite as much effect as we suppose. The Boers have a wonderful knack of developing leaders as they want them & I am not by any means sure that if Botha or De La Rey were caught tomorrow Ben Viljoen or Kemp would not in a few weeks be found to do just as well or ill.[52]

In his desire to control all aspects of the settlement of South Africa it is not surprising to find that some members of the Cabinet were unable to agree with Milner, as he often sounded like Kitchener himself. But, at least Milner's efforts had woken ministers to the fact that Kitchener would have to oversee British policy throughout the region. Only Milner seemed reluctant to acknowledge this, although, eventually, even he had to admit there was nothing he could do either to change Kitchener's strategy, or have him removed.

Keeping Kitchener focused

The British government, now aware that it could not threaten Kitchener with the extreme option of sacking, instead sought to keep his mind firmly fixed on the task of rounding-up the Boer commandos. Having granted more reinforcements in October, ministers were determined that Kitchener should finish the war quickly. For the time being, all talk of troop reductions and cuts in expenditure was stopped, as the military campaigns became the focus of government attention. To this end, the Cabinet, at Roberts's suggestion,[53] decided to send General Ian Hamilton back to South Africa. Hamilton was given secret instructions to keep watch over Kitchener's handling of the war,

---

[51] Milner to Chamberlain, 27 Sept. 1901, and Chamberlain to Milner, 2 Nov. 1901, CO 879/73/650/260, 278.
[52] Milner to Chamberlain, 15 Nov. 1901, JC 13/1/201.
[53] Roberts to Brodrick, 2 Nov. 1901, RP 7101/23/122/2/fos 245–6.

and to report back about his methods and the state of the country as a whole. Brodrick told Kitchener that everyone was concerned about his health, and they hoped Hamilton would relieve him of some of his more onerous tasks. Nothing was said of Hamilton's secret instructions, but the government was now committed to keeping Kitchener's mind fixed firmly on resolving the conflict.[54]

Brodrick also became anxious lest Kitchener should fail to use the reinforcements, sanctioned in October, for operations in the Cape. Kitchener had told Roberts that the situation had stabilised somewhat and thought any fresh troops ought to be used in keeping the likes of De Wet, De La Rey and Botha out of the colony: he was ever mindful of the panic that had ensued in Natal following Botha's earlier invasion.[55] But Brodrick wanted to make sure Kitchener did not lose sight of the main objective: the clearance of Cape Colony. Although he was aware that the situation in the colony had improved, and that the new troops might be better employed elsewhere, Brodrick wanted Kitchener to finish the war in the Cape once and for all as this 'would be the best guarantee of future progress'. Only then could troop reductions go ahead, and mining and agriculture be resumed. Moreover, Brodrick was now thinking of the estimates for 1902–3, and Kitchener was the only one who could supply him with information as to when reductions in the army might be made: Brodrick suggested 30 June 1902 as a time when reductions might start to take place.[56]

Kitchener's forces were being systematically worn out by the repeated Boer hunts, and he consequently sent in a request for even more troops instead of ideas on reductions. He wanted more yeomanry and Australians, as many of the former were clamouring to go home, especially as they were paid less than those from Rhodesia and the colonial forces. The main problem for the government, however, was that Kitchener's demands threatened, once again, to reopen the disputes within the Cabinet. Hicks Beach had intimated that he would not accept raising more troops at 5s. a day, and Brodrick was certain he would find himself at odds with the Chancellor if Kitchener's demands were not met.[57] As it was, a drop in War Office expenditure enabled funds to last until February, and allowed Brodrick to press for the reinforcements to be sent; this request was granted sometime in late December.[58]

Brodrick was concerned by Kitchener's demands, and he suggested to Kitchener that he would be supported by the government if he followed

---

[54] Roberts to Hamilton, 22 Nov. 1901, RP 7101/23/122/2/fos 265–7; Brodrick to Kitchener, 16 Nov. 1901, KP PRO 30/57/22/Y104. Kitchener was quite relieved to hear Hamilton was returning, and added that he would not be surprised if the government had decided to recall him for not finishing the war quickly enough: Kitchener to Brodrick, 8 Nov. 1901, KP PRO 30/57/22/Y101. Hamilton, though, told Kitchener of his 'secret orders'.
[55] Kitchener to Roberts, 29 Nov. 1901, RP 7101/23/33/fo. 61.
[56] Brodrick to Kitchener, 7 Dec. 1901, KP PRO 30/57/22/Y110.
[57] Brodrick to Salisbury, 19 Dec. 1901, SJB PRO 30/67/8.
[58] Yakutiel, 'Treasury control', 203–5.

Salisbury's favoured option of holding only selected positions and using the extra troops to hunt down the Boers. Evidently Brodrick was anxious to impress on Kitchener how imperative it was to end the war quickly, especially as the government expected, 'a strong revulsion of feeling here. . . . We have great confidence here that when you have had time to alter the disposition of your troops the war will enter on a new phase.'[59]

Privately, ministers criticised Kitchener's tactics and strategy. Salisbury was clearly apprehensive about Kitchener's methods, and the adverse effect they were having on public opinion in Britain. He cited the arbitrary punishment of those whose guilt had not been fully established, such as in accusations of disrupting communications, where being in the neighbourhood was often considered guilt enough; nor was he satisfied that burning the house of a Boer commandant was justified simply because the man was still on commando. Both Lansdowne and Chamberlain agreed with Salisbury.[60] Ministers were acutely conscious of, and sensitive to, the growing political unpopularity created by Kitchener's methods. Moreover, these complaints also reflected ministerial frustration at their lack of authority, and an awareness, perhaps, that this criticism would have little or no effect on Kitchener.

Frustration and anger was growing in political circles. Having been constantly informed that the only way the war could be won was for the military situation to improve, every setback was likely to cause much irritation. When, on 7 March 1902, Lord Methuen was wounded and captured at Tweebosch, the politicians were incensed. 'It is really our worst since Colenso', Brodrick told Violet Cecil, 'His [Methuen's] mounted troops bolted, and I have to begin the old driving & harrying to get some one made accountable. The Cabinet are quite out of patience with it & I really don't wonder.'[61]

Brodrick pestered Kitchener immediately, demanding to know who was responsible. Methuen's disaster was the second in ten days (Von Donop's convoy had been taken at Yzer Spruit by De La Rey on 24 February), and followed too closely De Wet's victory at Tweefontein on Christmas Day. Information was now coming in which suggested that the Tweefontein disaster might have been avoided, because troops in the vicinity had been warned that de Wet was nearby. Brodrick told Kitchener that he wanted examples made: 'People here will stand anything now in the way of men & money; but they will not readily overlook carelessness in a small section of the force when you, all your officers & 99 out of every 100 men are undergoing immense exertions.'[62]

For Milner the government's inability to deal decisively with Kitchener

59 Brodrick to Kitchener, 22 Dec. 1901, KP PRO 30/57/22/Y115(a).
60 Salisbury to Brodrick, 28 Nov. 1901, SJB PRO 30/67/8. This also contains the comments of Lansdowne and Chamberlain.
61 Brodrick to Violet Cecil, 14 Mar. 1902, VMP VM36/C176/136.
62 Brodrick to Kitchener, 15 Mar. 1902, KP PRO 30/57/22/Y132, and Brodrick to Kitchener, 13 Mar. 1902, SJB PRO 30/67/9, for concern over the Tweefontein disaster.

must have come as a great disappointment, but he did not give in and continued to press his views on the government whenever he could. Although limited progress had been made on the Rand,[63] he remained unsatisfied. Between November 1901 and April 1902 he still tried to influence the conduct of the war, and continued to seek the support of the British government.

Milner's refusal to admit that nothing could be done while the war lasted, and his reluctance to concede anything to the military, was due in part to the anger felt at the army's continual hindrance of his plans. While certain high-ranking officers said they agreed with him, they claimed there was always a reason why they could not act upon his demands. Nothing it seemed could be done to alleviate the refugee problem at the Cape, or get more industry working on the Rand. This was the view of the chief of staff in Johannesburg who said Milner did not understand the real problem; the railways were already working at full capacity, but repeated attacks on the line kept it in a disorganised state. Milner was fobbed off with the remark that the difficulty of supply and transport was much greater than he realised. He remained, however, unconvinced. He informed Chamberlain that the railways could supply both the military and the civil population and felt they were being wasted. This was part of Milner's complaint to Chamberlain about Kitchener, and was another reason why he wanted him sacked. Milner said the railways should be worked under his authority.[64]

Kitchener had stopped political criticism of his own methods by continually referring to the difficulties in Cape Colony. It was a case that was difficult to argue with, and as long as Kitchener diverted all his resources to ending the problem, there was little Milner could do about it. But when he received messages from Hely-Hutchinson who, along with General French, felt Kitchener did not attach sufficient importance to the task of clearing Cape Colony, Milner's temper was hardly soothed. [65]

In addition, the situation in the concentration camps had reached an all-time low as child-mortality in particular had reached unprecedented levels in October. In November the mortality figures rose again, much to Milner's chagrin. While ordering his officials to do all they could to procure anything they needed in the way of food and medicines,[66] Milner was in no doubt who was to blame for this appalling state of affairs. Although he himself realised that excuses and explanations were no longer adequate to explain the terrible conditions in the camps:

---

63 Between May and December 1901 some 13,500 refugees had returned to the Rand; by December fifteen mines were operational: Diana Cammack, *The Rand at war 1899–1902: the Witwatersrand and the Anglo-Boer war*, London 1990, 173, 183.
64 COS, Johannesburg to Milner, 6 Nov. 1901, MP IV/A/175/fos 245–6; Milner to Chamberlain, 1 Nov. 1901, JC 13/1/191.
65 Hely-Hutchinson to Milner, 20 Nov. 1901, MP IV/A/174/fos 151–2.
66 Goold Adams, 4 Dec. 1901, 14 Jan. 1902, MP IV/A/173/fos 245–8, 249–52.

I should much prefer to say at once, as far as the Civil Authorities are concerned, that we were suddenly confronted with a problem not of our making,
with which it was beyond our power properly to grapple. And no doubt its
vastness was not realised soon enough. . . . The fact that it [mortality] continues, is no doubt a condemnation of the Camp system. The whole thing, I
think now, has been a mistake. At the same time a sudden reversal of policy
would only make matters worse. At the present moment certainly everything
we know of is being done, both to improve the camps and reduce the numbers
in them. I believe we shall mitigate the evil, but we shall never get rid of it.[67]

However, as Milner's opinions carried little weight in shaping military strategy, the influx of civilians to the concentration camps continued.

Milner's anger boiled over as Kitchener continued to pursue his own policies. Every quarrel or disagreement became magnified by Milner's intense
frustration at having to play second fiddle to Kitchener. Yet the more he complained, the greater the realisation that Kitchener, could not and would not
be moved. All Milner could do was to let off steam in his letters to Chamberlain, but this only increased the growing realisation of his own weakness. Milner admitted he could not agree with Kitchener on anything, even though
they remained on friendly terms:

You may say if you differ from him on a matter wh. concerns you, why not have
out, & if you can't carry your point refer to the Government for a decision?
The answer is two fold. Firstly, such a decision if contrary to the C-in-C's
views would only be formally obeyed. In the 101 small & devious ways in wh.
it is possible for a man in possession of all the sources of power & channels of
information, to avoid carrying out orders he does not agree with, things would
go on as before. And secondly, and this is my strongest reason, I am personally
quite determined to be no party to a domestic quarrel. I am too painfully
impressed by the odiousness of the exhibition of differences amongst ourselves. I mean amongst leading Englishmen out here by the handle they afford
the enemy.

Milner conceded that he and Kitchener were so far apart in their views that
no blame could be attached to the other. Yet this did not prevent him reiter-
ating his views on the best strategy to employ in the new colonies. Some
progress had been made to revive industry, but this had required a great effort
(and still did), to keep it going. What could be done to end this situation?
Very little according to Milner; Kitchener would not go until the war was finished and the only way Milner could see that happening was (as he said
'Heaven forbid'), by a 'compact' or by catching every last Boer still on commando, which would take years: this in itself did not matter as long as Milner's ideas were followed, but Kitchener would never do this. Milner could
only hope that some event would turn up which would oblige Kitchener and
half the army to be recalled to Britain by public demand. 'In that case, *if we*

---

[67] Milner to Chamberlain, 7 Dec. 1901, JC 13/1/204.

could get our SAC back, & a practicable General, I think the bulk of the country would soon be quite quiet & we could scare off a few desperate districts till the fire gradually burned itself out. It is doing that already in places.'[68]

Milner, of course, had used such outbursts before, during the pre-war crisis particularly in July 1899, following Chamberlain's apparent acceptance of Boer terms. Then he had tried to redirect the way the British government was handling the crisis, through his own correspondence and the press. In 1899 Milner's task was somewhat easier as he and the government were on the same wave-length and the distance between them was not great.[69] This time, however, he was dealing with an entirely different situation and the same tactics were neither applicable nor successful. He could no longer influence the British authorities as he had done previously. He was no longer in charge in South Africa: Kitchener was.

On 12 March, in response to Milner's complaints, Chamberlain attempted to soothe the high commissioner; but all he could do was re-emphasise the nature of the problem they faced. It was the same old story which in his heart of hearts Milner knew to be correct. After making some suggestions and then destroying their feasibility immediately, Chamberlain stated, 'On the whole I see nothing for it but patience and a stiff upper lip, but I would beg you not to be discouraged and in spite of difficulties to press forward on every possible occasion your scheme of resettlement and recultivation as well as developing the mining industries.' Then, more as an afterthought it seems than a concrete piece of advice, he concluded in an attempt to boost flagging spirits, 'If you find at any time that I can usefully intervene by bringing pressure to bear through the War Office, pray let me know. I might be able to do so without mentioning your name if it seemed desirable to keep you out of it.'[70]

Milner may ruefully have thought that Chamberlain's pressure had not achieved much in the past. This attempt to provide Milner with a tonic shows the paucity of the measures left open to the government. Milner had by now recognised this; his complaints had borne little fruit in the way of changing policies in South Africa. Over the past six months, he might have asked, when had the Cabinet intervened decisively on his behalf? When had they said he was right and that Kitchener must comply? Milner replied to Chamberlain that he was more disgusted with military conduct than discouraged: this may have been true. He knew, by then, that a peace settlement still had to be concluded and he could get what he wanted from that.[71] As long as he could control the aftermath and have a pliable general in command, who did not interfere in what he considered civil matters, then he could tolerate the pre-eminence of the military at this stage of the war. Milner was intelligent enough to know that he and Kitchener were the same type of person –

---

68 Milner to Chamberlain, 8 Feb. 1902, JC 13/1/209.
69 Porter, *Origins*, 230–3 .
70 Chamberlain to Milner, 12 Mar. 1902, JC 13/1/212.
71 Milner to Chamberlain, 6 Apr. 1902, JC 13/1/216.

ruthlessly dedicated to what they thought best and determined to pursue their immediate objectives to a successful conclusion – and unlikely to reach agreement on the issues at stake. Milner's recognition of his secondary position to Kitchener may have come late in the day, but it made him all the more determined to make the peace negotiations a success, and achieve after the war, that which he had patently failed to do during it.

In order to gain complete authority for himself, Milner had tried to persuade the British government that the war in South Africa was not a war in the conventional sense. He had attempted to convince London that the war could be left to the SAC and not the army. Given that Roberts regarded the Boers as bandits rather than soldiers, Milner's insensitive handling of the field-marshal was a great mistake. Essentially, his priority was to coax and cajole the government away from their reliance on Kitchener, to undermine Kitchener's prestige as the military expert and assume the mantle of civilian commander-in-chief in his stead. Owing to the government's uncertainty and loss of faith in Kitchener in June 1901 Milner nearly succeeded. In the end, when the government was faced with a choice of either Kitchener or Milner, they chose the former because, in reality, they had little choice. Kitchener not only held legitimate authority, he held the popularity of the British public; he was the new symbol of empire and he was getting the political authorities out of the mess they had created. In the face of such reasoning Milner just could not compete.

8

Managing the Peace:
The Treaty of Vereeniging:
December 1901 – June 1902

On 3 December 1901, General Hamilton, in a confidential report seen by both Lord Roberts and the Cabinet, stated that

> A year ago termination of the war was a matter of opinion. Now all I can say is that it appears a mathematical certainty that no high veldt country will remain to the Boers after six months, unless they succeed in transferring themselves to Cape Colony or Natal, or unless our Army is allowed to fall below strength – neither which contingencies seems probable.[1]

Much thought was now turning to the possibility that the end of the war was in sight. Milner had already discussed the issue before the end of 1901, when he told Chamberlain of his opposition to peace talks and his own reliance on all-out victory.[2] Although much contemplative energy was expended on the future of a British South Africa, significant divisions remained within the British ranks. A number of historians have written about the general course of the peace negotiations.[3] This chapter, however, concentrates on the British approach, as it was affected by the continuing tension between the civil and military authorities. It stresses the fact that Kitchener represented a general military perspective and, more importantly, emphasises that Milner lost the peace. Having failed to get his schemes implemented in 1901, Milner sought to obtain a settlement favourable to his long-term plans. This too he failed to achieve. It was the peace settlement itself which effectively ended Milner's hopes of creating a South Africa in his own image, because he was unable to discredit the Boer leadership and secure their future political exile. This chapter, therefore, examines the various viewpoints and opinions which shaped the civil and military approach to the peace process. It will also examine the course of the negotiations to show that the settlement which emerged reflected the army's viewpoint and not Milner's. Consequently, three major

---

[1] Hamilton to Roberts, 3 Dec. 1901, CAB 37/59/124.
[2] Milner to Chamberlain, 20 Dec. 1901, JC 13/1/206.
[3] J. D. Kestell, *Through shot and flame*, London 1903, 283, passim; Le May, *British supremacy*, 125–54; Pakenham, *Boer war*, 551–71.

issues emerged from the negotiations: how soon would the Boers be granted self-government; the question of amnesty for rebels; and, lastly, the amount of 'compensation' to be awarded to the Boers for the rebuilding of their farms.

The military view

It is often found in warfare that one side will come to respect a determined and resourceful foe. Civilians do not always appreciate this and can remain, as Ian Hamilton later wrote, 'so ignorant of the heart of the fighting man and of the chivalrous side of the psychology of war'.[4] By 1902 many British army officers felt sympathy for their opponents and openly admired their ability to defy overwhelming odds.[5] Moreover it was not, as others have suggested, a recent phenomenon, which appeared at the time of the peace talks in 1902.[6] Indeed, a year earlier Altham had stated that Britain could not win the war by 'purely military methods'. He suggested that the Boers be allowed to surrender if they gave up their arms and recognised British authority, after which, following a probationary period, they might be given self-government. Money would have to be provided to rebuild farms and replenish livestock and from the point of view of political economy 'the money will be well spent if it terminates the war, and thus leads to the permanent settlement of South Africa. . . . The Boers spring from the same Teutonic stock as ourselves, and have the same ingrained traditions and passion for self-government.'[7] Similar views were expressed closer to headquarters. Colonel Rawlinson had spoken to Kitchener on the subject of negotiations and echoed Kitchener's views on the need to negotiate and promise self-government after a reasonable time, otherwise 'you will *never* have what we call peace'. Just as important was the need to have friendly Boer institutions to oppose the influence and power of Johannesburg and the 'goldring'.[8] Rawlinson was not impressed by Milner's speech in January 1902 to the Johannesburg business community quoted below: he told Roberts, 'We all understand that "unconditional surrender" is to be the keyword and that there is to be no thought of amnesty for the rebels. We shall therefore have to catch every Boer that is now out on commando.'[9] In his diary Rawlinson was more forthright. 'Milner's speech has declared the policy of himself and the Govt. He has identified himself irrevocably now with the gold party at Johannesburg.'[10]

4   Victor Sampson and Ian Hamilton, *Anti-commando*, London 1931, 26n.
5   For more on this see Keith Surridge ' "All you soldiers are what we call pro-Boer": the military critique of the South African war 1899–1902', *History* lxxxii (1997), 582–600.
6   Pakenham, *Boer war*, 561.
7   Altham to Ardagh, 7 Dec. 1900, CO 417/307/fos 619–24. Chamberlain wanted a copy sent to Milner: 'It is really an argument and a strong one against his view': ibid. fo. 619.
8   Diary, 27–31 Dec. 1901, National Army Museum, Rawlinson papers (RD) 5201/33/5.
9   Rawlinson to Roberts, 10 Jan. 1902, RP 7101/23/61.
10 Diary, 8–11 Jan. 1902, RD 5201/33/5.

Following his return to South Africa in December 1901, General Hamilton apparently saw his task as not only to help Kitchener, but to help bring the Boers to the negotiating table, where they would be offered generous terms. Hamilton's views offer a particularly clear insight into the mood of army headquarters and, while his enthusiasm appeared to get the better of him at times, his correspondence reveals that 'pro-Boer' opinions were already entrenched amongst elements of the officer corps. Hamilton's letters provide the only detailed views of an officer at headquarters, complemented solely by the few remarks left by Colonel Rawlinson.[11] Those staff officers who published, or had published by others, autobiographical material hardly mentioned any political views pervading Kitchener's headquarters. Their aim was to emphasise consensus and provide anecdotes for the general public.[12] Consequently, there is a dearth of material related to the workings and opinions of the general staff in Pretoria and, as a result, Hamilton's correspondence is important for the light it sheds on those around Kitchener. As his opinions often matched those of the officers mentioned above and, as he states below, many officers in Pretoria, it is likely Hamilton became, in his own eyes at least, an unofficial spokesman for a general viewpoint pervading the officer corps. However, Kitchener's own correspondence mentions nothing about life at headquarters and it is impossible to say if Hamilton's opinions influenced Kitchener. Nevertheless, Hamilton's views offered an articulate and persuasive viewpoint that complemented Kitchener's own ideas.

Hamilton's beliefs fell into two main categories: the favouring of a negotiated settlement; and an intense distrust and dislike of Milner and Johannesburg. Hamilton had definite objections to the policy of 'unconditional surrender', and here he seems to have followed Kitchener's reasoning.[13] In December 1901 he felt the Boers would never settle under British rule if they were forced into surrendering. If they were offered terms, Hamilton believed the Boers, as a law-abiding people, would then keep their promises embodied in a peace treaty. Having made no promises under 'unconditional surrender', Hamilton said the Boers would consider they had every right to rise again. He based these opinions on recently captured letters of Steyn and De Wet, but at the same time considered a more practical reason for showing leniency. 'I should not be at all surprised if we did not require their aid someday to steady the Johannesburgers who will be very apt to run riot.'[14]

---

11 Others, such as Kitchener's two aides, Captains Marker and Maxwell, tell us little of events at headquarters. Both men were devoted to Kitchener however, for example: Marker to his sister, 17 Jan. 1902, Marker papers, 6803/4/4/31.
12 For example see Lord Birdwood, *Khaki and gown: an autobiography*, London 1941, ch. xi.
13 Kitchener believed the Boers favoured unconditional surrender 'to preserve their legal right to give trouble later': Kitchener to Roberts, 18 Oct. 1901, RP 7101/23/33/fo. 53.
14 Hamilton to his wife, 19 Dec. 1901, King's College London, Hamilton papers (HP) 25/12/2/12. See also the letter from Frank Maxwell to his mother, 12 May 1902, in which he

After familiarising himself with the operations and personnel of headquarters, and the political situation in South Africa, Hamilton detected two differing perspectives regarding a future settlement. On one side stood Milner, Johannesburg, 'and some of the loyalists of Cape Colony and Natal'; whilst on the other side stood Kitchener,'with nearly every soldier of any standing or experience that I have spoken to on the subject up to date'. The first group wanted to crush the Boers utterly, just as the Burmese and Punjabis were crushed; the second group felt this policy would prove too costly, especially against 'a fine, hitherto, independent white race'.[15]

Hamilton proclaimed his antipathy towards South African capitalists and Jews and became suspicious of Milner's associations with the mining industry: the power and influence of Johannesburg in a post-war South Africa was a favourite theme. To him the Johannesburgers were an impediment to the peaceful absorption of the Boers into the empire. He believed they meant 'to run the show' and would not pay any subsidy towards the cost of the war. Equally, Milner's association with the mining interest also impeded a peaceful solution. Hamilton felt the Boers would never negotiate with Milner because he was regarded as a 'Johannesburger', whereas Kitchener was seen by them as a plain military man – disliked but not hated. Hatred of Milner and Johannesburg kept the Boers in the field, not enmity for Kitchener and the army. He advised that 'when you come to make peace it should be engineered through the military, and not through the political channel'.[16] After all, as Hamilton explained to Winston Churchill, 'I cannot tell you how strongly I feel that if we could incorporate these Boers into the Empire, we should be doing a vast deal more for the future of our race and language, than by assimilating a million Johannesburg Jews.'[17] Thus Hamilton embodied prejudices and values that coursed through the officer corps and, like many officers, he had little sympathy for the loyalists, regarding them as narrow-minded, parochial and selfish.[18]

Kitchener himself was taking notice of what the politicians were saying, and was especially pleased with Chamberlain's comments in the House of Commons. On 20 January Chamberlain had outlined the views of the

echoes the opinions of Hamilton and Kitchener on this point, in Charlotte Maxwell, *Frank Maxwell: a memoir and some letters edited by his wife*, London 1921, 101.

15 Hamilton to Roberts, 27 Dec. 1901, HP 24/7/10/7. On 31 December Hamilton dined with Milner and discussed the situation with him. Hamilton felt Milner might be 'too keen a Johannesburger': Hamilton to Roberts, 1 Jan. 1902, HP 24/7/10/8.

16 Hamilton to Brodrick, 16 Jan. 1902, HP 24/7/10/10/2. This letter was sent first to Roberts who never showed it to Brodrick. However, copies were sent to George Wyndham and Winston Churchill.

17 Cited in R. S. Churchill and M. Gilbert, *Winston S. Churchill*, II. *Companion*, i. *1901–7*, London 1969, 116. Hamilton told Churchill: 'Do let us profit by our experience when we smashed the Zulus for the Boers, and not repeat the mistake by annihilating the Boers for the Jewburghers': cited in Pakenham, *Boer war*, 562.

18 'Loyalists from conviction are, in this country, few and far between': Hamilton to Brodrick, 16 Jan. 1902, HP 24/7/10/10/2.

government regarding a future settlement. Unconditional surrender was still the linchpin of British policy, but Chamberlain explained this was not as draconian as it sounded. It meant the government would not make promises in the surrender document; instead, the Boers would have to rely on the good faith of the British. There would be no confiscation of property, and the government would be prepared to grant a large amnesty, but only after the interests of the loyalists and British security had been taken into consideration first. Primarily, the British government wanted the Boers to acknowledge the fact of their defeat.[19]

Kitchener thought Chamberlain's words would have a sobering effect on the Boer leadership in the field, particularly on Botha, and was impressed by Chamberlain's hints that the government might consider the question of an amnesty for rebels. To Kitchener, this was the 'crux of the situation' because the Boers were kept fighting on a 'point of honour' not to desert the rebels.[20] But, as he explained to Roberts, 'Milner still thinks there will be no final surrender but I cannot agree with him and if I could only deal with Steyn and de Wet I believe they would all give in at once.'[21] Kitchener realised that Milner wanted the army to keep on grinding away Boer resistance until none was left, something Milner hoped would finish off any resistance to his plans for the future. Kitchener believed, however, that if the war was to end satisfactorily the Boer leaders would have to be brought to the negotiating table first, an opinion which had first surfaced during the abortive Botha talks and to which he still adhered. Nevertheless, he was informed by Brodrick that 'anything which the Boers here or in Europe could interpret as "caving in" would never do'.[22]

Kitchener did have one factor in his favour: his position as commander-in-chief meant he would be the first official the Boers would approach, either to end the fighting, or to come to some other arrangement. Moreover, because the Boer generals were also the political leaders of the Boer forces and represented a 'nation-in-arms', the political and military aspect of any negotiations would be virtually inseparable. This meant Kitchener would be a necessary part of those negotiations, making the army 'the arbiter of the settlement'.[23] In the end, both Milner and Kitchener took part, but it was not Kitchener who needed confirmation that he would be required at the negotiations; his presence was taken for granted.

So when it became known that the Boers were coming together in order to send the British government peace proposals, Kitchener reminded Brodrick

---

19 *Hansard*, 4th ser. ci. 20 Jan. 1902, 360–83.
20 Kitchener to Brodrick, 24 Jan. 1902, KP PRO 30/57/22/Y121. Hamilton told Roberts that Chamberlain's speech had caused a great stir at headquarters: 'Of course, if this information is correct, I should think that Lord Kitchener and Botha, between them, could come to terms before very long': Hamilton to Roberts, 21 Jan. 1902, HP 24/7/10/11.
21 Kitchener to Roberts, 31 Jan. 1902, RP 7101/23/33/fo. 71.
22 Brodrick to Kitchener, 25 Jan. 1902, KP PRO 30/57/22/Y122.
23 Amery, *Times History*, v. 92.

of his own ideas as to what would constitute a lasting settlement in South Africa. Certain aspects were fairly obvious; Kitchener recognised the need for an amnesty and money for the rebuilding of farms; the most important point, however, would be how long before the Boers were granted self-government. Kitchener was of the opinion that the leaders would have to save face and it was necessary therefore to treat them with some generosity, because, 'none of them like the idea of being handed down to posterity as traitors who gave their country away'. Kitchener thought that if a period of two or three years could be fixed, it would help the peace process immensely: he did expect the Boers to pledge their best behaviour in the meantime.[24] He was determined to ease the path towards assimilating the Boers into a British South Africa, to create the best climate and framework to end the antagonism between Briton and Boer. He was still of the same opinion which he had expressed at the time of the talks with Botha in 1901; once the Boers gave up their independence and laid down their arms then the main military and political objective had been achieved.

On 12 April 1902, three days after the Boer delegates had come together at Klerksdorp, Kitchener met them on his own, as this was merely to accept the Boer proposals. The government had briefed him – through Brodrick – as to what was expected of him at this meeting, as concern had been expressed over his advocacy of a fixed term for crown colony government. Although Kitchener was not explicitly told to drop this idea, Brodrick stated that the government was unlikely to agree to a set date, because, 'It is the one quid pro quo we get for all our trouble & expenditure.'[25]

Milner's views

As industry and agriculture began to revive in the occupied territories, and the blockhouse system began to bite, views on a lasting settlement began to take shape. Milner, perhaps more concerned about the practicalities of peace than ever before, began a campaign to sound out opinion and impress on his listeners his own ideas and opinions. Reconstruction was already being tackled under Milner's guidance. A Johannesburg Municipal Area, including the mines, was being created, and studies made with a view to increasing agriculture through improved irrigation. Milner was preparing the ground for *his* reconstruction of British South Africa; the only problem now was to make sure the eventual peace facilitated the development he so desperately wanted to see.[26]

Milner was not averse to sharing his dream of a British-dominated South

---

24 Kitchener to Brodrick, 30 Mar. 1902, KP PRO 30/57/22/Y136.
25 Brodrick to Kitchener, 12 Apr. 1902, KP PRO 30/57/22/Y139.
26 Denoon, *A grand illusion*, 43–58; *Milner papers*, ii. 273–87; Cammack, *Rand at war*, ch. x; Le May, *British supremacy*, 125–7.

Africa. In a speech delivered to the representatives of the Johannesburg Town Council and business community on 8 January 1902, Milner left his audience in no doubt as to what he expected after the war. For one thing there would not be another 'post-Majuba settlement'; for another the only way to end the war properly was to apply, and keep on applying, steady military pressure on the Boer commandos. 'It is no use to wheedle', he said, 'the only thing is imperturbably to squeeze, and to keep our clemency and our conciliation – both excellent qualities in their place – for the Boers who surrendered, instead of lavishing our blandishments on those who still continue to fight.' Milner revealed publicly his annoyance at the way the pro-Boers ignored the loyalists in South Africa, and continued to call for talks with the irreconcilables. He was obviously drawing up his battle-lines for the time when peace became a real issue. The loyalists in South Africa, he hoped, would be his main constituency.[27]

To Milner any thought of negotiating with the Boers was anathema: he wanted to impose his own conditions and leave no obstacles to impede the progress of reconstruction. Yet, on reflection, he realised that Kitchener's cumbersome methods were actually working. The life force of the Boer war effort was being steadily strangled by the blockhouse system and the constant harassment by British columns. He wrote, 'The advantage for the future of a war ending as it is ending is enormous. I can see my way to a settlement with a free hand, but if we are to be hampered by terms, I shall be happy to hand the impossible tangle to somebody else.'[28] Milner feared that events such as the meeting of the British parliament on 16 January would provide sudden tonics for the Boers still in the field. The parliamentary airing of grievances, particularly against the concentration camps, would provide that tonic, although Milner remained sanguine that party political wrangling would not give the Boers too much hope.

Milner's difficulty, though, remained in the fact that to get the type of settlement he wanted, he had to acknowledge the efficacy of Kitchener's methods. This of course made a mockery of his earlier attempts to get Kitchener removed. But if he continued his attacks on Kitchener and gave the impression that his methods were not working quickly enough, then it was likely the government might feel obliged to offer terms to the Boers, and thus deny him the settlement he craved. He therefore had to tread a careful path when seeking support for his ideas.

Chamberlain reassured Milner that a parliamentary session was unlikely to provide any succour to the Boers, stating that German press attacks on the conduct of British troops had strengthened opinion in favour of the war effort. Moreover, he said colonial opinion was unwavering in its support of the war, and added:

---

[27] *Milner papers*, ii. 319–23.
[28] Milner to Clinton Dawkins, 16 Jan. 1902, MP IV/B/221/fos 172–6.

As regards the future, I do not think there is any influential opinion in favour of approaching the Boers, or indeed of anything but unconditional surrender, although many men dislike the particular words used to describe an inevitable result. There seems to be a flavour of medieval cruelty about unconditional surrender from which we shrink, but after all they mean the same thing as we do, and they would bitterly resent any concession that might be misunderstood or would leave any chance for a revival of contest hereafter. I hope there will be no negotiations except such negotiations between the military commanders as may precede a general laying down of arms; but in any case you may rely upon me to refuse any terms which seem to me likely to embarrass us hereafter.[29]

So far then, there was quite substantial support for Milner's point of view. He had assured the loyalists that he would not betray them and had the assurance from Chamberlain that he would not betray Milner.

However, as the possibility of peace became apparent, so did the strain on the Cabinet and the divisions within. Apart from concerns over the Education Bill, the Cabinet remained at loggerheads over aspects of Brodrick's army reforms, especially the need to increase the number of reservists and the cost. These divisions were not helped when in March Hicks Beach had suggested to Salisbury that Chamberlain might oversee negotiations without consulting Salisbury or the Cabinet. Obviously, Beach was frightened of losing another opportunity to terminate the war and so get back to more orderly and traditional finance. Chamberlain, however, reacted angrily to such a suggestion; he knew that both the king (for his coronation) and Beach (for his budget) were

> too eager for 'Peace of a Sort'. I have spoken several times to the King and thought each time that I had satisfied him that while we were all most anxious to finish the War, nothing would be more dangerous for the country and for his own popularity than that any responsible person should appear ready to sacrifice essential points and show weakness at this stage.[30]

For Milner too, the strain was having some effect; his somewhat contradictory position of having to uphold Kitchener's military system in order not to undermine confidence at home placed him in an awkward situation. For one thing, Kitchener himself told Brodrick that his attempts to strike hard at De Wet and De La Rey had not succeeded to the extent he had wished.[31] Chamberlain reminded Milner that the military situation was not as good as he had hoped; Methuen's recent defeat at Tweebosch was still fresh in the memory and nothing had been done to capture Boer leaders – Cronje being the only

29 Chamberlain to Milner, 20 Jan. 1902, JC 13/1/207.
30 Hicks Beach to Salisbury, 26 Mar. 1902, Salisbury correspondence, fos 284–5; Salisbury to Chamberlain, 29 Mar. 1902, JC 11/30/225; Chamberlain to Salisbury, 1 Apr. 1902, JC 11/30/226.
31 Kitchener to Brodrick, 30 Mar. 1902, KP PRO 30/57/22/Y136.

one of note and that was as far back as February 1900. Chamberlain's opinion on the issue of negotiations was also less than comforting. The news of the Boer governments meeting in Klerksdorp on 9 April, to discuss an approach to the British authorities, had obviously excited much speculation about peace.[32] While affirming his adherence to the idea of 'unconditional surrender', he cautioned Milner about sticking too rigidly to this concept because, 'this is not the opinion of everyone, & unless the issue was clear and supported by strong argument we should be seriously attacked if we allowed the negotiations to go off on what could with any show of reason be alleged to be an insufficient cause'. Faced with the prospect of peace Chamberlain was prepared to shift his position and take up a more flexible standpoint than that indicated in his letter to Milner of 20 January. Chamberlain was now willing to be generous on the question of money and amnesty, but he reiterated his conviction that to set a date for Boer self-government was both impossible and dangerous.[33]

This despatch seemed cold comfort to Milner; his hope of solid support from Chamberlain was being undermined. Milner's one main hope for his settlement of South Africa had been to get the Boers to surrender unconditionally; yet his chief support in the Cabinet was telling him this was now negotiable. It looked as if the main pillar of Milner's hopes was in the process of being sabotaged. If this could be done what would the government position on other questions be? Chamberlain's willingness to discuss the money and amnesty positions boded ill for the future.

Since the beginning of the year, Milner had been actively encouraging Rhodes and members of the Cape legislature to petition for the suspension of the Cape constitution. The war had revealed the depth of anti-British feeling in the Cape, and Milner had become determined to bring the colony to heel. The last thing he wanted was a disaffected colony interfering with his reconstruction of the Transvaal and ORC. He considered the Cape irredeemable; he believed the Afrikaners were far too entrenched there to become model citizens of his South Africa; it was essential therefore that Cape Colony should not hamper the start of the settlement. Consequently, Milner was reluctant to be lenient in negotiating just so that masses of British troops could be sent home quickly: he wanted a peace he believed would ensure British domination from the start. He even told Colonel Rawlinson over dinner that unless the Colonial Office agreed to suspend the Cape Constitution he could not see his way to agreeing to an amnesty or fixing a date for future

---

[32] The British government had Kitchener inform Botha and Schalk Burger of the Dutch government's attempt to broker a peace in January. In Lansdowne's reply to the Dutch he said if the Boers wanted to talk peace they only had to approach Kitchener first. The Transvaalers seized on this and were allowed to communicate with Steyn and De Wet. Eventually the two Boer governments agreed to meet in Klerksdorp, under British protection (ironically it was also the headquarters of Kitchener's latest drive in the Transvaal): Amery, *Times History*, v. 509–12, 517, 526–7.

[33] Chamberlain to Milner, 9 Apr. 1902, JC 13/1/219.

self-government. If the Colonial Office did agree to suspension, then Milner too would be agreeable; he felt that this would permit the whole of South Africa to be garrisoned by only 20,000 men. The prospect of another Afrikaner Bond ministry in Capetown filled him with dread.[34]

Meeting the Boers

So too did the news of Kitchener's unilateral meeting with the Boer leaders. Following their meeting at Klerksdorp, the Boer representatives decided to approach Kitchener. On 12 April they met him at Pretoria and presented their terms for a settlement.[35] Milner told Chamberlain he hardly relished the idea of Kitchener meeting the Boers alone as he knew this 'interview' would probably be the start of the negotiating process. He was profoundly suspicious that Kitchener would begin talking about political issues:

> Kitchener is not a good judge of the effect of such proposals, and he is extremely anxious to end the war and to get away. Under these circumstances he is very likely to make dangerous concessions without quite realizing the extent of them, and though of course this would not bind His Majesty's Government, who will reserve decision, it might be very compromising.

Milner's main objection was that he knew Kitchener was in favour of fixing a time period before Boer self-government: this Milner found intolerable, and in any case he realised Kitchener was 'inclined to be very lax'.[36] Milner was now extremely concerned to ensure that he would control the peace process; only then would there be no deviation from the tough stance he considered vital for the future. Some degree of reassurance arrived from Chamberlain who informed him that proper negotiations would not begin without him.[37]

The meeting between Kitchener and the Boer delegates resulted in the Boers presenting a seven-point list which they wished conveyed to the British government. This Kitchener agreed to do but remarked they were unacceptable, as the terms merely intended to restore the *status quo ante*, with a few minor adjustments in favour of the British.[38] If Milner was concerned about Kitchener giving anything away, then the absurdity of the Boer proposals relieved him of that anxiety for the moment. At least the next time they met, he would be there to present the answer of the British government.

Before the next meeting, Milner received his instructions from Chamber-

---

34 Rawlinson to Roberts, 29 Mar. 1902, RP 7101/23/61.
35 Captain Marker told his father that 'If you were to go to a market . . . especially in the South of Scotland, & pick the first half dozen farmers you meet you would get a very excellent idea of what the bulk of the representatives of both governments are like': Marker to his father, 14 Apr. 1902, Marker papers, 6804/4/4/34.
36 Milner to Chamberlain, 10 Apr. 1902, JC 13/1/220.
37 Chamberlain to Milner, 12 Apr. 1902, CAB 37/61/71.
38 Minutes of meeting, 12 Apr. 1902, WO 32/8103.

lain, and they did not make pleasant reading. It was becoming clear that there was a definite shift in Chamberlain's views on the idea of negotiations. As these instructions also reflected the views of the Cabinet, it was evident that there was a move toward leniency on the part of the government. While telling Milner to stick to the lines of policy set out in his speech in the House of Commons on 20 January, Chamberlain wrote, 'but if you think it wise to go further to secure peace I shall not shrink from charge of inconsistency especially if moderate and influential local opinion justifies change'. It was all right for Chamberlain to then state that it would be 'better to . . . arrange terms of surrender than conditions of peace', but his earlier remarks had clearly shown that there was a definite softening in his attitude, and by association – the government's. There was a growing realisation that the British public might not see the negotiations in the same light as certain politicians. Chamberlain reminded Milner that:

> The enormous cost of the war and the continuous strain upon the Army make peace desirable but we cannot buy it by concessions which may encourage future rebellion or which would justify the loyal section in saying that they had been betrayed. In this connexion the question of compensation to loyalists may be important as they ought to be placed in a better position than those who have fought against us.[39]

It seems then that the loyalists were to be bought off in order to secure a reasonable settlement, and not therefore the domination of British South Africa, as promised by Milner. Although Chamberlain might state that concessions cannot be bought, the very fact of actually negotiating with the Boer leaders was, in Milner's eyes, a concession in itself. His plans were already coming apart at the seams.

Moreover, Chamberlain's reference to going further to secure peace, was picked up by others more inclined to go further than either Chamberlain or Milner. Hicks Beach seemed quite taken by Chamberlain's instructions (they had been circulated during a three-man Cabinet meeting on 12 April, as it was a weekend – the other member being Brodrick). For once, he approved of Chamberlain's recommendations and pointed out that going further than the speech of 20 January, or Kitchener's letter to Botha during the abortive negotiations of 1901, was not a sign of inconsistency. More ominously he suggested Milner should be told that the desire for peace was strong, especially amongst those who had remained faithful throughout the war; and that the state of the army required immediate peace in order to facilitate Brodrick's reforms. He stated that:

> though our people would decidedly support us in resisting any proposals that could be clearly shown to be dangerous for the future, they would, I think take a very different view if we rejected an agreement with the Boers on what they

[39] Chamberlain to Milner, 13 Apr. 1902, JC 13/1/222.

would consider merely minor grounds. If I am right in this, Milner might see, more than I imagine he does now, that Kitchener's desire to get away from S. Africa is not the only reason for not being too stiff on the present occasion.[40]

The talks of 14 April, at which Milner was present, were fairly inconclusive. Milner and Kitchener presented the government's reply which stated that peace talks on the basis of Boer independence were out of the question, and that further proposals were necessary. To this Steyn replied that it was imperative for the Boer representatives to consult the people if they were to give up their independence and wanted to know exactly what the British would offer. In the end, Milner and Kitchener agreed to ask the government to outline their terms.[41]

Milner appeared dissatisfied: in writing to Chamberlain afterwards he flatly refused to place any confidence in negotiations and still thought the best solution was to keep on grinding down Boer resistance, which, he believed, was progressing satisfactorily. But, importantly, Milner was prepared to acknowledge that certain terms should be offered, even though they went against what he really wanted. Although his belief in his own views was as strong as ever, his telegrams and despatches reveal a certain uneasiness about opinion at home, and he may have already detected a shift in the Cabinet, and especially in the views of Chamberlain. Chamberlain's support was crucial to Milner because his was the only support he could really count on: but Milner probably began to suspect that Chamberlain's backing was not as strong as it once had been. This can be seen in the fact that Milner began to compromise his earlier pronouncements on the need to stand firm. This is not surprising when it is remembered how much was at stake for him. While urging there should be no retreat from the position mentioned in Chamberlain's speech of 20 January, he wanted the Boers reminded of the terms outlined in Kitchener's letter to Botha on 7 March 1901 (although with some modifications rendered necessary by altered circumstances). This in itself is quite revealing: when Kitchener began negotiating with Botha, Milner had been annoyed at talks ever taking place and felt relief after they failed. Then, Milner had recognised that he was up against the war weariness of the public – although it was not extensive enough to be too dangerous – and Kitchener, but had gauged the mood of the Boers correctly and had realised peace was impossible. For all his talk about wearing down the Boers, Milner must have realised that they were in earnest about peace this time; and that *now* he could no longer count on public opinion to carry on supporting a war deemed virtually over, just to satisfy his own grandiose schemes for South Africa. Consequently, he would have to compromise his own hopes, and this can be seen in his communications with Chamberlain.

The Boers, he wrote, should not be offered peace in the form of a treaty or

---

[40] Hicks Beach to Chamberlain, 13 Apr. 1902, JC 11/18/20.
[41] Minutes of meeting and Kitchener to Brodrick, 14 Apr. 1902, WO 32/8103.

a convention, they 'must be content to trust H. M. G. to do what they declare that they intend to do'. Thus he had modified his position on the desirability of negotiations. He stuck to the point that there must be no time scale for the reintroduction of self-government, but he was on firmer ground here and knew the Cabinet were of the same mind. He was prepared to concede that ordinary rebels, having surrendered and not having committed any crimes 'under the cloak of war', be disfranchised for life rather than face the death-penalty for treason. This could then be offered to loyalist opinion, especially in the Cape, as a sign of leniency, but as a measure that would still be effective in keeping out an Afrikaner ministry.[42] Milner's desire to be firm but fair was quickly responded to by Chamberlain, and Milner's suggestions were virtually accepted verbatim.[43]

On 17 April these terms were offered to the Boer delegates, who were then granted permission to go back and consult their commandos. If acceptable as a basis for negotiation, the commandos would then elect special delegates for a Boer conference to be held under British protection, so that the final peace terms could be decided upon. In the meantime, Milner, having got from the Boer delegates an official promise that they *would* be presenting the British government definite terms, had to wait some three weeks before negotiations could be resumed.[44]

This interval gave him the chance to attempt to undermine the negotiations and prepare opinion at home for their possible failure. While Kitchener remained ever hopeful, Milner expected the Boers to drop their demands for independence but only in return for 'unacceptable conditions'.[45] He wanted Kitchener told emphatically that the government was not prepared to make concessions on points of policy. Milner was intensely suspicious of Kitchener, especially as he was able to talk with Boer generals in a 'military capacity' – a situation which could quite possibly turn into political discussions. But what concerned Milner at this stage was the thought of offering the Boers some form of monetary compensation for the destruction of their farms; this would be a controversial measure and could upset the loyalists, especially those in the Cape, just when the suspension movement was at a critical stage. Although Kitchener remained Milner's main cause of concern, the money factor was intruding on his peace of mind.

He continued to doubt the strength of public opinion at home, especially with regard to this aspect of the negotiations; and feared the public's 'thoughtless generosity'. Milner was determined to put his foot down. 'If I am

[42] Milner to Chamberlain, 14 Apr. 1902, JC 13/1/225.
[43] Chamberlain to Milner, 16 Apr. 1902, JC 13/1/226–7.
[44] Milner did not like Kitchener granting the Boers an armistice of a sort to allow the leaders to get back to their commandos: Pakenham, *Boer war*, 553. Milner's attitude disgusted Captain Maxwell, 'Milner nearly spoilt the whole show by [getting] on the high stool & K. said it made his blood run cold for fear he should ruin everything': diary, 17 Apr. 1902, National Army Museum, Maxwell papers, 7807/25.
[45] Milner to Chamberlain, 17, 21 Apr. 1902, JC 13/1/229, 234.

once more represented as the evil genius, who always prevents peace & conciliation, I can't help it. I know I am right.' He was certain the loyalists would not stand for it, and would not accept the Boers being treated better than them. Moreover, in many cases Milner felt it would be throwing money away on farms that were already inefficient before the war, and always would be, 'the point is, & everybody sees it, that all our liberality is necessary out of the pockets of our friends'.[46]

Milner was also uncertain about the amnesty question. His somewhat lenient views had been readily accepted by the government, but he remained doubtful whether the loyalists would find them acceptable. Milner knew an amnesty for rebels might be a sticking-point: it had been during Kitchener's negotiations with Botha; but he needed something to offer the loyalists. His emphasis was thus on disfranchisement as an 'absolute essential'. In fact Milner attempted to sound as if he was more conciliatory on the subject – more so than the loyalists. He told Chamberlain the loyalists were against an amnesty of any kind, but said this problem could be solved if amnesty was applied to those who surrendered at once, and that they were disfranchised for life; those who committed outrages, of course, would be excepted.[47] Milner it seemed was desperate to get a concrete guarantee from the government that loyalist opinion would be catered for. His continual reiteration of the need to offer the loyalists something, betrayed his anxiety that the government might just deprive the loyalists of everything, simply to make the Boers more amenable at the conference table. Obviously, Milner now had serious doubts as to the reliability of the government at home, and, even that of Chamberlain.

'K. is of course the danger'

It was at this time that Milner requested definite statements of loyalist opinion regarding peace terms, doubtless to bolster his own position. Until now, Milner had spoken for the loyalist interest. In early May, however, he felt it necessary for the colonial governments to present their own views. Their main concern was that rebels should be punished. The Cape authorities wanted the rank and file disfranchised and the rebel leadership tried for high treason, although punishment would not include the death-penalty.[48] This was particularly important because disfranchising a large number of Afrikaners might ensure almost perpetual election victories for the British element in Cape Colony. In Natal this was not so vital, although the government maintained the same position as it had during the Middelburg talks. Essentially,

---

46 Milner to Chamberlain, 21, 23 Apr. 1902, JC 13/1/235.
47 Milner to Chamberlain, 29 Apr. 1902, JC 13/1/244.
48 Ministers to Hely-Hutchinson, 1 May 1902, CO 48/560/fos 522–6.

Natal wanted to try rebels as it saw fit and ensure all rebels were brought before the law.[49]

As Percy FitzPatrick shared the same ideas as Milner, and was the Uit- lander spokesman, he ensured their views were given wide publicity. On 5 May the Uitlanders told Milner to insist on unconditional surrender and not grant any concessions which the Boers might use as rallying-points for future opposition, particularly the announcement of a date when the Boers might be granted self-government.[50] FitzPatrick was already convinced Kitchener would 'betray' them. He argued with Kitchener after the latter showed him a document outlining various terms. When FitzPatrick said the Boers would exploit every ambiguity, Kitchener was supposed to have replied. 'You are one of Milner's men. You think he's everything here. I am going to settle this.'[51] FitzPatrick believed talks only gave hope to the Boers: 'it is the same old fight, the same old points, the same old "Kaffir" bargain again and that once more we have to put our backs into it if we don't want the long-sighted obstinacy of the Boer to preserve . . . the foundations upon which they hope to uprear the structure in the future'.[52] Thus the loyalist position centred on two principal factors: rebels should face punishment; and the Boers should be given no indication as to when they might be granted self-government.

As for Kitchener, Brodrick informed him on 19 April that the Cabinet would not countenance fixing a time period for Boer self-government, but was prepared to be liberal with regard to the money settlement, as they were to an amnesty for rebels. Although a week later Brodrick expressed the view that to be unduly lenient to rebels, 'would be a misfortune', he concluded by saying, 'You will however be able to judge better than we are whether our feeling is correct.'[53]

Indeed, Kitchener needed little prompting to know that he was the better judge. His recent 'drives' were beginning to have a notable effect on the Boers, through their sheer persistence rather than as a result of any clear-cut military victory. He was sure the end of the war was in sight, and believed the military pressure on the Boers would create the right impression on the dele- gates by the time they came to the conference table. Kitchener hoped the constant stress and strain of trying to avoid the British columns would make the Boers amenable and more willing to negotiate. And for all Kitchener's extreme solutions regarding the guerilla problem, such as the banishment of the entire irreconcilable population to Fiji or Madagascar, he knew that any settlement in South Africa depended on their acquiescence. It was even

[49] Ministers to Governor McCallum, 2 May 1902, and McCallum to Milner, 3 May 1902, CO 179/223/fos 348–9, 354. For the view of ministers during the Middelburg talks see Bale to Hime, 18 Apr. 1901, CO 179/218/fos 296–7; Le May, British supremacy, 140.
[50] Ibid. 140–1; FitzPatrick papers, 496–7 n. 5.
[51] A. Duminy and Bill Guest, Interfering in politics: a biography of Sir Percy FitzPatrick, Johan- nesburg 1987, 96.
[52] FitzPatrick to E. T. Cook, 24 Apr. 1902, in FitzPatrick papers, 316.
[53] Brodrick to Kitchener, 19, 26 Apr. 1902, KP PRO 30/57/22/Y141, Y144.

likely that if the banishment proclamation had worked and the burghers had surrendered, their leaders would still have been dealt with as their true representatives, as the only way to ensure lasting peace.[54] Moreover, with the Boer leadership split between those in Europe and those on the veldt, talks with the latter were the only way to secure peace: for those sitting comfortably in Europe could quite easily refuse to negotiate, even though the commandos were on the brink of defeat. Without valid discussions with those in the field, a secure settlement would be out of the question. This issue had been acknowledged by both Kitchener and the British government, and told to the Boer delegates. In effect, this undermined any attempt by Milner to weaken their position as negotiators, as he strove to have the negotiations put on ice. Kitchener was determined to get the Boers in a certain frame of mind, and then offer them lenient terms. For the future well-being of South Africa, Kitchener was not going to allow Milner to impose harsh conditions, wreck the negotiations or convince his superiors that he knew best.

On the eve of the meeting of the Boer delegates at Vereeniging, Milner knew that now would be the make or break of his political dreams. He stiffened his resolve by declaring that he would not surrender anything he considered vital for future development, and 'If a bad peace is to be made, it must be over my political corpse.'[55] He needed little reminding from Violet Cecil that, 'K. is of course the danger, he is offering the Government what seventeen of them want.'[56] Furthermore, the petition for the suspension of the Cape Constitution had been presented to Hely-Hutchinson and would soon be on its way to London.[57]

The outcome of the talks on 19 and 21 May was that Milner and Kitchener beat down Boer attempts to salvage some form of independence. However, the sticking-point which now emerged was how much compensation was to be offered to the Boers. Botha wanted receipts given by his officers, for the purchase of goods, repaid in full. These were not notes drawn under Transvaal Law, but requisitions for goods obtained whilst on commando, and not provided for by law. Botha added that, 'Our honour is bound up in the matter as we have signed receipts, and it would be a great point if we could come to the representatives with this point guaranteed', and, of course, avoid a civil–military breach on the Boer side. Milner might have sensed the potential for discrediting the Boer leadership. He thought this idea preposterous and complained that the 'proposal virtually is that the British Government should pay for all money borrowed by the two Republics in order to fight it'. It was at this stage that Kitchener openly sided with the Boers and suggested a

---

[54] Amery, *Times History*, v. 573. In fact, the army had promised minor leaders they would not be banished if they surrendered with their men: Kitchener to Brodrick, 20 Dec. 1901, KP PRO 30/57/22/Y113(b).

[55] Milner to Hanbury Williams, 30 Apr. 1902, in *Milner papers*, ii. 341–2.

[56] Lady Edward Cecil to Milner, 17 May 1902, ibid. 342.

[57] The petition was presented on 10 May 1902.

sum of £2m. be set aside to meet these payments. He explained later that he judged the issue 'vital to peace' and wanted the Boer leaders to keep their prestige. After some discussion, owing to the fact that the Boers could not make up their minds as to how much was needed, they eventually asked for £3m., and this was added to Clause Eleven of the draft treaty.[58]

Milner was not satisfied. Clause Eleven threatened to undo his careful lobbying about upsetting the loyalists, something he had already mentioned on 23 April. He realised the loyalists in the Cape and Natal, many of whom also had had property destroyed, would resent the Boers being offered what seemed like a gift to restore their farms. And secondly, he believed the money would have to come from South Africa. He explained to Chamberlain that Clause Eleven

> is detestable, and in my opinion in the nature of an audacious try-on. . . . As the clause stands, we shall be virtually paying for conduct of war against us, and this extravagant liberality to enemy will certainly involve corresponding extravagance in dealing with compensation to loyalists and cost many millions. For all this the . . . British Transvaal, will have to pay.[59]

Indeed Clause Eleven had all the ingredients for upsetting the loyalist applecart, just when Milner was staking a great deal of his political reputation on the suspension of the Cape Constitution, because how could he promote himself as the loyalist champion on one issue, when he might be seen as undermining their interests on another? But it was not just the amount of money that was causing the problem; the political implications of the grant were of far more importance. Milner might also have feared that if the Boers were allowed to dole out money they had *won* from the British at the negotiations, it would enhance the political standing of the Boer leaders, and cement their leadership of their own people. Milner's wish to have the money spent through his office probably had little to do with good financial management; more likely it was intended to bypass the Boer leadership and freeze them out of the business of reconstruction. That way Milner could neutralise the potential of the Boer generals to become political leaders in his South Africa.

Milner was annoyed by the implications of Clause Eleven. Even so, he still hoped the talks might founder on Boer intransigence. Possibly, Milner was trying to convince himself, as well as the British government, that Boer obduracy was insurmountable: in a despatch written on 21 May, he tried to make the government face the prospect of the talks failing. 'My own conviction', he wrote, 'is that the Boers are done for, and that if the assembly at Vereeniging breaks up without peace they will surrender right and left. The men here

---

[58] Minutes of meeting, 21 May 1902, WO 32/8108; Milner to Chamberlain, 21 May 1902, JC 13/1/255; *Milner papers*, ii. 349.
[59] Milner to Chamberlain, 21 May 1902, JC 13/1/254.

are either anxious to upset negotiations or bluffing, in reliance on our weakness, probably the latter.'[60]

If Milner wanted any solace from Chamberlain then he was disappointed. Chamberlain – expressing his own view – stated that the mere question of money should not stand in the way of a settlement, especially as Kitchener thought the matter vital.[61] Chamberlain argued that 'There should be some argument more cogent than the money cost to justify risking a failure on this point.'[62] Nor was Chamberlain alone in thinking this; Ritchie – the home secretary – was concerned lest the talks break down over the financial issue because restarting the war might cause difficulties with public opinion, and increase those difficulties once the talks were published.[63] Brodrick told Kitchener that he supported him on this issue, the only anxiety being that 'we must find a way . . . to put it which will be less crude & offensive to loyalist sentiment both here & in S. Africa than that originally sketched out'.[64] Now that peace was in sight the government was becoming fearful that the talks would break down, especially over money. Ministers knew full well that no matter how they justified it, the public would never forgive them for throwing away a good opportunity for peace. Thus, as Lord Salisbury reported to the king, though ministers recognised that the financial element might prove difficult in relation to the loyalists and the Boers who had surrendered (and joined the National Scouts), they nevertheless accepted the proposal to advance £3m. and hoped the formula they had worked out would be accepted by all sides.[65] The government decided that a commission be set up to oversee the spending of the money for those who needed to rebuild farms and to resupply those unable to help themselves. At least they managed to avoid the impression that they were throwing money at the Boers to pay off their war debts; even so the amount was substantial, especially as it was obviously intended for the use of the burghers themselves and no one else in South Africa. In addition, the government was prepared to offer interest-free loans for two years. To this final draft, the delegates at Vereeniging had to answer yes or no.[66] Three days later the terms of peace were signed.

Milner did manage to salvage something from the talks: he gained the amnesty terms desired by both colonial ministries,[67] and the money clause had been made slightly easier to accept. However, he recognised he had not really achieved what he had set out to accomplish; as early as 11 May he

[60] Milner to Chamberlain, 21 May 1902, JC 13/1/255.
[61] Milner to Chamberlain, 23 May 1902, in *Milner papers*, ii. Milner retorted that Kitchener said this about 'every other Boer demand' (p. 354).
[62] Chamberlain to Milner, 22 May 1902, CAB 37/61/95.
[63] Ritchie to Chamberlain, 26 May 1902, JC 11/27/5.
[64] Brodrick to Kitchener, 24 May 1902, KP PRO 30/57/22/Y151.
[65] Salisbury to the king, 27, 29 May 1902, CAB 41/27/19, 20.
[66] Minutes of meeting, 28 May 1902, WO 32/8107.
[67] These clauses were not embodied in the final treaty. This was part of Milner's desire not to have promises put in a surrender document.

wrote, 'My political dreams may be done for, but I am not done for.'[68] And again on 30 May, 'It has been an awful ten days, but I saved more than I expected. . . . What with our sentimentality, our party system, our Government by Committee, our "Mandarins", our "Society" and our Generals . . . the game is just hopeless.'[69] Milner knew well enough that his achievement fell far short of the complete and decisive victory he had hoped and campaigned for, prior to and during the talks. As Ian Hamilton succinctly put it, 'K. feels a mountain off his chest. Milner feels his troubles are going to begin.'[70]

Unable to impose his own policy in South Africa, Milner waited to influence the peace talks instead. But here he came up against war weariness and the British government's concern with other issues. Owing to the nature of the conflict, he was unable to conduct the negotiations on his own, principally because the Boers despised him and the British government was uncertain about his commitment to a rapid peace. His long-term plans rested on replacing a Boer heartland by a British one in the Transvaal, and the gradual removal of Boer influence from South Africa. This, like his military ideas, was based on a premise that relied too much on unknown factors – in this case British immigration on a large scale. But, he also needed to eliminate possible Boer interference and therefore sought to destroy the Boer leadership: hence his reluctance to talk; his attempts to undermine their political credibility by making no concessions of any practical value; and his reliance on Kitchener's despised military system. However, Milner lacked the support of the British government, who, in the end, wanted the war to end more than they wanted to see Milner's vision of a British South Africa become a reality.

Kitchener saw better than Milner that the immediate reconstruction of South Africa needed the support of the Boer leadership, not their hostility. And for once his views dovetailed neatly into sentiments prevalent in Britain. His victory speech in Johannesburg summed up both his policy and those sentiments: 'judged as a whole, I maintain that they [Boers] are a virile race and an asset of considerable importance to the British Empire, for whose honour and glory I hope before long they may be fighting side by side with us'.[71]

However, to describe the final settlement merely as Kitchener's peace fails to account for the climate of opinion which pervaded headquarters, and was personified by General Hamilton. Kitchener's handling of the negotiations reflected not only his personal opinions, but those of many of his officers. In this respect, therefore, the peace concluded at Vereeniging was just as much the army's peace as it was Kitchener's.

As for Milner, he never accepted the situation created by the Treaty of

---

68 *Milner papers*, ii. 330.
69 Ibid. 364.
70 Hamilton to his wife, 31 May 1902, HP 25/12/2/27.
71 Cited in G. H. Cassar, *Kitchener: architect of victory*, London 1977, 135.

Vereeniging; for him, the South African struggle continued: 'It has changed its character: it is no longer war with bullets, but war it still is. . . . It is quite true we hold the winning cards, but it is not true that we have won the game, and we cannot afford to lose a single trick.'[72]

[72] Milner to Wilkinson, 27 Apr. 1903, National Army Museum, Spenser Wilkinson papers, 9011/42/17.

Conclusion

I

The South African War was a conflict of immense proportions; it was fought over a vast area, with nearly 500,000 British soldiers, against an enemy who posed a direct threat to the security of the empire. Moreover, owing to better communications it afforded the political authorities – both imperial and local – the opportunity to influence military operations on a scale hitherto unknown. Consequently, this book has attempted to answer the controversial question of control: how far were the political authorities determined to extend their constitutional supremacy into areas which the generals considered their own; and how far were soldiers willing to resist such interference or extend their own influence. Overall, the conclusion drawn by this book is that by 1902 the generals had managed to frustrate undue political hindrance and increase their own influence and authority over events in South Africa. Essentially, the book has argued that the army played a far greater role in shaping British attitudes and decisions during the war, and influenced the settlement to a far greater extent than has previously been acknowledged.

Britain's parliamentary system provided the framework within which civil–military relations operated. The civil–military balance firmly favoured the politicians, as Britain's generals, unlike many of their European counterparts, acknowledged the supremacy of their political superiors.[1] However, British civil–military relations were rarely harmonious owing to the disputes over army administration and reform, and these antagonisms carried over into the formulation of policy against the Boer republics.

The measures designed to deal with Boer intransigence during the period 1895–9 reflected the priorities of the government and ultimately the political dominance of civil–military relations. Although the government constantly consulted their military advisers as Anglo-Boer relations deteriorated, ministers usually modified advice to suit political requirements. During the 1897 crisis, for instance, the government adapted military advice to suit the vagaries of foreign and British public opinion. The military failed to appreciate that the government had to consider the political implications of the advice offered: public opinion, financial costs and electoral survival determined how the government would react to a particular crisis. Consequently, there was no real consensus between politicians and generals. Final decisions regarding the

---

[1] Spiers, *Late Victorian army*, 155, 175.

military support of political demands were usually compromises which displeased the generals even though they appeared to work.

The need to appease public opinion and a Gladstonian attitude towards costs ensured the government used the same methods to deal with Boer intransigence during the final crisis in 1899. Despite constant demands by the soldiers for the mobilisation of a strong force, the government prevaricated until the last moment, a fact which had a detrimental effect on the military situation in South Africa. Until then the government had controlled its relations with the generals: it had accepted military advice when compatible with political interests, and had not allowed the military either to assert undue influence, or to pressurise ministers into hasty decisions. However, with the outbreak of war and a succession of defeats arising from British military weakness in South Africa, government control of the generals began to slip.

British imperialism had greatly popularised the army and its successful generals, and practically immunised the military from criticism; for example, G. W. Steevens wrote that the officer who ordered the charge of the Twenty-First Lancers at Omdurman could not be punished because 'the populace had glorified the charge of the 21st for its indisputable heroism'.[2] This fervour undermined the government's ability to control the generals. The army was considered the victim of ministerial irresponsibility and procrastination during the pre-war crises, and political interference was blamed for the defeats in Natal. Although the government had tried to cultivate public opinion, it was not enough to absolve ministers from blame. The formulation of policy was the responsibility of government and that policy had failed. A nation accustomed to victory could not contemplate the fallibility of its military heroes. Instead, public opinion preferred to blame the politicians.

Domestically, the Unionist government had not been a great success before 1899. The conquest of the Boer republics in 1900 helped redeem its reputation, and enabled the government to win the general election that year, but it was only one of several factors contributing to the government's electoral success.[3] Yet even this success failed to revive an almost moribund ministry. The strain caused by the war, by events elsewhere in the world, and by domestic difficulties drained the government. Contemporaries noted how the war had exhausted leading ministers: Gibson Bowles, a prominent backbencher noted, 'Souls, Cecils . . . are alike found wanting and there has arisen the most profound exasperation with the Ministry, which, when so well provided, has done so ill.' Churchill realised, 'The Government is not very

[2] Trevor Royle, *War report: the correspondents' view of battle from the Crimea to the Falklands*, London 1987, 56.
[3] M. Bentley, *The climax of Liberal politics*, London 1987, 107; Price, *An imperial war*, 98–132; Blanch, 'British society and the war', 222–5.

strong. . . . The whole Treasury bench appears to me to be sleepy and exhausted and played out.'[4]

The government's appointment of Roberts was a last ditch measure by a ministry which had lost the confidence of the public and many of its own supporters. Ministers had performed badly as war leaders and needed Roberts to restore some faith in their ability. Consequently, Roberts was given *carte blanche* to correct the military situation. Only after he had conquered the Boer republics did the government feel confident enough to try and reassert its views and priorities.

However, the government could never insist the generals take note of their demands. In dealing with Roberts ministers were inhibited by public opinion and, in Lansdowne's case, by too much personal regard.[5] The government could not afford to become involved in a public dispute with Roberts over policy in South Africa. As a result, ministerial calls for the reduction of troop numbers and costs were hints and suggestions rather than direct orders. The government had to be circumspect in dealing with Roberts and had to gently cajole 'the greatest hero since Wellington'. By promoting him to commander-in-chief in Britain, the government felt able to start afresh with his successor, Kitchener.

Kitchener's appointment, however, marked the nadir of political control. This is not to say that the government meekly surrendered their authority. Kitchener had to fight hard to maintain his influence in order to fight the war his way. As his strategy relied on attrition to defeat the Boer commandos, Kitchener was dependent on large numbers of troops which kept costs high. In early 1901 outright victory seemed remote and progress was slow. Nevertheless, despite the prolonged guerilla war, the government remained fearful of public censure if it tried to interfere in Kitchener's management of the conflict. The main problem facing the government was that it had no alternative policy to offer. Instead, ministers were eventually forced to rely on Milner's scheme which promised large-scale reductions in costs and troop numbers.

Even so, Kitchener was able to thwart the implementation of Milner's scheme through a combination of sound military advice and the knowledge that the government had no other prominent general to replace him. Kitchener also had powerful support from Roberts, especially after the latter had clashed with Brodrick over army reform and discipline. Moreover, disputes between the service ministers and Hicks Beach weakened the government's

4 Cited in J. P. Cornford, 'The parliamentary foundations of the Hotel Cecil', in R. Robson (ed.), *Ideas and institutions of Victorian Britain: essays in honour of George Kitson Clark*, London 1967, 268–311 at p. 308; R. Churchill, *Winston S. Churchill: young statesman*, London 1967, 22–3.
5 Chamberlain remarked, 'while thoroughly agreeing with Lansdowne's principle of leaving the Generals a free hand, I always thought he might have asked a few more questions and occasionally have submitted his own views for consideration. No good official would ever complain or be discouraged by this': cited in Spies, *Methods of barbarism*, 300.

position still further. It was left to Lord Salisbury to acknowledge explicitly that the government was tied to Kitchener and was in no position to sack him, as Milner wanted. There was no guarantee that either a new general or different policy would end the war any faster. The government realised that Milner's policy, designed to protect occupied areas behind a screen of defences and mounted patrols, and to ignore the Boer commandos outside those screens until they accepted unconditional surrender, meant the war might continue indefinitely. Conversely, Kitchener's policy of attrition, followed by negotiations and lenient terms once the Boers had surrendered, offered the best hope of a rapid end to the war. By late 1901 the government preferred Kitchener's advice rather than that offered by Milner.

Relations between the British government and its generals throughout the period 1895-1902 reveal that a parliamentary government must rely on several factors when dealing with the military. First, it must have a system of consultation designed to harmonise the often conflicting priorities of politicians and generals. Secondly, it must have the support of public opinion whatever happens on the battlefield. Thirdly, it must have a sound scheme of its own for when it is dissatisfied with the current conduct of operations. Unfortunately for the British government it was unable to rely on these factors sufficiently to ensure it exercised complete control over the generals. Consequently, ministers were more dependent on the advice and opinions of those officers who dominated events in South Africa. Perhaps Lord Esher was correct when he wrote: 'In the long run, luck in War is on the side of statesmen, who by precedence and forethought bend it to their will.'[6]

II

For Milner it was essential from the beginning that the military should comply with political demands. In his dealings with Roberts, Milner was unable to assert his authority, to ensure the military conducted operations which suited his own aspirations. He was censured for expressing concern over the defenceless state of Cape Colony in 1900; and was frustrated by Roberts's reluctance to get the Uitlander refugees moved back to the Rand. The clash between Milner and Roberts was over priorities and whose should take preference. Roberts's needs were short-term and designed to help the immediate necessities of his army. Milner took the long-term view believing his priorities were essential for the future well-being of South Africa. Unfortunately for him, because of the continuation of the guerilla war, Roberts's requirements were deemed to be paramount.

Kitchener's appointment ended Milner's attempts to use the war as a means of reconstructing South Africa according to his own principles.

---

6 Cited in Hamer, British army, 174.

Kitchener was able to resist two attempts to undermine his authority, both
initiated by Milner. The first was an attempt to make him redirect his strategy
to suit political requirements. Milner convinced the British government that
the guerilla war was not 'proper' warfare: it was banditry and did not require
the services of high-ranking generals and large numbers of troops. Milner's
strategy meant that military operations might be scaled down to permit the
resumption of civilian life in the occupied areas. However, Kitchener's assertion that Cape Colony had to be cleared of guerillas first was virtually unargu-
able, particularly as Milner agreed this should be done. Kitchener was able,
therefore, to carry on fighting the war much as before without altering either
his strategy or methods. Milner's second attempt centred on his demand for
Kitchener's dismissal and replacement by a more pliable general. Forced to
choose between the two, the government opted for Kitchener and confirmed
that he was indispensable. The war had to be won and the government preferred to accept the advice and experience of the military expert. To change
the management of the war at this late stage offered too many uncertainties
and not enough hope. By 1902 Kitchener's position was secure; the British
government, exhausted by internal rivalries and problems elsewhere was in
no condition to back Milner and incur the odium of dismissing Kitchener.

In 1901 Milner had gained the support of the British government by offering an alternative strategy to Kitchener's relentless, and apparently fruitless,
pursuit of the Boer commandos. However, Kitchener and other officers began
to offer another policy of their own. This was tied into ideas about a peace
settlement then beginning to circulate. The alternative offered by the military was that to conclude peace the British authorities would have to negotiate with the Boers and drop the idea of 'unconditional surrender'. The Botha
talks revealed that Kitchener and Milner differed over the place of the Boer
leadership in a future South Africa. Kitchener favoured negotiations and
believed that a lasting agreement could only be achieved by including the
Boer generals in the peace process. In 1902 General Hamilton made himself
the mouthpiece of Kitchener's staff and nurtured the view that the British
should negotiate with the Boers, to preserve an anti-Johannesburg element in
the future South Africa.

Thus the army offered the British government the chance of an early and
lasting conclusion to the war, not the speculative ideas propagated by Milner,
who felt the war would peter out sometime in the future and that negotiations were unnecessary. As the British government needed a feasible scheme
to ensure peace, ministers inclined towards Kitchener's view and eventually
accepted his solution. During the final peace talks Milner remained isolated
and defensive, and tried desperately to salvage something from the negotiations. In 1897 he had described himself as a 'civilian soldier of the Empire',[7]
yet he lacked the soldier's view that the enemy could be worthy opponents.

7 Smith, *Origins*, 150.

He failed therefore because he was too rigid: he turned out to be neither soldierly nor politician enough to make his policies succeed.

Several historians have tended to dismiss the importance of the war and the eventual peace settlement in explaining the 'failure of Milnerism'.[8] However, this book has argued that Milner failed after the war because he was unable to obtain certain advantages during it. One of the most important was the exclusion of the Boer generals from the political leadership of the Boer people. Milner's relations with the generals were based on the prospect of the military providing a 'clean slate' for the reshaping of both South Africa and the Boer leadership. The first step for Milner had been to get the mines working again; the second step was the establishment of a para-military force designed to protect those willing to surrender to the British. Hence his clashes with Roberts over the refugees and the SAC. The third step was the isolation of the Boer generals as the new South Africa was created behind the SAC's protective screen. Kitchener's failure to provide this screen and his advocacy of talks with the Boer leadership undermined this third, and most important, step. Milner had even backed Kitchener's attempts to have the Boer leadership banished, but this revealed the underlying differences between Kitchener's and Milner's views. Kitchener believed the threat of banishment would induce the Boers to surrender; once achieved he then expected to negotiate terms; Milner wanted actual banishment and only decided the idea was a dead-letter in May 1902, at the conclusion of the peace talks.[9] The acknowledgment of the Boer generals as political leaders, which was implicit in the Treaty of Vereeniging, was the one thing Milner had fought hard to prevent throughout the war. The very fact that Botha and his colleagues had preserved their reputations and negotiated as leaders meant that in future their positions as rallying-points for an anti-Milner opposition was assured. For this the Boers had Kitchener and the army to thank. Milner never managed to turn the Transvaal into a 'British' colony. In the first place the economy took too long to recover, secondly the gold-mining industry suffered acute labour shortages which meant that it provided less income for Milner's reconstruction programme, and thirdly the expected influx of British settlers never materialised. Moreover, the decision made by

8 Le May sees the 'failure of Milnerism' coming after the treaty: *British supremacy*, ch. vii; Pakenham argues that as Milner prevented a date for self-government he had prevented a disastrous peace: *Boer war*, 570; Denoon is more explicit: 'We may confidently exclude the peace negotiations. . .as having any major bearing upon the failure of [post-war] imperial policy': *A grand illusion*, 230.
9 Denoon attributes Milner's abandonment of banishment to the idea that he wanted to secure the future peace of South Africa. This makes it seem that Milner was advocating leniency during the negotiations. Milner announced his 'conversion' on 27 May 1902, which seems rather late in the day to be thinking of future peace. Milner's advocacy was merely a face-saving formula and acknowledged that he had lost the struggle against the Boer generals. Leniency had nothing to do with it: Denoon, *A grand illusion*, 59; Milner to Chamberlain, 27 May 1902, in *Milner papers*, ii. 358.

Milner and the gold industry to import Chinese labour alienated opinion in Britain and among the British in South Africa, which weakened Milner's plans still further. With his schemes in tatters Milner eventually resigned in March 1905.

Meanwhile, the Boer generals helped coalesce Afrikaner resistance against the settlement and were instrumental in the formation of two political parties, Het Volk in the Transvaal and Orangia Unie in the ORC. Under Botha and Smuts, Het Volk's initial goal was responsible government for the Transvaal. Helped by a split in the Uitlander community caused by Milner's policies, Het Volk achieved its aim in 1907 when it won the colony's first post-war election. The following year, in the ORC, Orangia Unie secured the same result. In Britain the new Liberal government realised that Milner's schemes had largely failed and were prepared to grant concessions to a conciliatory Boer leadership. This culminated in 1910 with the establishment of the Union of South Africa which united the British colonies and the former republics. On 31 May 1910, exactly eight years after Vereeniging, General Louis Botha became the first prime minister of the new dominion.[10]

III

The greatest of the colonial conflicts closed a chapter in the way the British had conducted wars for nearly a hundred years, and immediately opened another as British policy-makers, civilian and military, were confronted by the lessons drawn from the South African War. One of the first realisations to emerge was the poor quality of many recruits, and was a major reason for the government's decision to address concerns about urban decay, establishing a royal commission to investigate the question which reported its findings in 1904.[11] Indeed, as I have suggested elsewhere, many army officers regarded the Boers as virtual replenishment stock and welcomed their addition to the empire.[12] In Britain the debate over the type of outsider deemed fit and ready to become British citizens reached a climax in 1905 with the passing of the Aliens Act. This legislation restricted the influx of Jewish immigrants into the country and was, in David Feldman's words, 'a revealing response to the creeping transformation of Britain's place in the world'. The act allowed into Britain only those considered to be healthy and wealthy, who would not be a burden on the taxpayer and not cause the national stock to deteriorate further. Unlike the Boers, who were lauded as a 'ruling race',[13] and accepted into

---

[10] For more see Warwick, The South African war, pt iii; T. R. H. Davenport, South Africa: a modern history, 4th edn, Basingstoke 1991, ch. ix.

[11] Parliamentary papers (1904), xxxii. Cd. 2175, 2210, 2186, 'Inter-Departmental committee on physical deterioration'.

[12] See ch. 8.

[13] G. W. Steevens, From Capetown to Ladysmith, London 1900, 64.

the imperial community, Jewish immigrants were excluded from the 'heart of empire'.[14]

The social inefficiency of immigrants was not the only area highlighted by the war and upon which social critics and commentators focused. The war inspired those involved in the growing cult of 'national efficiency' to call for a more business-like approach to politics, imperialism, social welfare and the conduct of war.[15] This last aspect was naturally a matter of great concern for the army and during the Edwardian period many officers expressed anxiety about the potential and ability of the working-class to fight a modern war.[16] For some, the most immediate requirement was healthier soldiers. Baden-Powell, perhaps the most famous officer pundit, brought his views and experiences to the public's attention by forming the Boy Scout movement. This drew upon the rural skills of the Boer commandos amongst others, and stressed the importance of the countryside for those confined within the inner cities.[17] Ian Hamilton endorsed Baden-Powell's work and also felt that the working-class would benefit from more outdoor exercise and military training.[18] For many officers, therefore, experience in South Africa influenced their thoughts about Britain's prospects in a future conflict and consequently helped fashion the doctrines with which the British army went to war in 1914.

The clash between the civil and military authorities over control in war is a constitutional problem most British governments have faced. It was not a new phenomenon encountered by politicians and generals in the First World War. The South African War caused serious problems between the civil and military authorities which anticipated those of 1914–18. In South Africa military influence over the course of the war was enhanced by the failure of the politicians to assert their authority. That is not to say that certain generals deliberately sought to strengthen their own power over the politicians. The enhancement of military authority and prestige during the South African War emanated from several factors, one of which was a defensive reaction to what the generals considered as undue political interference. The

[14] David Feldman, 'The importance of being English: Jewish immigration and the decay of liberal England', in David Feldman and Gareth Stedman Jones (eds), *Metropolis London: histories and representations since 1800*, London 1989, 56–84, and 'Nationality and ethnicity', 139–42.

[15] See G. R. Searle, *The quest for national efficiency: a study in British politics and British political thought, 1899–1914*, Oxford 1971, and *Country before party: coalitions and the idea of national government in modern Britain, 1885–1987*, London 1995, ch. iv.

[16] Travers, *The killing ground*, 37–42.

[17] Jeal, *Baden-Powell*, ch. x.

[18] General Sir Ian Hamilton, *National life and national training*, London 1913. For a more detailed look at publications by army officers during the Edwardian period see Travers, *The killing ground*, ch. ii. At the same time, the press also portrayed warfare in a positive manner and as beneficial for the British race: G. R. Wilkinson, ' "The blessings of war": depictions and images of war in Edwardian newspapers, 1899–1914', unpubl. PhD diss. Lancaster 1994, passim.

generals sought to preserve their professional authority and reputations, and were helped by the effects of imperialism, nationalism and the late nineteenth-century 'cult' of the military expert which produced a climate of opinion too ready to accept military expertise in army matters. The idea that war was too important to be left to the generals had not yet developed.

Kitchener was perhaps the most immediate beneficiary of this climate after 1902. Soon after taking office in India he clashed with the viceroy, Lord Curzon, over aspects of the military system. Eventually, the government in Britain was forced to choose between the politician and the war-hero. Curzon's resignation was duly accepted in London because not only was the expert's opinion taken at face value, but ministers also believed they would face the wrath of public opinion in Britain if Kitchener did not get his own way. Curzon, it seems, failed to appreciate the implications of the 'new imperialism' and the soldier's place within it.[19] Indeed, such was Kitchener's reputation and image of power and authority that in 1914 he became secretary of state for war, the first serving soldier to sit in the Cabinet since 1660.[20]

Nevertheless, very little had changed on the outbreak of war in 1914. Although this time certain plans existed, there still remained fundamental differences between politicians and generals (and amongst the generals themselves) over how those plans were to be interpreted. The crisis in 1914, like that in 1899, revealed, as John Gooch explains, that 'British soldiers . . . had no right of strategic authority and would always have to "sell" their preferred strategy to civilian politicians. Second, it revealed that the soldiers had neither an agreed strategy nor even an agreed reading of strategic principles.'[21] So much for the start of the war. Once hostilities opened and then bogged down in the trench stalemate, civil–military differences intensified, and this time they were further complicated by the need to take into account the interests of allies.[22] The relations between Lloyd George, after he became prime minister, and Field-Marshal Haig, who commanded British forces on the western front, and General Robertson, who was chief of the imperial general staff in London, mirrored in some ways the relations between Milner, Kitchener and Roberts. Although the relative positions and authority of each set of officials hardly bears comparison, the broad issues which embittered civil–military relations were much the same. Basically, just as Milner and Kitchener failed to agree on an overall strategy in South Africa, so too did Lloyd George and Haig. On the one hand Haig and Robertson wanted most, if not all, resources concentrated on the western front, and felt that the civil

19 For a recent account of the quarrel see David Gilmour, *Curzon*, London 1994, ch. xx.
20 Magnus, *Kitchener*, 332.
21 John Gooch, 'The weary titan: strategy and policy in Great Britain, 1890–1918', in Williamson Murray, MacGregor Knox, and Alvin Bernstein (eds), *The making of strategy: rulers, states, and war*, Cambridge 1994, 278–306 at p. 299.
22 For a recent appraisal of the alliance problem see W. J. Philpott, *Anglo-French relations and strategy on the Western Front, 1914–18*, London 1996.

authorities should meet their demands without let or hindrance. In this they were backed by the king and much of the press, especially that owned by Lord Northcliffe.[23] Lloyd George, on the other hand, as well as many other politicians, felt that if no clear-cut victories could be achieved on the western front then precedence should be given to the east, to the Balkan and Palestine fronts, in order to gain victories deemed necessary to sustain British domestic morale. Only when the Americans arrived in strength would the British then return to the offensive in the west.[24] The conflict between the two approaches reflected that age-old conundrum between politicians and soldiers in a parliamentary system, to which I have alluded throughout this book. Indeed, the quarrel between Lloyd George and Haig and Robertson demonstrated 'the extent to which Britain failed during the war to devise a political and military strategy acceptable to both civilians and military'.[25] And just like Milner with Kitchener, Lloyd George, at various times, contemplated Haig's removal, only to be told on one occasion that such a step would in all probability unseat the government. Indeed, Lloyd George faced problems similar to those encountered by Lord Salisbury's government when Kitchener's removal was discussed. Which general would have sufficient status to take over and thus be able to maintain confidence and morale, and would he be any more likely to finish the war? Would a change in strategy have the desired effect?[26] Unable to undermine the generals sufficiently (despite Lloyd George managing to remove Robertson) and, 'although they [the civilians] possessed the ultimate authority, [they] bowed almost without exception to the government's military advisers on all major strategic questions'. Lloyd George tried to buck the trend but 'he shrank from interfering directly with the generals' strategy because of the political consequences'.[27] It was, as Woodward and others have pointed out, left to Winston Churchill in World War Two to sort out and overcome the traditional divergence between the civil and military authorities.[28]

---

[23] French, *Strategy of the Lloyd George coalition*, 22–3, 51, 58–9, 153, 155, 164–5, 286–90; David Woodward, 'Britain in a continental war': the civil–military debate over the strategical direction of the Great War of 1914–1918, *Albion* xii (1980), 37–65 at p. 48; Blake, *Douglas Haig*, 41.

[24] French, *Strategy of the Lloyd George coalition*, 7–9, passim.

[25] Gooch, 'Weary titan', 306; French, ' "A one-man show"'?: civil–military relations during the First World War', in Smith, *Government and the armed forces*, 75–107 at pp. 89–90.

[26] Woodward, 'Britain in a continental war', 51; French, *Strategy of the Lloyd George coalition*, 59, 149, 164–5, 167–8, 218, 231–4.

[27] Woodward, 'Britain in a continental war', 65.

[28] Ibid. See also Woodward, *Lloyd George and the generals*, 335–6, and Alex Danchev, 'Waltzing with Winston: civil–military relations in the Second World War', in Smith, *Government and the armed forces*, 191–216.

Biographical appendix

The politicians

Balfour, Arthur James, 1st earl Balfour (1848–1930); educated Eton and Trinity College, Cambridge; Conservative MP Hertford (1874–85), East Manchester (1885–1906), City of London (1906–22); pres. local govt bd, 1885–6; chief secretary for Ireland, 1887; leader in the House of Commons and first lord of the Treasury, 1891–2, 1895–1902; prime minister, 1902–5; first lord of the Admiralty in the coalition govt, 1915; foreign secretary under Lloyd George, 1916–19; lord president of the council, 1919–22, 1925–9; earl, 1922.

Brodrick, William St John Fremantle, 9th viscount Midleton and 1st earl of Midleton (1856–1942); educated Eton and Balliol College, Oxford; Conservative MP West Surrey (1880–5), Guildford (1885–1906); financial secretary to War Office, 1886–92; under-secretary for war, 1895–8; under-secretary for foreign affairs, 1898–1900; secretary of state for war, 1900–3; secretary of state for India, 1903–5; viscount, 1907; earl, 1920.

Chamberlain, Joseph (1836–1914); educated University College school; chairman, National Education League of Birmingham, 1868; National Education League, 1870; mayor of Birmingham, 1873–5; Liberal MP Birmingham (1876), West Birmingham (1885–1906); Liberal Unionist 1886; joined Conservative (Unionist) government in 1895 as colonial secretary; resigned from office in 1903 to promote tariff reform.

Hely-Hutchinson, Rt-Hon. Sir Walter Francis (1849–1913); educated Harrow and Trinity College, Cambridge; served on colonial administrations in New South Wales and Fiji, 1874–7; colonial secretary of Barbados, 1877–83; served in Malta, 1883–9 (Lt-Gov. 1884–9); governor, Windward Islands, 1889–93; Natal and Zululand, 1893–1901; Cape Colony, 1901–10.

Hicks Beach, Sir Michael, 1st earl St Aldwyn (1837–1916); educated Eton and Christ Church, Oxford; Conservative MP East Gloucestershire (1864–85), West Bristol (1885–1906); parl. under-secretary, Poor Law Board, 1868; under-secretary Home Dept., 1868; chief secretary for Ireland, 1874–8; colonial secretary, 1878–80; chancellor of the exchequer and leader of the House of Commons, 1885–6; Irish secretary, 1886–7; pres. of Bd of Trade, 1888–92; chancellor of exchequer, 1895–1902; earl, 1915.

Lansdowne, Henry Charles Keith Petty-Fitzmaurice, 5th marquess of (1845–1927); educated Eton and Balliol College, Oxford; marquess, 1866; junior lord of the Treasury, 1869; under-secretary of state for war, 1872–4;

under-secretary of state for India, 1880; resigned from Liberal govt in 1880 over Irish policy; governor-general of Canada, 1883–8; viceroy of India, 1888–94; joined Unionist govt 1895; secretary of state for war, 1895–1900; foreign secretary, 1900–5; leader of Unionist party in the House of Lords, 1903–14.

Milner, Sir Alfred, Viscount (1854–1925); educated Germany, King's College, London, Balliol College, Oxford; joined staff of *Pall Mall Gazette*, 1882–5; secretary to George Goschen when chancellor of the exchequer, 1887–9; director of accounts and under-secretary for finance in Egypt, 1889–92; chairman of the Bd of Inland Revenue, 1892–7; high commissioner for South Africa, 1897–1905; governor, Cape Colony, 1897–1900; Transvaal and Orange River Colony, 1901–5; baron, 1901; viscount, 1902; joined war cabinet, 1916; war secretary 1918; colonial secretary, 1918–21.

Salisbury, Robert Arthur Talbot Gascoyne-Cecil, 3rd marquess of (1830–1903); educated Eton and Christ Church, Oxford; Conservative MP Stamford, 1853–68; succeeded brother as Viscount Cranborne, 1865; secretary of state for India, 1866–7, 1874–8; marquess, 1868; foreign secretary, 1878–80; prime minister and foreign secretary, 1885–6; prime minister, foreign secretary and first lord of the Treasury, 1886–92; prime minister and foreign secretary, 1895–1900; prime minister, 1900–2.

Selborne, William Waldegrave Palmer, 2nd earl of (1859–1942); educated Winchester and University College, Oxford; became Liberal Unionist 1886; MP Petersfield (1886–92), West Edinburgh (1892–5); earl, 1895; under-secretary of state for the colonies, 1895–1900; first lord of the Admiralty, 1900–5; succeeded Milner as South African high commissioner, 1905–10; prominent in House of Lords, 1911–14; president of the Board of Agriculture, 1915–16.

The soldiers

Altham, Sir Edward, lieutenant-general (1856–1943); educated Winchester and Christ Church College, Oxford; joined Royal Scots in 1876; served in Bechuanaland exp. 1884–5; intelligence division, War Office, 1897–9, 1900–4; passed staff college (psc), 1900; served in South Africa as asst. adjutant-general for intelligence, 1899–1900; general staff, South Africa, 1906–8; southern district command, in charge of administration, 1914; served in Dardenelles (Gallipoli), 1915; Egyptian Exp. force, 1916; quartermaster-general, India, 1917–19.

Ardagh, Sir John Charles, major-general (1840–1907); educated Trinity College, Dublin and Royal Military Academy, Woolwich; commissioned in Royal Engineers, 1858; deputy asst quartermaster-general, War Office, 1876; commanded intelligence dept Egypt, 1882; commandant, Cairo, 1884; asst adjutant-general for defence, War Office, 1887; private secretary to viceroy

(Lansdowne), 1888–94; director of military intelligence, 1896–1901; British army delegate at conference for revision of Geneva Convention, 1906.

Buller, Sir Redvers Henry (1839–1908); educated Eton; commissioned 1858; joined 60th Regt (King's Royal Rifle Corps), 1862; served in Red River exp. Canada, 1870; Ashanti, 1873; South Africa, 1878–9, 1881; won VC in Zulu war, 1879; Egypt, 1882; Sudan, 1884–5; under-secretary for Ireland, 1886; adjutant-general, 1890–7; Aldershot command, 1898; GOC-in-C (SA), 1899; GOC (Natal), 1900; resumed Aldershot command Jan. 1901; removed Oct. 1901.

Butler, Sir William Francis, lieutenant-general and author (1838–1910); no formal education; commissioned 69th Foot (The Welch Regt), 1858; served under Wolseley in Canada (Red River exp.), 1870; Ashanti, 1873; Natal, 1875; Egypt, 1882; Gordon Relief exp. Sudan, 1884–5; also served in Natal during the Zulu war, 1879; commanded garrison at Alexandria, 1890; commanded a brigade at Aldershot, 1893; south east district command, 1896–8; GOC(SA), 1898–9; western district command, 1899–1905. Married Elizabeth Thompson (Lady Butler) the famous battle artist, 1877.

Forestier-Walker, Sir Frederick, lieutenant-general (1844–1910); educated Royal Military Academy Sandhurst; commissioned in Scots Guards, 1862; served in Mauritius, 1866–7; on staff in Cape Colony, 1873–9, first as asst. military secretary to the GOC(SA), secondly as military secretary to the high commissioner; on active service in South Africa, 1875, 1877–8, 1879 (Zulu war); served on Bechuanaland exp. 1884–5; brigadier-general, Aldershot, 1889–90; major-general commanding, Egypt, 1890–5; western district command, 1895–9; replaced Butler in South Africa, Sept. 1899; GOC lines of communication, 1899–1901; governor of Gibraltar, 1905.

Hamilton, Sir Ian Standish Monteith (1853–1947); educated Wellington College and Sandhurst; posted to 92nd Foot (Gordon Highlanders), 1873; wounded at Majuba hill, 1881; ADC to Sir Frederick Roberts, 1882–90; asst adjutant-general musketry, Bengal, 1890–3; military secretary to General White, 1893–5; deputy quartermaster-general, Simla, 1895–7; commandant, musketry school, Hythe, 1898; at siege of Ladysmith, 1899–1900; commanded mounted infantry division, 1900; military secretary, War Office, 1900–1; chief of staff to Lord Kitchener, 1901–2; commanded final drive against Boers in western Transvaal, 1902; military secretary, War Office, 1902–3; quartermaster-general, 1903–4; southern district command, 1905–9; adjutant-general, 1909–10; Mediterranean command, and inspector-general of overseas force, 1910–14; central command, 1914–15; commanded Mediterranean expedition (Dardenelles and Gallipoli campaign), 1915.

Kitchener, Horatio Herbert, field-marshal, 1st earl Kitchener of Khartoum and Broome (1850–1916); educated Royal Military Academy, Woolwich; commissioned in Royal Engineers, 1871; served in French ambulance unit,

Franco-Prussian war, 1871; Palestine Exploration Fund, 1874; surveyed Cyprus, 1878; second in command, Egyptian cavalry, 1882; served in Sudan, 1884–5; governor-general eastern Sudan, 1886; adjutant-general of Egyptian army, 1888; Sirdar (C-in-C) of Egyptian army, 1892–9; commanded army which successfully conquered the Sudan, 1896–8; governor-general of Sudan, 1899; chief of staff to Lord Roberts in South Africa, 1900; C-in-C, South Africa, 1900–2; C-in-C, India, 1902–9; field-marshal, 1909; British agent and consul-general, Egypt, 1911–14; earl, 1914; secretary of state for war, 1914–16; drowned at sea on a mission to Russia, 1916.

Methuen, Paul Sandford, field-marshal, 3rd Baron Methuen (1845–1932); educated Eton; joined Scots Fusilier Guards, 1864; commanded Methuen's Horse, Bechuanaland exp., 1884–5; baron, 1891; home district command, 1892–7; commanded 1st Div. South Africa, 1899–1900; commanded at battles of Modder river and Magersfontein, 1899; column commander thereafter; wounded and captured at Tweebosch, 7 Mar. 1902; eastern command, 1905–8; GOC-in-C (SA), 1908–12; field-marshal, 1911; gov. and C-in-C Malta, 1915–19.

Rawlinson, Sir Henry Seymour, 2nd baronet and Baron Rawlinson (1864–1925); educated Eton and Sandhurst; joined King's Royal Rifle Corps, 1884; ADC to Sir Frederick Roberts, 1886 (served in Burma, 1886); transferred to Coldstream Guards, 1892; psc and appointed brigade-major at Aldershot, 1895; served on Kitchener's staff in Sudan campaign, 1897–8; on staff of Sir George White in Natal, siege of Ladysmith, 1899–1900; served on Kitchener's staff and as column commander in South Africa, 1900–2; commandant, Staff College, 1903–6; major-general, 1909; commander, 3rd Division, 1910–14; commander, 4th Army, 1915–19; C-in-C India, 1920–5.

Roberts, Frederick Sleigh, field-marshal, 1st Earl Roberts of Kabul and Kandahar (1832–1914); educated Sandhurst and Addiscombe; commissioned 1851 in Bengal artillery; served in Indian mutiny, 1857–8; won VC during the mutiny, 1858; served on Abyssinian exp., 1868; quartermaster-general India, 1875; successfully commanded operations in Afghanistan, 1878–80, including the famous march from Kabul to Kandahar, 1880; C-in-C Madras army, 1880; India, 1885–93; field-marshal, 1895; C-in-C Ireland, 1895–99; South Africa, 1899–1900; earl, 1900; C-in-C Britain, 1900–5; campaigned for national service, 1905–14; colonel-in-chief of Indian exp. force to France, 1914.

White, Sir George Stuart, field-marshal (1835–1912); educated Sandhurst; entered army 1853; served in Indian mutiny, 1857–8; won VC in Afghan war, 1879; served in Burma war, 1885–7; on North-West Frontier, 1889; Baluchistan, 1893; C-in-C India, 1893–7; quartermaster-general, War Office, 1897; GOC Natal, 1899, commanded garrison during the siege of Ladymsith; governor of Gibraltar, 1900–5; field-marshal, 1903.

Wolseley, Garnet Joseph, field-marshal, Viscount (1833–1913); commissioned 1852, joined 12th Foot (Suffolk Regt); served in Burma war, 1852–3; Crimea, 1854–6; Indian mutiny, 1857–8; China war, 1860; asst quartermaster-general, Canada, 1861; commanded Red River exp. Canada, 1870; asst adjutant-general, War Office, 1871; commanded Ashanti exp., 1873–4; administrator and GOC, Natal, 1875; first administrator, Cyprus, 1878; administrator of Zululand and Transvaal, 1879–80; quartermaster-general, War Office, 1880–2; adjutant-general, 1882; commanded Egyptian exp., 1882; Gordon relief exp., 1884–5; viscount, 1885; C-in-C Ireland, 1890–5; field-marshal, 1894; C-in-C Britain, 1895–1900.

Wood, Sir Henry Evelyn, field-marshal (1838–1919); joined Royal Navy, 1854; transferred to army and commissioned into 13th Light Dragoons, 1855; won VC in India 1859; psc, 1864; served in Ashanti, 1873–4; Zululand, 1879; Natal 1881; royal commissioner for settlement of the war with the Transvaal, 1881; served in Egypt, 1882; Sirdar of Egyptian army, 1882–6; eastern district command, Britain, 1886; Aldershot command, 1889; quartermaster-general, War Office, 1893; adjutant-general, 1897–1900; field-marshal, 1903.

Select Bibliography

Unpublished primary sources

Birmingham University Library
Joseph Chamberlain papers

Hatfield, Hatfield House
Third marquess of Salisbury papers

Hove, Hove Central Library
Wolseley papers

London, Liddell Hart Centre for Military Archives, King's College London
Ian Hamilton papers

London, National Army Museum
6803–4/4 Marker papers
7807/25 Maxwell papers
5201/33 Rawlinson papers
7101/23 Roberts papers
9011/42 Spenser Wilkinson papers

London, Public Record Office, Kew
CAB 37 Cabinet records, general papers
CAB 41 Cabinet records, letters to the monarch
CO 48 Colonial Office, Cape Colony files
CO 179 Colonial Office, Natal files
CO 224 Colonial Office, Orange River Colony files
CO 291 Colonial Office, Transvaal files
CO 417 Colonial Office, High Commission files
CO 879 Colonial Office, Confidential files
PRO 30/40 Ardagh papers
PRO 30/57 Kitchener papers
PRO 30/67 Midleton papers (St John Brodrick)
WO 32, 33 War Office, Miscellaneous papers on the South African war
WO 108 War Office, South African war papers
WO 105 War Office, Roberts papers
WO 132 War Office, Buller papers

Oxford, Bodleian Library
Alfred Milner papers
Violet Milner papers

Published primary sources

Official publications

Intelligence Dept., Section B. (War Office), *Military notes on the Dutch republics of South Africa, War Office June 1899*, York 1983

Hansard parliamentary debates, 4th ser. 1899–1902

Mercer, W. E. and A. E. Collins, *The Colonial Office list*, London 1899

Parliamentary papers

PP(1900), lvi

Cd.43, 'Further correspondence relating to affairs in South Africa' (in continuation of [c. 9530], 1899)

Cd.44, 'Correspondence relating to the defence of Natal'

Cd.261, 'Further correspondence relating to affairs in South Africa' (in continuation of [Cd.43], 1900)

Cd.264, 'Correspondence relating to affairs of the Cape Colony'

Cd.420, 'Further correspondence relating to affairs in South Africa'

Cd.426, 'Proclamations issued by Field Marshal Lord Roberts in South Africa'

PP(1901), xlvii

Cd.457, 'Despatches relating to the war in South Africa', vol. i

Cd.458, 'Natal Field Army', vol. ii

Cd.463, 'Supplementary despatches relating to the war in South Africa'

Cd.522, 'Despatches by General Lord Kitchener, dated 8th March 1901, relative to military operations in South Africa'

Cd.528, 'Papers relating to negotiations between Commandant Louis Botha and Lord Kitchener'

Cd.546, 'Letter from Commandant Louis Botha to Lord Kitchener, dated 13th February 1901'

Cd.547, 'Further correspondence relating to affairs in South Africa' (in continuation of [Cd.420], 1900)

Cd.663, 'Further papers relating to negotiations between Commandant Louis Botha and Lord Kitchener' (in continuation of [Cd.528] 1901 and [Cd.546] 1901)

Cd.732, 'Correspondence relating to the prolongation of hostilities in South Africa'

PP(1902), lxvii

Cd.903, 'Further correspondence relating to affairs in South Africa' (in continuation of [Cd.547] 1901)

Cd.1163, 'Further correspondence relating to affairs in South Africa' (in continuation of [Cd.903] 1902)

PP(1904) xl

Cd.1789, 'Report of His Majesty's Commissioners appointed to inquire into the military preparations, and other matters connected with the war in South Africa'

Cd.1790, 'Minutes of evidence taken before the Royal Commission on the war in South Africa', vol. i

PP(1904), xli

Cd.1791, 'Minutes of evidence taken before the Royal Commission on the war in South Africa', vol. ii

PP(1904), xlii
Cd.1792, 'Appendices to the minutes of evidence taken before the Royal Commission on the war in South Africa'

Published diaries and correspondence

The crisis of power: the imperial and naval papers of the second earl of Selborne 1895–1910, ed. D. G. Boyce, London 1990
FitzPatrick: South African politician: selected papers 1888–1906, ed. A. H. Duminy and W. R. Guest, Johannesburg 1976
In relief of Gordon: Lord Wolseley's campaign journal of the Khartoum relief expedition, 1884–1885, ed. A. Preston, London 1967
Journals and letters of Reginald Viscount Esher, ed. M. V. Brett, London 1934–8
The Leo Amery diaries, ed. J. Barnes and D. Nicholson, London 1980–8
The letters of Lord and Lady Wolseley 1870–1911, ed. Sir George Arthur, London 1922
The letters of Queen Victoria, 3rd ser., ed. G. E. Buckle, London 1932
The life and letters of George Wyndham, ed. J. W. Mackail and G. Wyndham, London 1926
The Milner papers, ed. C. Headlam, London 1931–5
The private papers of Douglas Haig 1914–1919, ed. R. Blake, London 1952
The pro-Boers: anatomy of an anti-war movement, ed. S. Koss, Chicago 1973
Roberts in India: the military papers of Field-Marshal Lord Roberts 1876–1893, ed. B. Robson, Stroud 1993
'Select documents from the Chamberlain papers concerning Anglo-Transvaal relations 1896–9', ed. E. Drus, Bulletin of the Institute of Historical Research xxvii (1954), 156–89

Contemporary works

'Administrator', 'The army and the administration', Fortnightly Review lxvii (1900), 353–61
Amery, L. (ed.), The Times history of the war in South Africa 1899–1902, London 1900–9
'An average observer', The burden of proof: or England's debt to Sir Redvers Buller, London 1902
'An Englishman' [H. W. Wilson], 'The causes of reverse', National Review xxxiv (1900), 830–42
'An officer', 'The government and the war', Contemporary Review lxxvi (1899), 761–73
Anon. [C. E. Callwell], 'A Boer war: the military aspect', Blackwood's Magazine clxvi (1899), 259–65
Anon. [G. F. R. Henderson], 'The war in South Africa', Edinburgh Review cxci (1900), 247–78
Anon. [J. F. Maurice], 'The South African war and its critics', Edinburgh Review cxcii (1900), 229–46
'A soldier' [W. E. Cairnes], 'Some reflections on the war in South Africa', MacMillan's Magazine lxxxi (1900), 313–20
Burleigh, B., The Natal campaign, London 1900
Cairnes, Capt. W. E., An absent minded war, London 1900

Callwell, Col. C., *Small wars: a tactical textbook for imperial soldiers*, 1906 edn, repr. London 1990

Churchill, W. S., *The Boer war: London to Ladysmith and Ian Hamilton's march*, first publ. 1900, repr. London 1990

Crosthwaite, Sir C., *The pacification of Burma*, London 1912

Doyle, Sir A. Conan, *The great Boer War*, London 1900–2

Evans-Gordon, Maj. W., *The Cabinet and war*, London 1904

Griffiths, A., 'The conduct of the war', *Fortnightly Review* lxvii (1900), 1–10

Hamilton, Gen. Sir Ian, *National life and national training*, London 1913

Hobson, J. A., *The war in South Africa: its causes and effects*, London 1900

—————— *The psychology of jingoism*, London 1901

—————— *Imperialism: a study*, 3rd edn 1902, repr. London 1938

The intelligence officer, *On the heels of De Wet*, London 1903

Iwan Muller, E. B., *Lord Milner and South Africa*, London 1902

Kestell, J. D., *Through shot and flame*, London 1903

Maurice, J. F. and M. H. Grant, *Official history of the war in South Africa*, London 1906–10

Phillipps, L. March, *With Rimington*, London 1901

Steevens, G. W., *From Cape Town to Ladysmith*, London 1900

The Times Newspaper

Wheeler, Capt. O., *The War Office: past and present*, London 1914

Wilkinson, H. Spenser, *British policy in South Africa*, London 1899

—————— *Lessons of the war*, London 1900

—————— *War and policy*, London 1900

Wilson, H. W., *With the flag to Pretoria*, London 1900–2

—————— *After Pretoria: the guerilla war*, London 1902

Worsfold, B., *Lord Milner's work in South Africa*, London 1906

Military memoirs and biographies

Arthur, Sir G., *Life of Kitchener*, London 1920

Ballard, C., *Kitchener*, London 1936

Birdwood, Lord, *Khaki and gown: an autobiography*, London 1941

Butler, L., *Redvers Buller*, London 1909

Butler, W. F., *An autobiography*, London 1911

Cassar, G. H., *Kitchener: architect of victory*, London 1977

Collier, B., *Brasshat: a biography of Field-Marshal Sir Henry Wilson*, London 1961

De Groot, G. J., *Douglas Haig 1861–1928*, London 1988

de Watteville, Lt-Col. H., *Lord Roberts*, London 1938

Durand, M., *The life of Field-Marshal Sir George White VC*, Edinburgh–London 1915

Farwell, B., *Eminent Victorian soldiers: seekers of glory*, London 1986

Fuller, J. F. C., *The last of the gentlemen's wars*, London 1937

Gardner, B., *Allenby*, London 1965

Hamilton, Gen. Sir Ian, *Listening for the drums*, London 1944

—————— *The commander*, ed. Maj. A. Farrar-Hockley, London 1957

Hamilton, Ian, *A life of General Sir Ian Hamilton*, London 1966

Hannah, W. H., *Bobs: Kipling's general*, London 1972

Holmes, R., *The little field-marshal: Sir John French*, London 1981

James, D., *Lord Roberts*, London 1954

Jeal, T., *Baden-Powell*, London 1989

Lehmann, J., *All Sir Garnet: a life of Field-Marshal Lord Wolseley*, London 1966

Lyttelton, Gen. Sir N. G., *Eighty years: soldiering, politics and games*, London 1927

McCourt, E., *Remember Butler: the story of Sir William Butler*, London 1967

Magnus, P., *Kitchener: portrait of an imperialist*, Harmondsworth 1968

Malmesbury, Susan, countess of, *The life of Major-General Sir John Ardagh*, London 1909

Maurice, Sir F., *The life of General Lord Rawlinson of Trent*, London 1928

—— and Sir G. Arthur, *The life of Lord Wolseley*, London 1924

Maxwell, C., *Frank Maxwell: a memoir and some letters edited by his wife*, London 1921

Melville, C. H., *The life of the Rt-Hon. Sir Redvers Buller*, London 1923

Powell, G., *Buller: a scapegoat?: a life of General Sir Redvers Buller VC*, London 1994

Royle, T., *The Kitchener enigma*, London 1985

Seely, J. E. B., *Adventure*, London 1930

Warner, P., *Kitchener*, London 1985

Williams, W. W., *The life of General Sir Charles Warren*, Oxford 1941

Wood, Field-Marshal Sir H. E., *From midshipman to field-marshal*, London 1906

Political memoirs and biographies

Amery, L. S., *My political life*, London 1953–5

Churchill, R. S. and M. Gilbert, *Winston S. Churchill*, London 1967–89

Curtis, L., *With Milner in South Africa*, Oxford 1951

Dugdale, B., *Arthur James Balfour*, London 1936

Duminy, A. H. and W. Guest, *Interfering in politics: a biography of Sir Percy Fitz-Patrick*, Johannesburg 1987

Egremont, M., *Balfour: a life of Arthur James Balfour*, London 1980

Fraser, P., *Joseph Chamberlain*, London 1966

—— *Lord Esher: a political biography*, London 1973

Garvin, J. L. and J. Amery, *The life of Joseph Chamberlain*, London 1932–69

Gollin, A. M., *Proconsul in politics: Milner*, London 1964

Hicks Beach, Lady V., *Life of Sir Michael Hicks Beach*, London 1932

Judd, D., *Radical Joe: a life of Joseph Chamberlain*, London 1977

Lee, Sir S., *King Edward VII: a biography*, London 1927

Mackay, R. F., *Balfour: intellectual statesman*, Oxford 1985

Marlowe, J., *Milner: apostle of Empire*, London 1976

Marsh, P., *Joseph Chamberlain: entrepreneur in politics*, London 1994

Midleton, the earl of, *Records and reactions 1856–1939*, London 1939

Newton, Lord, *Lord Lansdowne: a biography*, London 1929

O'Brien, T. H., *Milner*, London 1979

Wilkinson, H. Spenser, *Thirty-five years 1874–1909*, London 1933

Wrench, J. E., *Milner: the man of no illusions*, London 1958

Young, K., *Arthur James Balfour: the happy life of the politician, prime minister, statesman and philosopher 1848–1930*, London 1963

Zebel, S., *Balfour: a political biography*, Cambridge 1973

Secondary sources

[Some works cited in the footnotes have not been reproduced in the list below.
They are recommended for further reading on topics upon
which this book touches.]

Anderson, D. M. and D. Killingray, 'Consent, coercion and colonial control: policing the empire, 1830–1940', in D. M. Anderson and D. Killingray (eds), *Policing the empire: government, authority and control, 1830–1940*, Manchester 1991, 1–15

Bailes, H., 'Patterns of thought in the late Victorian army', *Journal of Strategic Studies* iv (1981), 29–45

Beckett, I., 'The Stanhope memorandum of 1888: a reinterpretation', *Bulletin of the Institute of Historical Research* lvii (1984), 240–7

Belich, J., *The Victorian interpretation of racial conflict: the Maori, the British, and the New Zealand wars*, Montreal 1989

Bentley, M., *Politics without democracy*, London 1984
———— *The climax of Liberal politics*, London 1987

Benyon, J., *Proconsul and paramountcy in South Africa*, Pietermaritzburg 1980
———— 'Overlords of empire? British "pro-consular imperialism" in comparative perspective', *JICH* xix (1990), 164–202

Blanch, M. D., 'British society and the war', in Warwick, *The South African war*, 210–38

Bond, B., 'The late Victorian army', *History Today* xi (1961), 616–24
———— 'The retirement of the Duke of Cambridge', *Journal of the Royal United Services Institution* cvi (1961), 544–53
———— *The Victorian army and the Staff College 1854–1914*, London 1972
———— 'Introduction', in B. Bond (ed.), *Victorian military campaigns*, 2nd edn, London 1994, 3–29
———— 'The South African War, 1880–1', in Bond, *Victorian military campaigns*, 199–240

Brookes, E. H. and C. De B. Webb, *A history of Natal*, Natal 1965

Burroughs, P., 'Imperial defence and the Victorian army', *JICH* xv (1986), 55–73

Cammack, D., *The Rand at war 1899–1902: the Witwatersrand and the Anglo-Boer war*, London 1990

Coleman, B., *Conservatism and the Conservative party in nineteenth-century Britain*, London 1988

Cornford, J. P., 'The parliamentary foundations of the Hotel Cecil', in R. Robson (ed.), *Ideas and institutions of Victorian Britain: essays in honour of George Kitson Clark*, London 1967, 268–311

Cunningham, H., 'The language of patriotism 1750–1914', *HW* xii (1981), 8–33

Danchev, A., 'Waltzing with Winston: civil–military relations in the Second World War', in Smith, *Government and the armed forces*, 191–216

Davey, A., *The British pro-Boers*, London 1978

Denoon, D. A., *A grand illusion: the failure of imperial policy in the Transvaal Colony during the period of reconstruction 1900–1905*, London 1973

Duminy, A. H., *Sir Alfred Milner and the outbreak of the Anglo-Boer War*, Durban 1976

Dunlop, J. K., *The development of the British army 1899–1914*, London 1938

Ehrman, J., *Cabinet government and war 1890–1940*, Cambridge 1958

Farwell, B., *The great Boer war*, New York 1977

Feldman, D., 'The importance of being English: Jewish immigration and the decay of liberal England', in D. Feldman and G. Stedman Jones (eds), *Metropolis London: histories and representations since 1800*, London 1989, 56–84

───── 'Nationality and ethnicity', in Paul Johnson (ed.), *Twentieth-century Britain: economic, social and cultural change*, Harlow 1994, 127–48

Ferguson, T. G., *British military intelligence 1870–1914*, London 1984

Finer, S. E., *The man on horseback: the role of the military in politics*, 2nd edn, London 1988

Flournoy, F. R., *Parliament and war*, London 1927

French, D., *British strategy and war aims, 1914–1916*, London 1986

───── *The British way in warfare 1688–2000*, London 1990

───── *The strategy of the Lloyd George coalition, 1916–1918*, Oxford 1995

───── ' "A one-man show"?: civil–military relations during the First World War', in Smith, *Government and the armed forces*, 75–108

Friedberg, A. L., 'Britain faces the burden of empire: the financial crisis of 1901–5', *War and Society* v (1987), 15–37

───── *The weary titan: Britain and the experience of relative decline 1895–1905*, Princeton 1988

Fuller, Maj.-Gen. J. F. C., *The conduct of war 1789–1961*, London 1979

Gibbs, N. H., *The origins of imperial defence*, Oxford 1955

Gooch, J., *The plans of war: the general staff and British military strategy c. 1900–1916*, London 1974

───── *The prospect of war*, London 1981

───── 'The weary titan: strategy and policy in Great Britain, 1890–1918', in W. Murray, M. Knox and A. Bernstein (eds), *The making of strategy: rulers, states, and war*, Cambridge 1994, 278–306

───── 'Adversarial attitudes: servicemen, politicians and strategic policy in Edwardian England, 1899–1914', in Smith, *Government and the armed forces*, 53–74

Gordon, D. C., *The Dominion partnership in imperial defense, 1870–1914*, Baltimore 1965

Gordon, H., *The War Office*, London 1935

Green, E. H. H., *The crisis of Conservatism: the politics, economics and ideology of the British Conservative party*, London 1995

Grenville, J. A. S., *Lord Salisbury and foreign policy: the close of the nineteenth century*, London 1964

Grundlingh, A., ' "Protectors and friends of the people"?: the South African Constabulary in the Transvaal and Orange River Colony, 1900–08', in Anderson and Killingray, *Policing the empire*, 168–82

Gwynn, S., 'The writings and opinions of General Sir William Butler', *The Nineteenth Century and After* lxix (1911), 314–28

Halperin, V., *Lord Milner and the empire*, London 1952

Hamer, W., *The British army: civil–military relations 1885–1905*, Oxford 1970

Harries-Jenkins, G., *The army in Victorian society*, London 1977

Howard, M. (ed.), *Soldiers and governments*, London 1957

───── *The causes of wars and other essays*, 2nd edn. London 1983

Johnson, F. A., *Defence by committee: the British Committee of Imperial Defence 1885–1959*, London 1960

Judd, D., *Balfour and the British empire*, London 1968

———— *The Boer War*, London 1977

Kruger, R., *Goodbye Dolly Gray*, London 1967

Lehmann, J., *The first Boer War*, 2nd edn, London 1985

Le May, G. H., *British supremacy in South Africa 1899–1907*, Oxford 1965

Mackenzie, J., *Propaganda and empire*, Manchester 1984

———— (ed.), *Imperialism and popular culture*, Manchester 1986

———— (ed.), *Popular imperialism and the military 1850–1950*, Manchester 1992

Marais, J. S., *The fall of Kruger's republic*, Oxford 1961

Marks, S. and S. Trapido, 'Lord Milner and the South African state', *HW* viii (1979), 50–80

Marsh, P., *The discipline of popular government: Lord Salisbury's domestic statecraft 1881–1902*, Brighton 1978

Marshall, P. (ed.), *The Cambridge illustrated history of the British empire*, Cambridge 1996

Morris, J., *Farewell the trumpets*, Harmondsworth 1979

———— *Heaven's command*, Harmondsworth 1979

———— *Pax Britannica*, Harmondsworth 1979

Nimocks, W., *Milner's young men: the 'Kindergarten' in Edwardian imperial affairs*, London 1970

Omond, J. S., *Parliament and the army 1642–1904*, Cambridge 1933

Ovendale, R., 'Profits or patriotism: Natal, the Transvaal, and the coming of the second Anglo-Boer War', *JICH* viii (1980), 209–34

Pakenham, T., *The Boer war*, London 1982

Pelling, H., *Popular politics and society in late Victorian Britain*, London 1968

Porter, A. N., 'Lord Salisbury, Mr Chamberlain and South Africa, 1895–9', *JICH* i (1972), 3–26

———— 'Sir Alfred Milner and the press 1897–9', *Historical Journal* xvi (1973), 323–39

———— *The origins of the South African war: Joseph Chamberlain and the diplomacy of imperialism 1895–9*, Manchester 1980

———— 'Lord Salisbury, foreign policy and domestic finance, 1860–1900', in R. Blake and H. Cecil (eds), *Salisbury: the man and his policies*, London 1987, 148–84

———— 'The South African War (1899–1902): context and motive reconsidered', *Journal of African History* xxxi (1990), 43–57

———— (ed.), *Atlas of British overseas expansion*, London 1991

Porter, B. J., *Critics of empire: British radical attitudes to colonialism in Africa 1895–1914*, London 1968

———— 'The pro-Boers in Britain', in Warwick, *The South African War*, 239–57

———— *The Lion's share: a short history of British imperialism 1850–1983*, 2nd edn, London 1984

Price, R., *An imperial war and the British working-class: working-class attitudes and reactions to the Boer War 1899–1902*, London 1972

Robinson, R. and J. Gallagher, with A. Denny, *Africa and the Victorians: the official mind of imperialism*, 2nd edn, London 1981

Royle, T., *War report: the correspondents' view of battle from the Crimea to the Falklands*, London 1987

Sampson, V. and I. Hamilton, *Anti-commando*, London 1931

Satre, L. J., 'St John Brodrick and army reform 1901–3', *Journal of British Studies* xv (1976), 117–39

Schreuder, D. M., *Gladstone and Kruger: Liberal government and colonial home rule 1880–5*, London 1969

Searle, G. R., *The quest for national efficiency: a study in British politics and political thought 1899–1914*, Oxford 1971

Shakow, Z., 'The defence committee: a forerunner of the Committee of Imperial Defence', *Canadian Historical Review* xxxvi (1955), 36–44

Sixsmith, Maj.-Gen. E. K. G., 'Kitchener and the guerrillas in the Boer War', *Army Quarterly* civ (1974), 203–14

Skelley, A. R., *The Victorian army at home*, London 1977

Smith, I. R., *The origins of the South African war 1899–1902*, London 1996

Smith, P. (ed.), *Government and the armed forces in Britain 1856–1990*, London 1996

Spiers, E. M., *The army and society 1815–1914*, London 1980

—— 'Reforming the infantry of the line 1900–1914', *Journal of the Society for Army Historical Research* lix (1981), 82–94

—— *The late Victorian army 1868–1902*, Manchester 1992

Spies, S. B., *Methods of barbarism?: Roberts and Kitchener and civilians in the Boer republics January 1900–May 1902*, Cape Town 1977

Springhall, J., *Youth, empire and society*, London 1977

Stearn, R. T., 'G. W. Steevens and the message of empire', *JICH* xvii (1989), 210–31

—— 'War correspondents and colonial war, c. 1870–1900', in Mackenzie, *Popular imperialism and the military*, 139–61

Stockwell, A. J., 'Power, authority, and freedom', in Marshall, *Cambridge illustrated history*, 147–84

Stokes, E., 'Milnerism', *Historical Journal* v (1962), 47–60

Summers, A., 'Militarism in Britain before the Great War,' *HW* ii (1976), 104–23

—— 'Edwardian militarism', in R. Samuel, (ed.), *Patriotism: the making and unmaking of British national identity*, London 1989, i. 236–56

Surridge, K. T., ' "All you soldiers are what we call pro-Boer": the military critique of the South African war 1899–1902', *History* lxxxii (1997), 582–600

Sweetman, J., (ed.), *Sword and mace: twentieth century civil–military relations in Britain*, London 1986

Symons, J., *Buller's campaign*, London 1963

Taylor, M., 'Imperium et libertas? Rethinking the radical critique of imperialism during the nineteenth century', *JICH* xix (1991), 1–23

Thompson, L., *A history of South Africa*, London 1990

Thornton, A. P., *The imperial idea and its enemies: a study in British power*, London 1959

Travers, T., *The killing ground: the British army, the western front and the emergence of modern warfare 1900–1918*, London 1990

Trebilcock, C., 'War and the failure of industrial mobilisation: 1899–1914', in J. M. Winter (ed.), *War and economic development: essays in memory of David Joslin*, Cambridge 1975, 139–64

Tucker, A. V., 'Army and society in England 1870–1900: a reassessment of the Cardwell Reforms', *Journal of British Studies* ii (1963), 110–41

———— 'Politics and the army in the Unionist government in England 1900–05', *Report of the Canadian Historical Association* (1964), 105–19

Walker, E. A., 'Lord Milner and South Africa', *Proceedings of the British Academy* xxviii (1942), 155–78

———— (ed.), *The Cambridge history of the British empire*, 2nd edn, Cambridge 1963

Warwick, P. (ed.), *The South African war: the Anglo-Boer war 1899–1902*, Harlow 1980

Wilde, R. H., *Joseph Chamberlain and the South African Republic 1895–9*, Pretoria 1956

Wilkinson-Latham, R. J., *From our special correspondent: Victorian correspondents and their campaigns*, London 1979

Williams, R., *Defending the empire: the Conservative party and British defence policy 1899–1915*, London 1991

Wilson, M. and L. Thompson (eds), *The Oxford history of South Africa*, Oxford 1969–71

Woodward, D. R., 'Britain in a continental war: the civil–military debate over the strategical direction of the Great War of 1914–1918', *Albion* xii (1980), 37–65

———— *Lloyd George and the generals*, Newark, Del. 1983

Unpublished theses

Kochanski, H., 'Field-Marshal Viscount Wolseley: a reformer at the War Office, 1871–1900', unpubl. PhD diss. London 1996

Moon, H. R., 'The invasion of the United Kingdom: public controversy and official planning 1888–1918', unpubl. PhD diss. London 1968

Page, A. H., 'The supply services of the British army in the South African war 1899–1902,' unpubl. DPhil. diss. Oxford 1976

Stearn, R. T., 'War images and image makers in the Victorian era: aspects of the British visual and written portrayal of war and defence c. 1866–1906', unpubl. PhD diss. London 1987

Stone, M. S., 'The Victorian army: health, hospitals and social conditions as encountered by British troops during the South African war, 1899–1902', unpubl. PhD diss. London 1993

Surridge, K. T., 'British civil–military relations and the South African war 1899–1902', unpubl. PhD diss. London 1994

Ward, P. J., 'Englishness, patriotism and the British left 1881–1924', unpubl. PhD diss. London 1994

Wilkinson, G. R., ' "The blessings of war": depictions and images of war in Edwardian newspapers, 1899–1914', unpubl. PhD diss. Lancaster 1994

Yakutiel, M. M., ' "Treasury control" and the South African war 1899–c. 1905', unpubl. DPhil diss. Oxford 1989

Index

Bold type indicates an entry in the biographical appendix

Admiralty, 19, 25
Adye, Col. J., 80
Akers-Douglas, Aretas, 146
Aliens' Immigration Act (1897), 26
Altham, Lt-Gen. Sir Edward, **186**: and
   pre-war planning, 21–2, 23, 35–6, 53,
   87; and views on Boers, 156
Ardagh, Maj-Gen. Sir John, **186–7**: and
   intelligence department, 21; and
   pre-war planning, 22, 23, 33, 34, 53;
   and 1897 crisis, 28, 30
Ashbourne, Edward Gibson, 1st baron,
   146

Baden-Powell, Maj-Gen. R. S. S., 91, 105,
   106, 125; and Boy Scouts, 182
Balfour of Burleigh, A.H. Bruce, 6th
   baron, 146
Balfour, A. J., 1st earl, **185**; and 1897
   crisis, 26, 29; and Manchester
   speeches, 61–2, 64; and appointment
   of Lord Roberts, 66–7; and Britain's
   defence, 70
Basutoland, 32, 35
Bechuanaland, 34, 35
Benson, Col. G., 143
Biggarsberg range, 38, 44, 52, 53
Bigge, Sir Arthur, 67
Bloemfontein, 81, 85, 95, 117, 121, 124,
   125; and talks at, 37, 40, 47
Botha, Gen. Louis, 87, 118, 134, 141, 145,
   148, 149; and peace talks (1901),
   120–3, 129; and Vereeniging talks
   (1902), 170; and post-war South
   Africa, 181
Boxer Rebellion (China), 88, 89, 90
Brackenbury, Lt-Gen. Sir Henry, 68, 70
British army garrisons: before 1897, 16, 21,
   23, 25; and 1897 crisis, 30; and
   pre-war, 34–5, 37
British colonists, 23. See also loyalists
British government, see Cabinet
British South Africa Company, 16
Brodrick, W. St J. F., **185**; and military

preparations, 55, 61; and outbreak of
   war, 69; and Wolseley, 71–2; and SAC,
   109–10; and Kitchener, 113–16, 118,
   126–7, 135–6, 138–42, 146, 149–50;
   and attitude of Hicks Beach, 116, 128,
   139, 140, 149; and government's
   attitudes towards peace (1901), 121,
   124; and final peace talks (1902), 165,
   169, 172
Buller, Gen. Sir Redvers, 18, 88, 99, **187**;
   and 1897 crisis, 27; and military
   preparations (1899), 41–2, 50, 52, 53,
   54, 55; as c-in-c (SA), 57, 58, 60,
   64–7, 76; and sacking, 146–7
Burgher Peace Committee, 115, 116, 120
Burleigh, Bennett, 64
Burma, 105
Butler, Lt-Gen. Sir William, 36–9, 41, 53,
   76, **187**

Cabinet: and 1897 crisis, 25, 30; defence
   committee of, 19, 67, 69, 70; and
   military preparations (1899), 41–3,
   46–8, 50–4; and Uitlander grievances,
   44, 48, 52; and criticism of, 55, 61–2,
   64, 65, 67, 75; anxiety within, 86,
   88–90, 110, 115, 116; and cost of war,
   90, 98–9, 107–8; and military situation,
   118; and peace talks (1901), 124; takes
   up Milner's schemes, 130; and
   Chamberlain's *corps d'élite* idea, 131,
   132; and possible removal of Kitchener,
   146–7; wants Kitchener focused, 148;
   strain upon, 162
Cambridge, George William Frederick
   Charles, 2nd duke of, 17–18, 19
Cape Afrikaners, 15, 17, 23; and 1897
   crisis, 26–7; and loyalty of, 44, 53, 55;
   and Milner's fears of, 41, 76–81, 100,
   119, 163–4
Cape Colony, 15, 16, 23, 107–8; and 1897
   crisis, 27, 29, 31; and transport debate,
   33–4; and military planning, 36–8; and
   military preparations (1899), 41–2, 44,

49, 55; and outbreak of war, 58, 60–1, 67; and Uitlander refugees, 92, 94, 96, 99, 100; Boer invasion of (1900), 113, 114–16, 139, 140; and rebellion in, 118, 127; and government's conditions for peace, 168

Cape Town, 15, 16, 17, 35, 52, 55, 60, 78

Chamberlain, Joseph, 16–17, 20, 23, 25, 33, 110, **185**; and 1897 crisis, 26–7, 29–30; and Butler, 37, 38; and Uitlander grievances, 40, 41, 43, 48; and Natal, 45; and military preparations, 49–51, 53, 55; and outbreak of war, 58, 60; and appointment of Roberts, 65, 66, 68; and defence of Cape Colony, 77, 79, 80; and Uitlander refugees, 96, 98, 101, 104; and SAC, 105, 107; and helping Kitchener, 115; wants Milner's views, 117–18; and possibility of peace, 119; and peace talks (1901), 122; rejects Kitchener's views, 137–8, 140; and Cabinet disagreements, 139, 141; and Cabinet's views on Milner and Kitchener, 146–7; tries to soothe Milner, 153; and peace talks (1902), 158–9, 162–3, 165, 167, 172

Chamber of mines, 94, 96, 100

Chaplin, Henry, 62

Childers, Hugh, 17

City Imperial Volunteers, 65

Clements, Maj-Gen. R., 114

Clery, Lt-Gen. Sir Cornelius, 89

Colenso, battle of, 61, 64, 66, 150

Colonial defence committee (1878), 19

Colonial Office, 19, 25; and 1897 crisis, 26, 30; and transport debate, 32, 33, 35; and Uitlander grievances, 41; and defence of Natal, 45, 59–60; and SAC, 106, 107, 109, 110, 125.

Committee of Imperial Defence, 73–4

Crabbe, Lt-Col. E., 139

Cradock, action at, 139

Curzon of Kedleston, G. N., 1st marquess, 183

Dawkins, Sir Clinton, 73

De Aar, 38

Delagoa Bay, 30, 130

De La Rey, Gen. Koos, 92, 120, 141, 148, 149, 150, 162

De Montmorency's Scouts, 95

De Wet, Gen. Christian, 84, 90, 92, 116, 149, 150, 157, 159, 162; invades Cape Colony, 118; considered fanatical, 120

Drifts crisis, 16

Dundee (Natal), 45

Durban, 22, 44, 59

East London (Cape Colony), 78

Elandslaagte, battle of, 60

Elgin Commission, 74

Esher, R.B. Brett, 2nd viscount, 74

Esher Committee, 74

Everett, Col. Sir William, 54

Fiddes, George, 23, 89

First World War: civil–military relations, 183–4

Fitzpatrick, Percy, 100, 102, 103; and peace talks (1902), 169

Fleetwood-Wilson, Sir Guy, 106

Forestier-Walker, Lt-Gen. Sir Frederick, 39, 53, 80, 100, 103, **187**

Fourteen Streams, 35

France, 16, 35

French, Maj-Gen. Sir John, 151

Gatacre, Lt-Gen. Sir William, 60, 61, 76

Gell, Philip, 67

Germany, 16, 29, 123

Girouard, Lt-Col. P., 95, 100, 103

Glencoe, 38, 45, 58, 59, 60, 77

Goodenough, Lt-Gen. Sir William, 22, 34, 36, 37

Goold-Adams, Maj. H., 124

Goschen, George, 26

Gough, Lt-Col. H., 141

Graham, Frederick, 106

Grahamstown, 35

Greene, Conyngham, 31, 33, 49

Griffiths, Maj. Arthur, 61

Hamilton, Edward, 46

Hamilton, Lord George, 146

Hamilton, Maj-Gen. Sir Ian, **187**: sent back to South Africa, 148–9; and views of, 155–8; and peace treaty (1902), 173; and working-class health, 182

Hanbury, R. W., 146

Hartington Commission, report (1890), 74

Hely-Hutchinson, Sir Walter, 45, **185**; and military operations in Natal, 58–60, 77, 100, 103; on military situation in Cape Colony, 126, 151; and Cape suspension movement, 170

Henderson, Col. G., 78
Hicks Beach, Sir Michael, **185**; and 1897 crisis, 26, 28, 29; and reinforcements to Natal, 46; and cost of war, 90, 107–8, 109, 110, 115, 116, 126; and conflict with Brodrick, 140, 141, 149; and clash with Chamberlain, 162; and peace talks (1902), 165
Hildyard, Maj-Gen. Sir Henry, 99
Hobson, J. A., 63
Holland, 29
Houwater, action at, 80

Imperial Light Horse, 95, 99
India, 18, 21, 48–9, 65, 138, 147
Intelligence department, 18; its functions, 20–1; and pre-war planning, 25, 35, 36, 54; and confiscating Boer property, 134
irregulars, see Uitlanders, regiments

Jagersfontein, 117
James of Hereford, Sir Henry James, 1st lord, 146
Jameson raid, 16–17, 25, 26, 27, 29
Johannesburg, 16, 27, 40, 53, 54, 90, 93, 100, 118, 151, 157, 173; and British capture, 86; and return of Uitlander refugees, 92, 94–9, 101–3

Kekewich, Lt-Col. R., 141
Kelly-Kenny, Lt-Gen. T., 85
Kimberley, 26, 38, 60, 77, 78, 79, 80
King Williamstown, 35
Kitchener of Khartoum, H. H., 1st earl, field-marshal, 64, 66, 68, 78, 80, 109, 111, **187–8**; early career, 12–14; and Uitlander refugees, 95, 98, 100–1, 103; and military situation, 113–16, 118; and peace talks (1901), 120–4; and SAC, 125; his pessimism, 126, 127; agrees to change strategy, 131–2; and confiscation of Boer property, 134–5; and banishment proclamation, 129, 135; rejects Milner's schemes, 137, 139, 142–4; and peace talks (1902), 158–60, 164, 166–7, 169–70, 173; and Lord Curzon, 183; secretary of state for war, 183
Kleinfontein, action at, 141
Klerksdorp, 160, 163, 164
Komati Poort, 85, 89, 91, 92, 96, 97, 98, 99, 104, 112
Kronspruit, action at, 115
Kruger, Paul, 16, 17, 31, 32, 37, 40; and

1897 crisis, 26, 27, 29, 30; pressurised by British government, 41, 42, 43, 45, 46, 49, 51, 52, 54

Labour movement, 57. See also working-class
Ladysmith, 34, 38, 46, 58, 59, 72; and siege of, 60, 61, 66, 77, 79, 80
Laingsburg, action at, 139
Laing's Nek, 22, 38; and 1897 crisis, 28–30; and pre-war crisis, 44–6, 53; and outbreak of war, 58
Lansdowne, H. C. K. Petty-Fitzmaurice, 5th marquess, **185–6**; and army garrisons in South Africa, 19, 21, 22, 23, 25; and 1897 crisis, 26–30; and transport debate, 32–5; and Butler, 38–9; and military preparations (1899), 41–2, 46–50, 52–4; and outbreak of war, 58, 61–2; and appointment of Roberts, 65–6; and Britain's defence, 69–70; defends military system, 72; and Roberts, 75, 78–80, 104, 108; and guerilla war, 86, 88–90; and cost of war, 90–1, 101; replaced by Brodrick, 109; backs Kitchener, 146
Lindley, action at, 84
London Convention (1884), 26, 31, 33
Long, Walter, 146
Lotter, Commandant, I.C., 139
loyalists, 26, 27, 51, 118, 157; and peace talks (1902), 161, 162, 167, 168, 171, 172
Lyttelton, Maj-Gen. N., 145, 146, 147

Magersfontein, battle of, 61
Majuba Hill, battle of (1881), 21, 48
Marker, Capt. R., 112
Mauritius, 35
Methuen, P. S., 3rd baron, field-marshal, 60, 61, 150, 162, **188**
militia, 63, 69, 122, 131, 138
Milner, Sir Alfred, **186**; and 1897 crisis, 27–8, 31; and transport debate, 32, 34; and Butler, 38–9, and Uitlander grievances, 40, 41; and military preparations (1899), 43, 49–52, 55; and defence of Natal, 44–6, 48, 53; and early campaigns, 60, 62, 67–8; and Cape Colony, 75–81, 116, 138; and OFS, 81–5; and guerilla war, 86, 89, 91–2, 97–8, 109–10; and Uitlander refugees, 92–104; and Uitlander regiments, 95–6, 99, 101–2; and SAC,

104–9, 111; and military situation, 112, 117–18; complains to Pretyman, 117; and peace talks (1901), 119–24; and Kitchener, 124–6, 144–7, 150–4; in London, 127–9; confiscation of Boer property, 134–5; banishing Boer leaders, 136; and Roberts, 136–7; weakened authority, 147–8; and suspension of Cape constitution, 163–4, 170–1; and peace talks (1902), 160–2; 164–8, 170–4; and post-war South Africa, 180–1

Moedwil, action at, 141

Molteno, 38

Morning Post, 58

Murray, Maj-Gen. J., 100

Naauwpoort, 38

Natal, 15, 16, 22, 23; and 1897 crisis, 27–31; and pre-war planning, 34–8; and defence of, 42, 44–52, 53, 54, 55; military operations in, 57–61, 64, 66, 76, 77; and Uitlander refugees, 92, 93, 96, 98, 99, 103; and government's conditions for peace (1902), 168–9

Newcastle (Natal), 45, 46

Nicholson's Nek, action at, 60

Niger valley, 20

Nooitgedacht, action at, 114

Orange Free State, 22; and 1897 crisis, 26–30; and British military planning, 34, 36–8, 42, 44, 49, 50, 51, 53–4, 60, 78; and invasion of Cape Colony (1899), 76; and British invasion, 80, 81–85

Orange river, 22, 26, 37, 38

Orange River Colony, 84, 92, 93; guerilla war in, 85, 86, 87, 117, 124, 127, 139; self-government, 181

order-in-council (1895), 18, 72

Paardeberg, battle of, 80

Pietermaritzburg, 22, 38, 59

Pietersburg, 113

popular patriotism, 62–4

Port Elizabeth, 78

Pretoria, 16, 22, 27, 31, 42, 53; and fall of, 86, 87; British occupation of, 89, 90, 94, 96, 99, 100, 102, 104, 157, 164

Pretyman, Maj-Gen. G., 85, 117, 118

Prieska, rebellion at, 79–80

public opinion: and 1897 crisis, 26, 29, 30; and military preparations, 40, 41, 47,

49, 50, 54, 55; and outbreak of war, 57, 58, 61, 62, 67, 75, 76, 79; and invasion scares, 69

Railway Pioneers, 95

Rawlinson, Col. Sir Henry, 2nd baronet and baron, general, 122, 156, 157, 163, **188**

Reddersburg, action at, 82

Rhenoster river, action at, 84

Rhodes, Cecil, 16, 17, 38, 39, 163

Rhodesia, 54, 149

Rietfontein, action at, 60

Ritchie, C. T., 172

Roberts of Kabul and Kandahar, F. S., 1st earl, field-marshal, 18, 48, 57, 71, 74, 112, **188**; early career, 10–12; popularity of, 64; appointment as c-in-c (SA), 65–8; and Cape Colony, 77–81; and OFS, 81–5; and guerilla war, 86–92; and Transvaal, 93; and Uitlander refugees, 95–104; and Uitlander regiments, 95–6, 99–103; and SAC, 105–11; as go-between government and Kitchener, 114, 115; and peace talks (1901), 124; and Kitchener, 130–2; rejects Milner's schemes, 137; supports Kitchener, 140–1

Roodewal, action at, 84

Rouxville, 84

Royal Irish Constabulary, 105

Russia, 35, 126

St Helena, 136

Salisbury, R. A. T. Gascoyne-Talbot, 3rd marquess, 15, 17, 20, 107, 109, 110, **186**; and 1897 crisis, 26, 29; and military preparations (1899), 41, 43, 46–8, 51; and outbreak of war, 62; and appointment of Roberts, 66–7; and Britain's defence, 70; and Wolseley, 71, 73; agrees to send reinforcements, 115; and peace talks (1901), 121; and Kitchener, 146–7, 150; and peace talks (1902), 172

Sannah's Post, action at, 82

Scheepers, Gideon, 139

Scobell, Col. H., 139

Selborne, W. W. Palmer, 2nd earl, 17, 23, 31, 78, **186**; and military preparations, 41, 44, 46, 50, 55; at the admiralty, 113; supports Milner, 146

Smithfield, 84, 117

Smuts, Gen. Jan Christian, 141; and post-war South Africa, 181
Smuts proposals, 48, 49, 50
South African Constabulary (SAC), 107–8, 109, 110–11; under military command, 116; and Gen. Ridley's strategy, 117
South Rand Mine, action at, 115
Standard Bank, 94
Stanhope Memorandum (1888), 69
Stead, W. T., 69
Steevens, G. W., 64
Steyn, Martinus, 51, 54, 82, 83, 120, 145, 148, 157, 159; and peace talks (1902), 166
Stopford, Col. F., 36, 37
Stormberg, 60; battle of, 61, 76
Sudan, 20, 112
Symons, Maj-Gen. Sir William Penn, 45–6, 59–60

Talana, battle of, 60
The Times, 58, 61, 67
Transvaal, 15–16, 22; intelligence services, 21; and 1897 crisis, 26, 28–31; and transport debate, 32–4; and British military planning, 35–7, 53–4; and Uitlander grievances, 40, 43, 48; British military pressure upon, 43–4, 47, 51; and outbreak of war, 58; British invasion of, 81, 83, 85–7, 89, 92; under British occupation, 105, 127, 139; and self-government, 181
Treasury, 19–20, 30, 46; and cost of war, 90
Tugela river, 46
Tweebosch, action at, 150
Tweefontein, action at, 150

Uitlanders, 16–17, 22, 36; and 1897 crisis, 26, 30; and grievances, 40–1; and refugees, 93–7, 99, 101–4, 107; and regiments, 95–6, 99–103; and peace talks (1902), 169

Vaal river, 16, 85
Vereeniging, peace talks at, 170–4
Victoria, queen, 66, 67, 71

volunteers, the, 63
Von Donop, Lt-Col. S., 141, 150
Vredefort, action at, 84

Walrond, Osmond, 117
War Office: and reforms (1895), 17–19, 23, 25; and 1897 crisis, 26, 29, 30; and transport debate, 32–4; and pre-war planning, 35–9; and military preparations (1899), 41, 48; criticism of, 64, 75; and appointment of Roberts, 66; and Wolseley, 70–2; and reform (1901), 73; reform (1904), 74; and SAC, 105–7, 109, 125, 127
Warren, Lt-Gen. Sir Charles, 25
Weil & Co, 34
Wepener, 84
White, Field-Marshal Sir George, 53, 59, 60, 61, 67, 77, **188**
White-Ridley, Sir Matthew, 62
Wilkinson, Spenser, 58, 61, 64
Witwatersrand (or Rand), 15, 102; and restarting of, 98, 101, 104, 113, 115, 130, 151; and defence corps, 116–17
Wolseley, G. J., Field-Marshal Viscount, **189**; early career, 8–10; and order-in-council (1895), 18; and intelligence department, 18–21; and military situation, 21, 23, 34, 35; and 1897 crisis, 27, 30; and military preparations, 40–3, 46, 48–53, 54; and early campaigns, 58; popularity of 63–4; and appointment of Roberts, 65–7, 75; and Britain's defence, 68–71; defends reputation, 71–2; retirement, 104
Wood, Field-Marshal Sir Henry Evelyn, 19, 27, 28, 30, 34, 55, 70, **189**
Wools-Sampson, Col. A., 99
working-class, 63; and health of, 181–2
Wyndham, George, 69

yeomanry, 63, 105, 116, 131, 138, 139, 149; imperial yeomanry, 84
Yule, Brig-Gen. J., 60
Yzer Spruit, action at, 150